Modern Language Association of America

Approaches to Teaching
World Literature

Joseph Gibaldi, Series Editor

26. Robin Riley Fast and Christine Mack Gordon, eds. *Approaches to Teaching Dickinson's Poetry*. 1989.

27. Spencer Hall, ed. *Approaches to Teaching Shelley's Poetry*. 1990.

28. Sidney Gottlieb, ed. *Approaches to Teaching the Metaphysical Poets*. 1990.

29. Richard K. Emmerson, ed. *Approaches to Teaching Medieval English Drama*. 1990.

30. Kathleen Blake, ed. *Approaches to Teaching Eliot's* Middlemarch. 1990.

31. María Elena de Valdés and Mario J. Valdés, eds. *Approaches to Teaching García Márquez's* One Hundred Years of Solitude. 1990.

32. Donald D. Kummings, ed. *Approaches to Teaching Whitman's* Leaves of Grass. 1990.

33. Stephen C. Behrendt, ed. *Approaches to Teaching Shelley's* Frankenstein. 1990.

34. June Schlueter and Enoch Brater, eds. *Approaches to Teaching Beckett's* Waiting for Godot. 1991.

35. Walter H. Evert and Jack W. Rhodes, eds. *Approaches to Teaching Keats's Poetry*. 1991.

36. Frederick W. Shilstone, ed. *Approaches to Teaching Byron's Poetry*. 1991.

37. Bernth Lindfors, ed. *Approaches to Teaching Achebe's* Things Fall Apart. 1991.

38. Richard E. Matlak, ed. *Approaches to Teaching Coleridge's Poetry and Prose*. 1991.

Approaches to Teaching Coleridge's Poetry and Prose

Edited by

Richard E. Matlak

The Modern Language Association of America
New York   1991

Library of Congress Cataloging-in-Publication Data

Approaches to teaching Coleridge's poetry and prose / edited by
  Richard E. Matlak.
      p.   cm. — (Approaches to teaching world literature ; 38)
    Includes bibliographical references and index.
    ISBN 0-87352-549-3 (cloth)   ISBN 0-87352-700-3 (paper)
    1. Coleridge, Samuel Taylor, 1772–1834—Study and teaching.
  I. Matlak, Richard E., 1944–   . II. Series.
  PR4487.S78A66   1991
  821'.7—dc20   91-21906

Cover illustration of the paperback edition: Peter Vandyke, *Coleridge* (1795), and Washington Allston, *Coleridge* (1814). By courtesy of the National Portrait Gallery, London.

Published by The Modern Language Association of America
10 Astor Place, New York, New York 10003-6981

To Meegan, Mandy, and Maura

CONTENTS

PREFACE TO THE SERIES

In *The Art of Teaching* Gilbert Highet wrote, "Bad teaching wastes a great deal of effort, and spoils many lives which might have been full of energy and happiness." All too many teachers have failed in their work, Highet argued, simply "because they have not thought about it." We hope that the Approaches to Teaching World Literature series, sponsored by the Modern Language Association's Publications Committee, will not only improve the craft—as well as the art—of teaching but also encourage serious and continuing discussion of the aims and methods of teaching literature.

The principal objective of the series is to collect within each volume different points of view on teaching a specific literary work, a literary tradition, or a writer widely taught at the undergraduate level. The preparation of each volume begins with a wide-ranging survey of instructors, thus enabling us to include in the volume the philosophies and approaches, thoughts and methods of scores of experienced teachers. The result is a sourcebook of material, information, and ideas on teaching the subject of the volume to undergraduates.

The series is intended to serve nonspecialists as well as specialists, inexperienced as well as experienced teachers, graduate students who wish to learn effective ways of teaching as well as senior professors who wish to compare their own approaches with the approaches of colleagues in other schools. Of course, no volume in the series can ever substitute for erudition, intelligence, creativity, and sensitivity in teaching. We hope merely that each book will point readers in useful directions; at most each will offer only a first step in the long journey to successful teaching.

Joseph Gibaldi
Series Editor

PREFACE TO THE VOLUME

There were times when it seemed this project would be delayed interminably. Beginning with my letter of inquiry to the series editor in late 1985, the project went ahead, with direction, though haltingly, through the temporal interweaving of semester breaks with plans, submissions, revisions, late submissions, further revisions, and editorial phases. It seemed the Man from Porlock himself had blessed the volume. Today, however, Porlock is withdrawn, and these useful essays may begin to influence our understanding and teaching of Coleridge.

The substance of part 1, "Materials," derives from responses to the MLA's survey of teachers of Coleridge. If part 1 ignores a particular pedagogical or critical perspective, that is due to its apparent omission in the undergraduate teaching of Coleridge by survey respondents. I have not tried to fill or to obscure these perhaps meaningful lacunae.

There are fewer essays in part 2, "Approaches," than one finds in many teaching volumes, because I opted to restrict submissions to allow contributors developmental space. Beyond attempting to ensure that significant areas of Coleridge's poetry and prose were treated in at least one essay, I have not asked contributors to superimpose approaches or concerns onto or into their teaching to enhance inclusiveness.

To all who contributed to the development and completion of this volume—respondents, essayists, readers, reference librarians from Holy Cross and Clark universities, and editors, especially Joseph Gibaldi—I wish to conclude with my respectful appreciation.

REM

Part One

MATERIALS

Introduction: Coleridge, Patron Teacher

Coleridge would have been an enthralling undergraduate teacher. We know, of course, from familiar anecdotes, that he could be a charismatic lecturer: high-minded, impassioned, devastatingly quick-witted, a speaker who could send a hissing opponent to an early exit with a pointed retort: "I am not at all surprised, when the red hot prejudices of aristocrats are suddenly plunged into the cool water of reason, that they should go off with a hiss!" (Cottle, *Recollections* 1: 178n). But there is evidence that he would have accomplished even mundane, often averted, pedagogical tasks with a positive attitude and happy results. He would have scrutinized student writing with a good-natured rigor to exalt a young ego while introducing a dash of sanity: "the *five first Lines* of the Poem—they are very, very *beautiful*; but (pardon my obtuseness) have they any *meaning*?" (*CL* 1: 291); or, "Your sonnet— (as you call it—& being a free-born Briton who shall prevent you from calling 25 blank verse lines a Sonnet, if you have taken a bloody resolution so to do)—your Sonnet I am much pleased with—but the epithet 'downy' is probably more applicable to Susan's upper lip than to her Bosom. . . . A little *compression* would make it a beautiful poem. *Study compression*" (*CL* 1: 351); or, consider this judicious handling of a problematic persona: "the pamphlet is . . . warm, not fiery; well-reasoned without being dry; the periods harmonious yet avoiding metrical harmony; . . . I account for it's slow sale partly from your having compared yourself to Christ . . ." (*CL* 1: 307).

In a lecture on education, Coleridge made explicit the embedded objectives of such instances of mentoring: "Stimulate the heart to love, and the mind to be early accurate, and all other virtues will rise of their own accord. . ." (*CC* 5.1: 107). Knowledge, humor, concern, enthusiasm, brilliance would have made Coleridge a legend of undergraduate instruction at any university. We surely cannot do much better than to apply Coleridgean pedagogy to the teaching of Coleridge.

Prefatory Note   See Works Cited at the end of this volume for abbreviations of primary Coleridge texts. Coleridge's Mystery (or supernatural) poems are *The Rime of the Ancient Mariner*, *Christabel*, and "Kubla Khan"; the major Conversation poems (or Greater Romantic lyrics) are "Eolian Harp," "Reflections on Having Left a Place of Retirement," "This Lime-tree Bower My Prison," "Frost at Midnight," and "The Nightingale: A Conversation Poem."

What We Teach and How

Keeping with tradition in categorizing Coleridge's important poetry as the Mystery poems and the Conversation poems, we find that survey respondents use the Mystery poems and occasionally "Dejection: An Ode" to introduce the poet in freshman-level courses and introductory surveys. In period surveys and beyond, they include more Conversation poems, especially "Frost at Midnight" and "This Lime-tree Bower My Prison," and sometimes "Eolian Harp" and "The Nightingale."

Instructors limit the prose selections of introductory surveys to *Biographia Literaria*, chapters 13 ("On the Imagination") and 14 ("Occasion of the *Lyrical Ballads*"), with more *Biographia* added at the period level, usually the chapters on Wordsworth's poetry, 17 and 22. From "Lectures on Belles Lettres," the often printed passage on mechanic and organic form (*CC* 5.1: 494–95) is also commonly taught, at which point we reach the demarcation between standard and unique advanced courses. From here on, prose assignments depend on the selection of anthology or on the instructor's plundering of *The Collected Works of Samuel Taylor Coleridge*, a mammoth publishing enterprise of the Bollingen Foundation and Princeton University Press under the general editorship of Kathleen Coburn that is freshly editing and adding voluminously to the Coleridge canon.

The contexts instructors use most often in teaching Coleridge's poetry and prose are historical and intertextual. The renewed interest in historical criticism is not due to the *Collected Coleridge*, but its editions of Coleridge's political and religious lectures (*CC* 1) and journalism (*CC* 2, 3) provide for an exciting confluence with the period of the Conversation and Mystery poems (1795–1802). For many instructors, it is now inadequate to teach Coleridge apart from the active political role he played in the revolutionary milieu of his youth. The second most common pedagogical context, one that readily, though not necessarily, overlaps with the first, emphasizes the textual interrelation of Coleridge's poetry with Wordsworth's. As with the revival of historicism, recent scholarship provides influence criticism with new life, sophistication, and textual precision, in this case, by aligning Coleridge's works—*Collected Coleridge*, *Notebooks*, and *Letters*—with early manuscripts made available in the Cornell Wordsworth, under the general editorship of Stephen Parrish. Advocates of the intertextual approach argue as convincingly as historicists do that to read poems as if emitted ex nihilo is to risk misreading them and, many would add, to risk misunderstanding the poets as well. (A survey of one hundred American, British, and Canadian universities undertaken by G. Kim Blank revealed that one-third of their Romanticists teach Coleridge and Wordsworth dialogically.) In addition, if one teaches Coleridge and Wordsworth separately, one loses a signal opportunity to challenge students to seek evidence of poetic symbiosis through close reading. As several of the essays in this volume also show, feminist readers offer an even more unusual opportunity to teach the intertextuality of Coleridge's poetry with the works of contemporary women writers, such as Maria Edgeworth, Ann Radcliffe, and Mary Robinson. Among the many other contexts instructors use in presenting Coleridge, this volume provides examples of aesthetic, biographical, linguistic, philosophical, psychoanalytic, and sociological approaches.

The Choice of Texts

As one respondent to the survey on teaching Coleridge notes, "The progress of the Bollingen edition of Coleridge's works has rendered most other texts obsolete, and the constant growth of interest in Coleridge's journals, letters, and prose works has made the study of his poetry in isolation increasingly unattractive." Though it will be impossible to cull and thus to buy an ideal anthology until the Bollingen project is completed, one has to choose. Despite their grumbling about the paucity of prose and the modest helpfulness of notes in most anthologies, respondents prefer one anthology for introductory surveys, another for period surveys, and a choice of two for specialized courses.

The most popular general anthology for introductory surveys is volume 2 of *The Norton Anthology of English Literature*; the Romantic section is edited by M. H. Abrams, who is also the general editor. Instructors praise the clarity and usefulness of the introductions, the acceptability of the notes for the introductory level, the selection of texts and their reliability, and the currency of the bibliographies, made possible by Norton's frequent editions. Criticisms are minimal: skimpy coverage of Coleridge's difficult prose and the crowded appearance of texts on the page. It might be added that there is virtually no difference between the Coleridge selections in volume 2 and those in Norton's *Major Authors Edition*, which certainly contains enough material for even a year-long survey.

On the period-survey level, respondents use Russell Noyes's *English Romantic Poetry and Prose*, David Perkins's *English Romantic Writers*, William Heath's *Major British Poets of the Romantic Period*, and John L. Mahoney's *English Romantics: Major Poetry and Critical Theory*. One is not likely to choose a period anthology for its representation of a single author; however, more respondents are pleased with the Perkins, including its Coleridge selections, than with any other. That being said, it is worthwhile to note that each is suitable for different emphases.

If literary history is one's pedagogical inclination, the 1956 Noyes volume is probably still the best choice, though its bibliographies and some primary texts are dated. Noyes includes a wide representation of eighteenth-century Romantics—James Thomson, John Dyer, Edward Young, Robert Blair, Mark Akenside, Joseph and Thomas Warton, William Collins, Thomas Gray, James

Macpherson, Horace Walpole, Thomas Percy, Oliver Goldsmith, Thomas Chatterton, William Beckford, Ann Radcliffe, William Lisle Bowles, William Cowper, Robert Burns; several of the political and intellectual luminaries of the Romantic context—Thomas Paine, William Godwin, Mary Wollstone-craft; and generous sections on the six major poets as well as selections from twenty-six of their contemporaries. Noyes provides a topical essay to intro-duce the volume, a chronology of personally significant events and an in-troduction for each writer, and, for some, a selection of letters. The volume closes with a wide-ranging general bibliography and then author bibliogra-phies, both of which offer a sentence or two of annotation for almost all entries. The selection of thirty-seven poems from all periods of Coleridge's life rivals the choices in Perkins. Noyes includes the chapters from the *Biographia Literaria* on the background of *Lyrical Ballads* and on the crit-icism of Wordsworth's poetry and several pages from *Shakespearean Crit-icism*, but no religious, political, or aesthetic essays and no informal prose, such as letters, marginalia, or notebook entries.

Perkins shifts emphasis from literary history to biography. The ancillary materials offer a rich biographical context for the six major Romantic poets. The quality of the introductory essays is what one expects of a major critic, and Perkins is especially good on Coleridge. The authors included published their principal works between 1798 and 1832, except for several authors chosen to offer a perspective or anecdote on a major figure. Besides the major poets, Perkins prints selected works of George Crabbe, Dorothy Wordsworth, Francis Jeffrey, Walter Scott, Robert Southey, Walter Savage Landor, Charles Lamb, Thomas Campbell, William Hazlitt, Thomas Moore, Leigh Hunt, Thomas De Quincey, Thomas Love Peacock, Benjamin Robert Haydon, Edward John Trelawney, John Clare, Charles Cowden Clarke, Benjamin Bailey, Richard Woodhouse, J. G. Lockhart, and Thomas Lovell Beddoes. The Coleridge section consists of thirty-seven poems, the third essay from *On the Principles of Genial Criticism*, "On Poesy and Art," selections from *Biographia Literaria* (chs. 4, 13, and 20 in part; 14, 15, 17, 18, and 22 complete), *Shakespearean Criticism*, *The Statesman's Manual*, the *Friend*, *Essays on His Own Times*, *Aids to Reflection*, *Specimens of the Table Talk*, *Anima Poetae*, and twenty-one well-chosen letters from 1796–1828. The only general weaknesses of the anthology are its dated biblio-graphical essays, its lack of women authors—Dorothy Wordsworth is the only woman included—and, with respect to Coleridge, its paucity of political and religious prose.

An alternative to both Noyes and Perkins is Heath's anthology, of equal length, that eliminates all ancillary writers to more fully represent the six major poets. This, of course, allows for greatly expanded selections of formal and informal prose, but especially of the poetry, including more major works, many minor poems, important drafts, and even unpublished works. For each author, Heath provides an introductory essay, which is shorter than Perkins's; a chronology, longer than Noyes's; and a selected bibliography of the works, biographical references, and important criticism. Poetry from Coleridge's entire life is treated very fully, with seventy-eight selections, including several drafts and three versions of "Dejection: An Ode." Heath does not favor Coleridge's prose, printing only ten pages of letters, several pages from *Notebooks*, part of chapter 13 and all of 14 from *Biographia Literaria*, and the brief essay "On Method" from the *Friend*. Heath's anthology is most conducive to an emphasis on an author's poetic development, although the earliest forms of the poems are not generally offered unless they are the only texts.

The latest of the major Romantic anthologies is John L. Mahoney's. Its distinctive feature is the inclusion of twenty-one critical essays on the period and the seven authors anthologized, the six major poets and Hazlitt. In contrast with the anthologies of Noyes, Perkins, and Heath, which can be used for both undergraduate and graduate classes, Mahoney's is intended for an undergraduate course that focuses on the major works of major writers, to the exclusion of minor writers and even biographical materials, such as letters, except for Keats's on poetry. For Coleridge, Mahoney includes twenty poems, all of which are in Perkins, and slightly more of the aesthetic prose than Noyes provides; the prose includes *Biographia* 14 and 17 complete and parts of 4, 13, and 22 and selections from *The Statesman's Manual, Shakespearean Criticism*, and "On Poesy and Art." The critical essays on Coleridge are Walter Jackson Bate's "Coleridge: Transcendentalism, and the Organic View of Nature," reprinted from *Criticism: The Major Texts*; a selection from Robert Penn Warren's commentary for his 1946 edition of *Ancient Mariner*, "Sin and Redemption in *The Ancient Mariner*"; and Bate's "*Christabel* and 'Kubla Khan,' " excerpted from his biography, *Coleridge*. Needless to say, if the instructor finds major poems sufficient for the undergraduate classroom and tends to require the purchase of critical essays (and finds Mahoney's selections satisfactory), this text is economically efficient and convenient.

Of the anthologies devoted exclusively to Coleridge, and thus for advanced courses, more instructors now prefer the 1985 volume edited by H. J. Jackson, *Samuel Taylor Coleridge*, over Donald A. Stauffer's 1951 Modern Library edition, *Selected Poetry and Prose of Samuel Taylor Coleridge*, which may soon be out of print. After these, the field is open.

Jackson organizes her selection of fifty-eight poems chronologically: thirteen from the period 1789–97; twenty from 1797–1802; and twenty-five from 1803–33/34. Her prose selections include *Biographia Literaria* complete; 60 pages of letters from 1794 to 1832; some 60 pages of informal prose from *Notebooks, Marginalia*, and *Table Talk*; and 90 pages of lectures and essays, including excerpts from the *Friend, Lectures on Shakespeare* (on *Romeo and Juliet* and *Hamlet*), *The Statesman's Manual, Aids to Reflection,* and *On the Constitution of the Church and State.* The anthology closes with 22 pages of notes in small print; a brief guide to further reading; and two indexes— one to the poems by first line and one to the prose by topic and name. Jackson uses the prose texts from *Collected Coleridge* whenever available.

The Stauffer edition contains 104 pages of poetry and about 500 pages of prose, including *Biographia Literaria* (complete), five essays on Shakespeare and one on Milton, seven essays from the *Friend,* excerpts from *Aids to Reflection,* and a selection of miscellaneous religious essays from what used to be called *Literary Remains.* There is an index of titles, but no notes or index to the prose.

Several respondents use I. A. Richards's *Portable Coleridge,* but, though it has Richards's often reprinted essay on Coleridge as its introduction, it lacks notes and sufficient commentary. For graduate courses several use the two volumes of the poetry edited by Ernest Hartley Coleridge, which contain detailed bibliographical information on the first publication of Coleridge's poems. Some who teach *Biographia Literaria* entire select George Watson's Everyman edition, but the standard text is now volume 7 of the *Collected Coleridge* (ed. Bate and Engell), which is also available in a single-volume paperback edition. Its irreplaceable introduction on *Biographia's* ideas and compositional history and its abundance of informative notes— which should not be neglected as an extra dimension of knowledge—are sure to make this edition the standard for teaching as it is for scholarship.

Those wishing to use an edition of *Lyrical Ballads* for focusing on the Coleridge-Wordsworth enterprise have two excellent paperback choices: W. J. B. Owen's *Wordsworth and Coleridge:* Lyrical Ballads *1798,* which contains the Preface of 1800 with 1802 variants, and R. L. Brett and A. R. Jones's edition, which contains the additional poems of the 1800 edition and the Preface, also with 1802 variants. Both offer excellent notes to the poems, to which the Brett and Jones volume adds an appendix, "Contemporary Criticisms of *Lyrical Ballads.*"

The Teacher's Library

Regardless of the edition chosen as a class text, the teacher of Coleridge will find it helpful to have within arm's reach three of the above: E. H. Coleridge's edition of the poetry, Bate and Engell's *Biographia,* and either edition of *Lyrical Ballads.* Beyond these, it becomes a matter of interest, money, and the tolerance of one's institutional library in permitting the extended holding of books. The recommendations for scholarly reading that follow represent works that respondents have found fundamental for their understanding of Coleridge. Much is missing, which is the point. Those who seek comprehensive bibliographical guidance can refer to the extensive bibliographical essays on Coleridge in the third and fourth editions of the MLA's *English Romantic Poets: A Review of Research and Criticism* (ed. Jordan), the latest of which provides a long and masterly bibliographical essay by Max F. Schulz, and to Garland Press's annual *Romantic Movement: A Selective and Critical Bibliography*, compiled by David V. Erdman et al. The review essays of Wordsworth-Coleridge scholarship in *Studies in Romanticism* and in the Summer (1971–84) and Autumn (1985–) issues of the *Wordsworth Circle* keep one current.

The work respondents recommend most often is Walter Jackson Bate's woefully brief but still standard biography, *Coleridge*. One respondent assesses its interpretation of Coleridge's life and major poetry as being "somewhere between common sense and profundity." A definitive biography may not emerge until the Bollingen project is completed, as Erdman predicts: "there is so much new Coleridge in [*Collected Coleridge*] that only when the collecting is finished will it be possible for some presently matriculating student, in his maturity, to prepare the first critical biography of the man portraying all the facets of his streaming flashing mind and his multiple careers" ("Coleridge as Editorial Writer" 183). Nevertheless, Bate's book is and will remain an ideal introduction precisely for its succinctness. The first volume of Richard Holmes's biography of Coleridge, *Coleridge: Early Visions*, provides an engaging narrative of Coleridge's emotional life and relationships to 1804 but considers the poetry and some prose as biographical materials, instead of interpreting them biographically. An essay that expertly interprets a wealth of biographical detail from a psychoanalytic perspective is Thomas McFarland's "Coleridge's Anxieties," in John Beer's *Coleridge's Variety: Bicentenary Studies*; it is reprinted in McFarland's brilliant study of Romantic fragmentation, *Romanticism and the Forms of Ruin*. Finally, on a topic of special biographical interest to an undergraduate audience, Coleridge's addiction, several respondents recommend Alethea Hayter's *Opium and the Romantic Imagination*, which devotes a chapter to Coleridge.

The most highly recommended study of the metaphysical issue synonymous with Romanticism is McFarland's *Coleridge and the Pantheist Tradition*, a work of vast learning but dense with a richness of reference and philosophical argument that could make it difficult for readers not philosophically inclined. This being said, it should be noted that besides its four main chapters—on Coleridge's plagiarisms, Spinoza's influence, pantheism, and Coleridge's Trinitarian resolution—McFarland includes "Excursus Notes" on nineteen subtopics of philosophical interest (e.g., "Panentheism," "The New Cosmology," "Berkeley's Idealism and Pantheism," and "Existential

Shipwreck in Coleridge's Thought and Life") that are lucid and useful. An alternative book-length account of pantheism, which may be more applicable pedagogically because it contains readings of the poetry, is H. W. Piper's *Active Universe: Pantheism and the Concept of Imagination in the English Romantic Poets.*

M. H. Abrams's still very influential scholarly masterpieces *The Mirror and the Lamp: Romantic Theory and the Critical Tradition* and *Natural Supernaturalism: Tradition and Revolution in Romantic Literature* lead the next group of recommended works. *The Mirror and the Lamp* offers an excellent historical account of the Romantic imagination and the substance of the debate between Coleridge and Wordsworth over poetic diction. One can go further into the diction issue in Stephen M. Parrish's *Art of the Lyrical Ballads,* Don H. Bialostosky's "Coleridge's Interpretation of Wordsworth's Preface to *Lyrical Ballads,*" and James Engell's half of the introduction to *Biographia* (*CC* 7). What *The Mirror and the Lamp* does for Romantic aesthetics and literary history, *Natural Supernaturalism* does even more impressively for Romanticism's central political and metaphysical endeavors, especially "the secularization of inherited theological ideas and ways of thinking" (12) in Germany and England. It has also served as the target of opportunity for postmodern critics, especially deconstructionists who seek to alter Abrams's theologically based theory of Romanticism.

Norman Fruman's *Coleridge, the Damaged Archangel* is the respondents' most often recommended book after those of Abrams's. Originally making its reputation as a project of demystification—"Coleridge plain is a far more absorbing figure than the exalted seer fitfully glimpsed through the painted mists of illusion" (xix)—*The Damaged Archangel* can always be read profitably for its thorough marshaling of both old evidence and new in support of provocative readings of Coleridge's works and life.

"Demystification" has indeed taken its toll of Coleridge's rhapsodic reputation and the transcendental concepts identified with his thought, such as imagination, creativity, originality, and organicism. Although it will always be important to understand the historical significance of the ideas of Coleridgean aesthetics, readers have come self-consciously to avoid explicating texts as if they believed those ideas. The following disclaimer in a recent study of Wordsworth and Coleridge represents this critical stance: "Within these pages figurative language is granted its effects but allowed no miracles. The study consequently does not rely for its explanations on such terms as *imagination, organic unity,* or *natural supernaturalism . . .*" (Ruoff 3). It is difficult to know what the position of most teachers may be; however, contributors to this volume and respondents to the pedagogical survey seem to share this position of recent scholarship.

The next most frequently recommended group of book-length works includes the studies of John Beer generally, including *Coleridge the Visionary* and *Coleridge's Poetic Intelligence*; Humphrey House's *Coleridge: The Clark Lectures*, often excerpted on the Mystery poems; John Livingston Lowes's *Road to Xanadu: A Study in the Ways of the Imagination*, the still indispensable source study on "Kubla Khan" and *Ancient Mariner*; and the introductions to the Bollingen Coleridge volumes. Among the essays of substantial scholarly importance in the last category are Lewis Patton and Peter Mann's essay on Coleridge's youthful political and religious radicalism, in *Lectures 1795 on Politics and Religion* (*CC* 1); Patton's discussion of Coleridge's earliest attempt at religiopolitical journalism in his short-lived miscellany *The Watchman*, of 1797 (*CC* 2); David V. Erdman's thorough survey and interpretation of Coleridge's politics and political journalism from 1798 to 1823 for the London newspapers the *Morning Post* and the evening *Courier*, in the three volumes of *Essays on His Times* (*CC* 3); R. A. Foakes's balanced accounting in *Lectures 1808–1819 on Literature* (*CC* 5) of Coleridge's critical thought and its importance and of the development of Coleridge's literary lectures—including issues related to his reading, such as his plagiarisms and indebtedness to Schlegel; and, as discussed above, the important introduction to the compositional history and ideas in *Biographia Literaria* by Bate and Engell (*CC* 7). Other volumes and introductions are of undeniable value but perhaps of less general interest to the nonspecialist, though George Whalley's edition of *Marginalia* (*CC* 12), a cornucopia of unpredictable, lyrical commentary by Coleridge on everything, undoubtedly has something for everyone.

On the topic of Coleridge's politics broached by the introductory essays of Patton, Mann, and Erdman, one might also refer to Carl R. Woodring's *Politics in the Poetry of Coleridge* and Nicholas Roe's *Wordsworth and Coleridge: The Radical Years*. For a briefer treatment of Coleridge's political radicalism and his religious beliefs one might turn to Leonard W. Deen's "Coleridge and the Radicalism of Religious Dissent" and to Robert Sayre's "Young Coleridge: Romantic Utopianism and the French Revolution."

The many remaining works respondents recommend deal with the Mystery poems, the Conversation poems, the prose, and the relationship with Wordsworth and include general collections of important essays.

Receiving special notice for helpfulness with the Mystery poems were Arthur H. Nethercot's *Road to Tryermaine: A Study of the History, Background, and Purposes of Coleridge's* Christabel; Elisabeth Schneider's *Coleridge, Opium, and "Kubla Khan"*; Edward E. Bostetter's *Romantic Ventriloquists*; The Rime of the Ancient Mariner: *A Collection of Critical Essays*, edited by James D. Boulger; and The Rime of the Ancient Mariner: *A Handbook*, edited by Royal A. Gettmann. The last two contain classic essays and statements from an earlier generations of scholars (e.g., John L. Lowes, Irving Babbitt, Kathleen Coburn, Maud Bodkin, Austin Warren, E. E. Stoll). Of course, there are always article-length studies and chapters too important to ignore. Many will be mentioned in the essays that follow, but of special interest on *Ancient Mariner* are Jerome J. McGann's "Meaning of the *Ancient Mariner*" and Stanley Cavell's "In Quest of the Ordinary: Texts of Recovery." Anne K. Mellor's "Guilt and Samuel Taylor Coleridge" is excellent on the function of the gloss in perpetuating the unresolvable ironies of *Ancient Mariner*.

Highlighted for their helpfulness with the Conversation poems are Albert S. Gérard's *English Romantic Poetry: Ethos, Structure, and Symbol in Coleridge, Wordsworth, Shelley, and Keats*; Reeve Parker's *Coleridge's Meditative Art*, which is particularly good on "Frost at Midnight"; and M. H. Abrams's classic essay "Structure and Style in the Greater Romantic Lyric."

For guidance in appreciating the art of Coleridge's prose, a relatively new scholarly emphasis, one might turn to a distinguished series of essays on *Biographia Literaria*, headed by McFarland's "Coleridge's Plagiarisms," the first chapter in *Coleridge and the Pantheist Tradition*; Jerome C. Christensen's "Coleridge's Marginal Method in the *Biographia Literaria*," reprinted in *Coleridge's Blessed Machine of Language*; and Donald H. Reiman's "Coleridge and the Art of Equivocation." Laurence S. Lockridge, in *Coleridge the Moralist*, offers a wide reading of Coleridge's prose and, to a lesser extent, his poetry as both bear on Coleridge's moral thought. Lockridge's "Explaining Coleridge's Explanation: Toward a Practical Methodology for Coleridge Studies" establishes sensible structures for organizing and advancing one's understanding of Coleridge through his prose.

One interested in pursuing the Coleridge-Wordsworth connection could begin again with McFarland, this time with his influential essay "The Symbiosis of Coleridge and Wordsworth"; read Harold Bloom's brief but suggestive "Coleridge: The Anxiety of Influence" and the shrewd chapter "Partnership" in Parrish's *Art of the* Lyrical Ballads; examine Gene W. Ruoff's *Wordsworth and Coleridge: The Making of the Major Lyrics, 1802–1804*, the best intertextual analysis of Coleridge's "Dejection" and Wordsworth's "Resolution and Independence" and "Ode: Intimations of Immortality"; and conclude with Paul Magnuson's *Coleridge and Wordsworth: A Lyrical Dialogue*, the fullest state-of-the-art treatment of this complex literary partnership.

Receiving no small measure of respondents' respect and gratitude for permanent usefulness are collections of essays. M. H. Abrams's *English Romantic Poets: Modern Essays in Criticism* contains essays by G. M. Harper on the Conversation poems, G. W. Knight on the Mystery poems, Humphrey House on *Ancient Mariner*, and Reeve Parker on Coleridge's art of analogy. Kathleen Coburn's *Coleridge: A Collection of Critical Essays* gathers other important essays—on Coleridge's life, by I. A. Richards; on *Ancient Mariner*, by George Whalley, D. W. Harding, and Edward E. Bostetter; on the Conversation poems, by Gérard; on "Kubla Khan," by Elisabeth

Schneider; and on Coleridge's poetics, aesthetics, and politics. J. R. de J. Jackson provides a fine anthology of reception criticism of all Coleridge's works in *Coleridge: The Critical Heritage.*

Student Reading

Most respondents assign outside readings on Coleridge to their undergraduate classes. Leading the list of references are Bate's *Coleridge*; Lowes's *Road to Xanadu*; essays from the collections of Abrams, Gettmann, Boulger, Bloom, and Coburn; *The Annotated* Ancient Mariner, by Martin Gardner; and a selection of works on drug dependency—most frequently, Hayter's *Opium and the Romantic Imagination* and Schneider's *Coleridge, Opium, and "Kubla Khan."* Some assign Molly Lefebure's *Samuel Taylor Coleridge: A Bondage of Opium*, to which might be added a drop of M. H. Abrams's *Milk of Paradise: The Effect of Opium Visions on the Works of De Quincey, Crabbe, Francis Thompson, and Coleridge.* (This last can be of unique interest to ambitious undergraduates since it is Abrams's senior honors thesis at Harvard.) About equally recommended are Abrams's *Natural Supernaturalism*, Christensen's *Blessed Machine of Language*, notes and essays from the Bollingen *Collected Coleridge*, and Fruman's *Damaged Archangel.* Others described in the preceding section but assigned less frequently are House's *Coleridge*, Jackson's *Critical Heritage*, McFarland's *Coleridge and the Pantheist Tradition*, McGann's "Meaning of the *Ancient Mariner*," Nethercot's *Road to Tryermaine*, and Parker's *Coleridge's Meditative Art.*

Audiovisual Materials

Fewer than half the respondents use audiovisual materials. Those who do use them prefer visual works, which consist mainly of personal slides of excursions in the Lake District. Though the camcorder hasn't yet provided peripatetic re-creations, two films mentioned have tried to do so: *Coleridge: The Fountain and the Cave*, which one respondent claims his students love, and Ken Russell's interesting, though heavy-handed, *Samuel Taylor Coleridge*: The Rime of the Ancient Mariner, which uses *Ancient Mariner* as a frame for telling a drug-drenched story of Coleridge's life. To make the point about Coleridge's prolific career, one respondent carries all the volumes of poetry, the *Notebooks*, the *Letters*, and the *Collected Coleridge* to class. Another respondent uses poster panels from the 1988 traveling exhibition "William Wordsworth and the Age of English Romanticism." Related to this, one might consider having students purchase as a supplementary text the exceptionally fine catalog of the exhibition, by Jonathan Wordsworth, Michael C. Jaye, and Robert Woof; it is the most satisfying visual as well as textual "aid" that can be purchased for a Romanticism course and has recently been reduced in price for classroom use. Rutgers has also published a film on the exhibition narrated by Richard Kiley.

Audio aids, mentioned less frequently, include a reading of *Ancient Mariner* by Ralph Richardson, a weird rendering of *Ancient Mariner* by the heavy-metal group Iron Maiden on the album *Powerslave*, and some lectures on *Biographia Literaria*, *Christabel*, and *Ancient Mariner* by Stephen Prickett.

Whether or not one is attached to audiovisual aids, one might wish to consider a related visual pedagogical strategy, namely, the blackboard sketching of landscape poems—"Eolian Harp," "Frost at Midnight," especially "Kubla Khan," and so on—to encourage more precise literal reading. Also, comparing sketches of compatible poetry, such as "Kubla Khan" and Wordsworth's Vision on Snowdon, effectively illustrates visual and verbal relations. If one dares, students can be asked to sketch poem landscapes on the blackboard to compare emphases and, surreptitiously, to look for missing elements from the poems. Students will condescend to perform the task, with a bemused air, of course, but the wise instructor may be vindicated on asking pertinent questions, such as "Where's the pleasure dome?" or, in an advanced class, "Where's the shadow of the pleasure dome that's supposed to be floating midway on the waves?"

Part Two

APPROACHES

Introduction: Coleridge, Patron Student

If we can imagine the older Coleridge to be an ideal teacher of undergraduates, it is even more likely that our students would find young Coleridge an undergraduate hero: a sparkling, iconoclastic wit; the bane of dull teachers; as confused about vocation, love, religion, and family as one could wish of an interesting confidant; an enthusiastic debauchee, certainly the life of many a loud, wet, and smoky gathering and a sometime habitué of "a house of ill fame," where he admitted to "ruminating in a chair" (Godwin, qtd. in Roe 109).

Many students share the adolescence of this Coleridge but lack his saving curiosity. They ruminate in classroom chairs, with inert gaze, often distant in proportion to our enthusiasm and understanding. In well-earned moments of self-pity, we may be wont to interpret our situation romantically, feeling that Coleridge, in "Frost at Midnight," correctly diagnoses our need to seek "companionable form[s]." If he is right, our teaching had better address the making rather than the finding of intellectual correspondents. Our knowledge and enthusiasm require an equally inspired pedagogy to enhance the development we desire for our students and the curiosity and love for literature we wish to arouse.

The essays that follow begin with purposeful revisions of Coleridge's life and times to prepare us for understanding and valuing his lifelong achievements. Arguing against the failed-poet syndrome of single-self biographies, Max F. Schulz shows to great advantage a "multivaried Coleridge," whose "quick change of fictive personalities" reveals (and permits an equable assessment of) achievements commensurate with all stages of his life. Also looking at Coleridge's entire career, but from the wider end of the funnel, Donald H. Reiman's "Coleridge and British Society" emphasizes the macroinfluences of social structures on Coleridge's political and religious prose and his poetry.

The second group of essays, "Teaching the Prose and Literary Criticism," is intended partly to offer guidance and direction in assigning unfamiliar prose and partly to provide a new perspective on standard, necessary assignments, for which, perhaps, "custom ha[s] bedimmed all the lustre" (*CC* 7.1: 80). Laurence S. Lockridge presents method and markers for adventurous students to follow in tracking the genius and spirit of Coleridge's informal prose. James C. McKusick's linguistic approach has the rare promise of unifying the prose and poetry through Coleridge's central and constant interest in language. Don H. Bialostosky examines a fundamental strain in Wordsworth's Preface to *Lyrical Ballads* and Coleridge's *Biographia* that will revive the assignment for many and send students out of the classroom with a keener awareness of knowledge and campus geography, or what one of my former instructors called the Edifice Complex of Higher Education. Finally, James Holt McGavran's essay "Building Domes in Air" is likely to make one wish to teach the next literary criticism course using "Kubla Khan" as a central point of reference for a variety of critical approaches.

The next group of essays, "Teaching the Conversation Poems," presents Coleridge's landscape meditations in blank verse as foci of genetic and thematic importance. Together the essays offer a way of framing an introduction to Coleridge. John A. Hodgson makes an important case for using "Eolian Harp" to introduce students to the tensions and ambivalences of Coleridge's thought and art. Paul Magnuson's "Teaching the Coleridge-Wordsworth Dialogue" offers a series of fascinating poetic groupings to argue for the need of a dialogic pedagogy to illustrate the creative interplay of poetic creation. John T. Ogden presents the retrospective value of "Dejection" in crystallizing the perplexities of Coleridge's art, biography, critical thought, and even his times.

The last group of essays is devoted to the most frequently taught works of Coleridge's canon, the Mystery poems. Norman Fruman's uncommonly commonsensical reading of "Kubla Khan" shows that there may be no better poem for considering with students "what principles have in the past and perhaps still may legitimately govern plausibility, not to mention validity, in interpretation." Richard E. Matlak emphasizes the epistemological quandaries of *Ancient Mariner* as a source of unfailing fascination for scholars and critics and offers a set of study questions to vex students into a condition of enlightened confusion. The essays on *Christabel* may well make that poem the most commonly taught Coleridge work of the future. Mary Favret finds purposeful inscrutability in *Christabel* through a close reading of the gender biases of its two parts: the first, bodily, sensory, female; the second, visionary, linguistic, male. Karen Swann reads *Christabel* as part of the *Lyrical Ballads* project to perplex readers over form and to examine strange states of mind, an approach that leads to provocative speculations on the relation between gender and genre in Coleridge.

Anya Taylor uses *Ancient Mariner* and *Christabel* to ponder deviant behavior with criminology students. In a different setting, Patricia L. Skarda's work with student groups on the fragmentary nature of "Kubla Khan" and *Christabel* capitalizes on the reader response of students as an enactment of the frustration and anxiety that exemplify Romantic indeterminacy. Anne Williams argues that the three Mystery poems illustrate *l'écriture féminine* in their violation of metaphysical priorities and narrative forms. Finally, Jeanne Moskal provides the context and a series of assignments for research papers on the Mystery poems that lead students through the labyrinths of scholarship they have inspired.

BIOGRAPHICAL AND SOCIAL BACKGROUNDS

The Many Coleridges

Max F. Schulz

Dealing with Coleridge is like dealing with not one person but a dozen. In view of his reputation for unsystematized metaphysics; his notoriety as opium eater, plagiarist, and failed genius; his slim poetic output vis-à-vis Wordsworth's, I like to remind students of Coleridge's successful avatars: playwright, London journalist, Anglican theologian, public lecturer, Shakespearean critic, and imperial civil administrator, to name some. Such an introduction places in perspective the dreary litany of self-flagellation, of guilt and remorse, that fills his notebooks and letters and spills over into his poetry and public utterances and, inevitably, into the biographies. To accent the positive achievements, minimizing, initially at least, the seeming and reputed failures one finds when using Coleridge as the guide through the labyrinth of his life and works, brings one face-to-face with a late eighteenth-century "Renaissance" man who played varied roles in his lifetime and assumed many personas in his poetry and prose and in his public stances.

In reviewing the many Coleridges, one can be as sketchy or as weighty as one wishes; but one should note both the guises he presented to his contemporaries and the changing image he has presented to subsequent generations down to our time.

Starting with his false, fumbling, faulty metamorphosis into an "indifferent horseman" (Carpenter) named Silas Tompkins Comberbache, he re-created himself anew as the Watchman and, ubiquitously, as the Friend, to name two personas he adopted for his periodical ventures. Invented anecdotes by, or letters from, a Friend (who is himself) become a favorite rhetorical device in his lectures (see *CC* 5.1: 278, 289) and, of course, in his criticism (the famous instance being the letter in chapter 13 of *Biographia Literaria* that he used to get himself out of the morass of transcendental metaphysics miring his effort to explain the working of the imagination). One might contend that Coleridge singularly preferred the activity of friend to the more socially approved and psychically mandatory roles of son, brother, husband, and father—if the tragedy of his life as a perennial "poor nigh-related guest, / That may not rudely be dismist; / Yet hath outstay'd his welcome while" ("Youth and Age" 46–48), were not so movingly lamented. Beyond question is that he luxuriated in the role in poems of 1794 and 1795 and in a variety of addresses and in all kinds of domestic situations throughout his life, celebrating the nomenclature and prizing the relationship in such fine late poems as "Youth and Age" (1823, 1828) and "The Garden of Boccaccio" (1828). He came to think of himself also (or others so saw him, and he accepted their judgments) as the Old Navigator (after the ancient Mariner of his most famous poem), as the Glossist interpreting the Mariner's tale for us, as the Hamlet of his critiques of Shakespeare (*CC* 5.1: 376; Morley 1: 57), as the Preacher of Lay Sermons to his compatriots. He gloried in the role of lecturer, so much so that his friends chortled over his being "the fittest man for a Lecturer [they] had ever known: [since] he was constantly lecturing when in company, only he did it [then] better" (George Dyer, *CC* 5.1: 233; see also 1: 283). The guise of preacher seems to have afforded Coleridge even more self-gratification. As a young man he preached in various Unitarian churches often garbed in what he proudly termed "coloured [that is, "Blue"] Cloths" (*CL* 1: 180) to indicate his political sympathies. As an old man and the Sage of Highgate, he greeted friends and celebrity seekers in his walks on Hampstead Heath and on his Thursday "at-home" hours resplendent in old-fashioned hose and all in black as a sign of his clerical aspirations.

That he mistranscribes/mistranslates the "Punic Greek" (*CL* 2: 867) transliteration of the etymon of his signature (Es-tee-see [ΕΣ-ΤΗ-ΣΕ] for STC) from the correct Greek word for "He hath placed" to the word for "He hath stood"—biographical "theft" Jerome Christensen terms it (" 'Like a Guilty Thing' " 785n6)—seems to suggest that Coleridge himself believed that he could switch selves with the swipe of his pen.

To his friends, family, and acquaintances, Coleridge epitomized the poet tuned to the highest pitch of "mystic sounds" (Hazlitt, "First Acquaintance" 107) anthropomorphized into human voice. Unfortunately, so the near unanimous lament went, the genius and "face of Poetry" (Hazlitt, "First Acquaintance" 115), as impersonated by Samuel Taylor Coleridge, appeared to most of them to drift over the course of thirty years into "the hazy infinitude of

Kantean transcendentalism" (Carlyle 56) or into predinner, dinnertime, and after-dinner "continuous flow of converse" (Lamb 199). By 1816 the poet, journalist, lecturer, and youthful part-time preacher to sparse Unitarian congregations had yielded to the middle-aged self-appointed Trinitarian teacher to the nation.

Then there are the historical transformations of the man. If Coleridge's contemporaries heard in the alcohol- or opium-tainted voice the damaged archangelic tones of the poet, the next generation—much to Carlyle's disgust—listened to him with the devoted respect and attention due a religious oracle. In the 1820s to such men as John Sterling, Julius Charles Hare, Frederick Denison Maurice, and others who would help determine the religious conscience of the Victorians, Coleridge offered the best and wisest positions on the theological controversies of their day. Armed with his commonsensical, person-oriented approach to belief and to such questions as the historical validity of the Bible, they did much to establish in England, as James Marsh did in America, well past mid-century, Coleridge's reputation as a religious thinker and defender of the Anglican faith. By the last quarter of the century, however, the image of Coleridge the philosopher-theologian had pretty much run its course.

Even as his reputation as a philosopher was falling in the second half of the nineteenth century, his star was reascending under the aegis of poet. The adulation that the Pre-Raphaelites accorded *Ancient Mariner*, "Kubla Khan," and *Christabel* prefigures the poet of "a handful of golden poems" (Chambers 331) celebrated in the early decades of our century and damned with faint praise by E. K. Chambers in his 1938 biography of Coleridge. This is the noble poet redivivus ruined once again by philosophical moonshine, and more's the pity, since, according to the holy writ of René Wellek, the philosophy was a structurally flawed House That Jack Built anyway, with "here a story from Kant, there a part of a room from Schelling" (Wellek, *Kant in England* 67). Then, in the decades preceding and following the Second World War Coleridge the literary critic and critical theorist was thrust to the fore, to the disgust of F. R. Leavis, who considered Coleridge's "currency as an academic classic . . . something of a scandal" (86).

And now begins "the age of Coleridge the thinker" (so a recent critic prophesied [Barth, Rev. 239]); and the *Collected Coleridge*, with its projected three volumes of poetry and twenty-three, twenty-four, or more of prose, threatens to bury the poet beneath the man of letters and of ideas— to the alarm of more than one lover of his poems.

Which brings one to the many Coleridges to be found among current Coleridgeans. To list them is both fun and instructive. There are the Romanized Anglo-Catholic of J. Robert Barth (*Coleridge and Christian Doctrine*); the incautious fell-walker, bad husband, and junky of Molly Lefebure; the early, if not first, courageous, poignantly enduring existentialist of Thomas

McFarland (*Romanticism*); the theologian of Basil Willey; the priest of polarity of Owen Barfield; the higher biblical critic of Elinor Shaffer; the sometimes rascally, sometimes devious, Fleet Street journalist of David V. Erdman ("Coleridge on Coleridge"; *CC* 3.1: lix–clxxix); the Pecksniffian comedian team of Mr. Box and Mr. Cox of Stephen Potter; the spiritual humanist, cabalist, and occultist of Anya Taylor (*Magic*) and John Beer (*Coleridge the Visionary; Coleridge's Poetic Intelligence*); the failed enfant terrible, liar, and plagiarist of Norman Fruman; the pseudo-Germanist of René Wellek (*Romantic Age; Kant in England*); the political theorist of John Colmer; the cultural conservative and social apologist of Raymond Williams; the political apostate of E. P. Thompson; the metaphysician of apostasy of Jerome C. Christensen (" 'Like a Guilty Thing' ").

Behind which, among this welter of masks, lurks the real Coleridge? On which identity should a student focus as an aid to understanding Coleridge the poet, the critic, the thinker, and man of letters? An answer is implicit in the form of my question. One Coleridge won't do. I urge students to live with the ambiguity, uncertainty, indeterminacy of many Coleridges, fitting the appropriate biographical facts and the successive stages in his personal and professional development to the appropriate piece of writing.

Nor do I, ordinarily, attempt an explanation for the multivisaged Coleridges. Coleridge criticism is already overloaded with psychological diagnoses—that he suffered some version of shaky identity, hesitant self-acceptance, excessive narcissism, ego-development disturbance, childhood mother rejection—to which the interested student can be referred. Instead, I inform students that James Clifford, the eminent biographer of the young Samuel Johnson, questions, as a suspect assumption, the biographical idea of an essential self. Biography as currently practiced, he contends, is the product of eighteenth- and nineteenth-century psychology. Governed by Freudian axioms, it assumes the need to deliver a coherent personality at "the expense of plenitude" out of the bits and pieces, the paradoxes and contradictions of a person's life. In the drive to render up artificially "a shaped life" consistent with the "myth of personal coherence," emphasizing "closure and progress towards individuality rather than openness and discontinuity," the biographer should not overlook "a concomitant myth of personal participation" that extends the boundaries of the Freudian self to include sociocultural determinants of personality. Such ethnological forces, Clifford says, foreground an individual "radically decentered" into a succession of constituents of personality, "forever losing, and re-creating himself in his social contexts, in his 'others,' and in language" (46–47).

What pedagogical purpose does a multivaried Coleridge serve? It corrects the myth that Coleridge was a poet destroyed by opium and metaphysics and reduces to a nonissue the question of why he did not live up to his promise as a poet. It allows us to read the poems as representative of one stage in his development, as the youthful product of an ardent imagination, whose effect on Hazlitt was like "the first welcome breath of Spring" ("First Acquaintance" 117). It helps one resist the temptation to read the poems from the perspective of the middle and late Coleridge. It accords an authenticity to the Coleridge of the *Friend*, of the *Morning Post* and *Courier* essays, of the *Lay Sermons*, of the *Biographia Literaria*, of the *Aids to Reflection*—honoring them as valid expressions of a man of letters who has profoundly influenced Anglo-American thought over the past two hundred years. It urges one to be cautious about hanging political tags on him. It supplements Coleridge's compositional peculiarities with a gloss of changing personalities. It places Coleridge and Wordsworth in a continuing relationship that is more complicated than their association as competitive poets, which has commanded our attention for so long. Without diminishing the poetic achievement of the annus mirabilis of 1797–98, it paradoxically affirms the middle and late poems, by providing them with more meaningful contexts than the sterile supposition that they represent a falling off from the magical three. It offers fascinating perspectives on a complex protean psyche, which reveals simultaneously Coleridge's impatience with a faulty self in his fictive readiness to assume other personas and respect for that self in his pertinacious hold on it through all his quick changes of fictive personalities (see Martin).

At this point I usually offer illustrations broadly representative of Coleridge the public activist, Coleridge the philosophical-religious guru, and Coleridge the erstwhile poet–man of letters.

There is much one can say on behalf of the inner coherent personality of Coleridge the untypical genius who is at the same time the typical British citizen of the Napoleonic era. Daniel Stuart valued Coleridge as a writer of newspaper editorials, because of his ability to analyze developing political and military situations in a historical frame of reference that suggested the governance of general laws of human behavior and political practice (*CC* 3.1: introd.). Coleridge's portraits of William Pitt (*CC* 3.1: 219–27) and General Washington (*CC* 3.1: 131–33, 228–32), his Plutarchan comparisons of Luther and Rousseau (*CC* 4.1: 131–43) and his comparison of France with Rome (*CC* 3.1: 311–39), his placement of the Spanish rebellion against French rule in a context of the Netherlands' revolt against Spanish rule in the sixteenth century (*CC* 3.2: 37–85)—his lifelong preoccupation with reconciling past and present, "truths of mind" and empirical facts, Platonic-Christian philosophy and quantifiable science—attest to the tensions necessarily engendered by his effort to be comprehensive and by his need to hold together the conflicting components of his being. His was a personality at once gregarious and contemplative, outgoing and inward-staring, reveling in a zeitgeist oriented toward the present and luxuriating in a life-style directed toward the past.

To demand of Coleridge that he stand outside his time is to expect an unnatural action of human beings who are nothing if not the embodiment of the "characteristic occasions of [the] historical period. . . . immanent in [their] lives" (Clifford 52). And as a desultory editorial writer for two of London's newspapers, the *Morning Post* and the *Courier*, Coleridge assumed on the world stage a role determined as much by the political, cultural, social, and historical situation as by the inner person. His responsiveness to the exterior patterned realities of the world, his readiness to lend his self to external events, explains without recrimination the anomaly, which so intrigued and amused David Erdman (*CC* 3.1: introd.), of the antiwar and anti-Pitt critic metamorphosing into the prowar, progovernment advocate. I point out to students how easy it is for armchair academics to scold Coleridge for his apparent apostasy from principled positions, when in fact he was responding, like the practical politician and the practicing journalist, with versatile energy to world events. Indeed, in his grasp of these events, one might with justice say that between 1800 and 1815 the individual person and society converge in him to embody the sociopolitical paradoxes of an island sea power in a desperate political and economic struggle with a mighty, seemingly invincible, land power. That is not to say that Coleridge avoids taking positions on specific issues; rather, his perceptions of England at war with France in the 1800s involve political realities at variance with the political stances of a youthful Bristol rebel of the 1790s. Instead of being charged against him as fallings away from internal intellectual consistency, his departures from earlier positions should be seen for what they may be, successive social loci and natural matrices, in the transitions of life.

Such public moments are scattered through Coleridge's life and pose interpretative pitfalls for students, teachers, and biographer-critics alike. To mention one: in 1804–05, during his year and a half on Malta, he appears to inch his way into the camp of Anglo-imperialists. However distressing, and perplexing, his seeming colonial imperialism may be to us 150 years later, grown, if not wiser, certainly more cynical, about the expansionist tendencies of nations, we should not forget that Coleridge was working at the time for Alexander Ball, one of Nelson's captains, who had commanded a ship at the Battle of the Nile (1798) and then conducted and won the siege of Malta (1798–1800). Ball, whom Coleridge admired (see "Sketch of the Life of Sir Alexander Ball," *CC* 4.1: 532–80), was an unapologetic militarist and eloquent defender of the principle of Pax Britannia. Nor should we forget that Coleridge spent his days and nights on Malta with men whose instincts, training, and public charge were to extend British hegemony and that the geopolitical idea of England as an island sea power ruling a far-flung empire of colonialized parcels of real estate was a hotly debated issue of the day.

Given the situation, how much of the several versions of the document arguing for English military occupation and commercial exploitation of Egypt, called variously "Defense of Egypt" and "Observations on Egypt," can we assume represents Coleridge's private tenets (see *CN* 2: xvii, 2297; Sultana 174–78, 234–36; see also Erdman, *CC* 3.1: cxxiv–viii)? The original version was a white paper prepared for Admiral Ball, who we know assigned Coleridge, first as his private secretary and then as the island's public secretary, the task of revising the paper for style and substance before submission to the British Colonial Office. Coleridge did better than that. He rewrote it, introducing new arguments and additional factual and theoretical matter for the old arguments.

So, is the revised essay a reliable index to Coleridge's political and economic beliefs? Or is it a civil servant's faithful record of his supervisor's beliefs? What bearing does it have on the answer to these questions that Coleridge, with a journalist's instinct for news, sent Stuart a copy of the paper to publish if it suited his "own opinion" (*CL* 2: 1149; cf. 1178)?

Plagiarism poses as many indeterminate questions about the hydra-headed Coleridge as the political and journalistic issues just raised do. Throughout much of his life Coleridge exhibited a sometimes inspired, at all times perversely addictive, habit of verbal annexation of another's identity, a practice that continues to call down on his head the ire of the morally outraged. A generic form that appealed to him was the travesty, which he practiced early and late in life, from "To a Young Ass" (1794) to "The Historie and Gests of Maxilian" (1822; see H. J. Jackson, "Coleridge's 'Maxilian' "). The travesty takes a less comic form when he elects in chapter 5 of *Biographia Literaria* to present his case against associationism by clothing his argument in the language of the obscure German philosopher-historian J. G. E. Maass and putting it in the form of a rejoinder to the detested Scottish philosopher-timeserver James Mackintosh (see Christensen, *Coleridge's Blessed Machine*).

As these metamorphoses and tergiversations suggest (and one can cite instance after instance), we are dealing with a master verbal shapeshifter, one who through the symbolic power of language (talking and writing) finds a self-conscious reflex of himself in aid of recovering his other "Halfness" and achieving "that absolute *Union*, which the soul sensible of its imperfection in itself . . . yearns after" (*CN* 3: 3325). Through language he cherishes "the 'multilayeredness' of the individual character" without endangering "the whole person" (Auerbach 9–10, qtd. in Taylor, *Coleridge's Defense* 191, 193). Even at mundane levels of aspiration he is forever cross-dressing his language; by the duplicitous alteration of a word here and there he fits an old representation snugly behind a new mask, as he does in the notorious letter "from a friend whose practical judgment," he cheekily assures us, "I have had ample reason to estimate and revere" (to wit, himself!). This well-known instance, which is not without its wry self-deprecatory humor, occurs in chapter 13 of *Biographia Literaria*. In it he proceeds to alter two and a half lines of his poem "To William Wordsworth" in praise of *The Prelude* so that he may allude appropriately to the *Biographia* as a "tale *obscure* [in lieu of "song divine"] of high and passionate thoughts / To a *strange* [in lieu of "their own"] music chaunted" (*CC* 7.1: 302).

Current critical theory places parody, plagiarism, copy-imitation, irony, and satire (some are favorite antitheses of Coleridge) in a perilous relation (see Hutcheon), making it risky for a writer to employ them, since the moral and verbal equilibrium among such literary feints is easily lost. Coleridge's compulsion to use another's verbal signature sometimes led to his falling on his head, at other times to his managing a marathon balancing act. *Aids to Reflection* is an instance of the latter.

Aids is a compound of the prudential, moral, and spiritual writings of seventeenth-century divines, principally Archbishop Leighton and, to a lesser extent, Henry More, Jeremy Taylor, and others. Extrapolations and aphorisms by Coleridge are interspersed, with his aphorisms increasingly foregrounded as the book proceeds. In the advertisement to the 1825 publication, Coleridge discloses that "the Work was begun as a mere Selection . . . under the usual title of The Beauties of Archbishop Leighton, with a few notes and a biographical preface by the Selector." That plan, however, yielded to the importunities of "various Reflections . . . that pressed on" Coleridge's mind while he was "considering the motives for selecting this or that passage." As a consequence, Coleridge writes, he was soon adding so many of his own words in "the desire for enforcing, and as it were integrating, the truths contained in the Original Author" that he was

> soon induced . . . to recognize and adopt a revolution in my plan and object, which had in fact actually taken place without my intention, and almost unawares. It would indeed be more correct to say, that the present Volume owed its accidental origin to the intention of compiling one of a different description, than to speak of it as the same Work. It is not a change in the child, but a changeling.
>
> (1825 ed., iii–iv)

The bilateral ingenuousness of Coleridge's self-reflexivity—note the "almost unawares" in his explanation of how he came to write *Aids*—should not blind us to the paradigmatic transformation of identity, as exposed by this explanation, of an editor struggling to elevate his subsidiary book-making role into the book's originating voice. Coleridge defines aphorism as a "two fold act of circumscribing, and detaching" (1825 ed., 15n). From literally "circumscribing, and detaching" Archbishop Leighton's truths from the inert reflections on the page in which they have been interred, to accord them due prominence and filial honor, Coleridge moves to supersede, that is, to circumscribe and detach from the words (in an equally fundamental but more self-aggrandizing sense) the initiating authority of Leighton's voice by (1) occasionally subsuming Leighton's voice into his and (2) attaching commentaries and aphorisms of his own, which multiply and grow ever longer, until Coleridge's words and viewpoint dominate the proceedings. The aphorisms of a Leighton, a Jeremy Taylor are still ostensibly accorded primacy of place, but such respect is increasingly honorific, as Coleridge's words (and "voice") assume priority. The role of authority has undergone transposition. As usual, Coleridge's explanation of what he has done seizes on language that is remarkably precise. He characterizes his displacement of Leighton as "not a change in the child, but a changeling." Why the careful semantic distinction? Because the book has become other than the work originally initiated, yet is not unconnected in intention to that earlier conception. In "changeling" Coleridge strives to incorporate the paradoxical identicalness and singularity, which he perceives to be coexistent with a twofold creation. In fact, twice twofold: Leighton's seventeenth-century utterances and Coleridge's contemporary book, and Coleridge's initial intentions and his final result. The changeling (*Aids*) has not been substituted for the child ("The Beauties of Archbishop Leighton"); rather, its separate form has been superimposed on the child's. In fact, *Aids* still retains genetic vestiges of the original child (hence one possible sense of "not a change in the child") both in the separately identifiable aphorisms of Leighton and the other seventeenth-century divines and in those instances in its new guise where Leighton's and Coleridge's contributions are inextricably intertwined. Yet, in these instances, as well as in those where Coleridge's voice is unambiguously identified, *Aids*, as Coleridge rightly acknowledges, has become another child, not least through the metamorphosis of the "parent." Coleridge the editor has usurped the identity and function of Archbishop Leighton the author, the man of print and letters has usurped those of the preacher of words. The repeated, and supplemented, words of Leighton have awakened a new voice, which also still echoes its own old voice. Students who wish to pursue the Leighton-Coleridge talisman relationship further, particularly that of the father-son displacement, in philosophical and linguistic rather than psychoanalytical terms, can be directed to the gloss provided by Jacques Derrida's deconstruction of the Thoth-Thamuz myth in his essay "Plato's Pharmacy."

The presence of the multimasked Coleridge in the great poems is axiomatic, offering, for example, an explanation for the layers of narrative points of view laminating the successive versions of *Ancient Mariner*. The superstitious late-medieval early-Renaissance bard of the 1798 literary pastiche, with its shaky orthography, yields in 1800 to the less ersatz eighteenth-century antiquarian recoverer of the ballad form and to the subtitular admission "A Poet's Reverie." For the brief life of the 1800 poem the laconic pseudoballadic argument of 1798 is retained, but revised to include a sophisticated sociomoral explanation of etiquette for "the strange things that befell" the Mariner. Dropped in all subsequent reprintings, the argument is eventually replaced in 1817 with a learned Latin epigraph from a 1692 work of Thomas Burnet, somewhat theologically bowdlerized by Coleridge, attesting to the prolixity of invisible spirits in the visible universe. In 1817 also appears the pedantic seventeenth-century narrative voice of the prose glossist reinforcing the poem's Christian causal underpinning of the otherwise mysterious events of the voyage, judging, for example, the "spell" (line 442), or trance, of the Mariner as a "curse," or cross, of guilt suffered by him for killing the albatross and expiable through penitential suffering. In the poem's transformational accretion from 1798 to 1817 of narrators and points of view—and I have by no means exhausted the possibilities—is imprinted the record of Coleridge's ideological development, artistic perceptions, and psychoreligious anxieties for those years. He is, in effect, co-opting successive versions of his self, while never quite effacing the trace of old personas and viewpoints. In its palimpsest the poem thus encodes prototypically the disguised signatures of the protean Coleridge: delver in old pre-Christian texts, acolyte of nature, hermeneutic formalist, philologist, Broad Church apologist, wandering Old Navigator, sophisticated balladeer-poet, literary theorist and critic.

The changeling nature of *Ancient Mariner* has raised the question of authoritative text. William Empson prescriptively dismisses what he perceives to be the 1817 poem's Christian allegory in favor of the more authentic neurotic guilt-ridden 1798–1800 ballads of nature and of geopolitical allusion (Empson and Pirie, sec. 3). Jerome McGann postmodernly treats the separate poems as endless alternative meanings of a Derridean text absorbing not only Coleridge's shifting avatars but also the layered identities of generations of critics' polyphonic and dissonant interpretations ("Meaning"). As a cautionary alternative to such traditional scholarly and canonical concerns, one can instructively posit the repetitive phenomenon of multiple personas in the Coleridgean corpus to justify the reading of each version of *Ancient Mariner* as a unique expression of one or more of the many Coleridges. This biographical perspective privileges a pluralistic perspective on Coleridge that balances the questionable psychological assumption of an "essential self" with the evidentiary hypothesis of a particular historical individual's personal plenitude of being.

Less familiar, but more biographically explicit and hence more readily elucidative to students of the point I'm making, is a post–West Country, postaddiction poem like "A Tombless Epitaph" (1809), which carries as part of its residual baggage the history of Coleridge's critical-biographical masking. The poem is ostensibly a laudatory "record of [his] worth"—"His wildwood fancy and impetuous zeal . . . passionate for ancient truths"—a portrait of himself in the guise of a youthful Satyrane, who had traced every "rill /

There issues forth from the fount of Hippocrine / . . . upward to its source," despite "Whole years of weary days" of sickness. The poem turns out on examination, however, to be a translation of the seventh epitaph of the late sixteenth-century Italian poet Gabriello Chiabrera, who is eulogizing one Ambrosio Sallinero (*PW* 413n). As if assimilating these two persons into his own self does not satisfy his appetite for clothing himself in layers of borrowed personalities, Coleridge multiplies the heteroglossia of voices, for the imitation "closely" follows "an earlier translation of Wordsworth," Norman Fruman records disapprovingly (269). In fact, Fruman's allegation applies to roughly a quarter of Coleridge's forty lines. The rest warrants Coleridge's characteristic claim, when he published it in the *Friend*, 23 November 1809, to have "imitated . . . the movements rather than the thoughts" of his model (*CC* 4.2: 184). The first appearance of the poem ("half" a representation of Wordsworth's pen, corrected and completed by Coleridge's) in Coleridge's periodical, then, is owed to the good offices of an editorial patronage posing behind the literary mask of yet another identity, that of Coleridge as the Friend of his fellow writers and readers.

Nor is that an end to the layers of personal and verbal signature through which Coleridge sifts to fix his own voiceprint as "studious Poet" and "Philosopher"—the self-portrait he is at pains to establish in the poem. Never mind the echo of Satyrane in the name of Spenser's character born to "A satyres sonne" (*Faerie Queene* 1.6.21), who is faithful to Una (Truth), or the complicated textual history of the Coleridge letters written home from Germany in 1798–99 and published in the *Friend* and the *Biographia* as Satyrane's, which are part of the background of the poem. Most beguiling is the way Coleridge masquerades simultaneously as Satyrane and as the eponymous Friend to establish the dead Satyrane as the phoenix of a Coleridge who rises out of the ashes of the 1797–98 annus mirabilis, when he was Wordsworth's poetic compeer, to fly again in the 1809 *Friend* despite the disapproving Wordsworths' expectations of his failure. In a biographical sketch introducing the Satyrane/Friend letter, which follows the poem, the narrational I (Coleridge? the Friend?) tells of a tour "a few Seasons ago, I made . . . of the northern Counties" with Satyrane, his "deceased Friend" (note the ambiguity of identity neatly encapsulated in the squinting duality of the epithet "Friend"). Still remembered, and now eulogized, is Satyrane's brilliant talk, which lightened the tiresome length of the walk so much that "a joint work to be entitled 'TRAVELLING CONVERSATIONS' " (*CC* 4.2: 185–86) was suggested to commemorate the tour. The proposed work was never written, presumably because of Satyrane's untimely death. Instead we are given what is ostensibly a literary epitaph to his memory by which Coleridge announces to the world the demise of his old poetic identity (in part, self-referentially and ironically, in the form of a poem) and the birth of a new literary and philosophical identity. The once-upon-a-time poet of Nether

Stowey is being reborn as the thinker-teacher and writer-friend to an English reading nation. Yet, as the (con)fusion of Satyrane and the Friend indicates, Coleridge's rebirth is not a simple case of identity replacement; rather, it is one of complex addition and superimposition of new on old, of two (or more) become another one. The dead Satyrane is being resurrected and bonded alphabetically and epistolarily, literally and literarily, to the Friend, man of letters and periodicals. The dead poet's words are being revived in the live essayist-editor's, and both integrated historically into the elegiac tradition of Western poetry. To gloss "A Tombless Epitaph" with this history of growth and loss, and of renewal through accretion in personas, is to epitomize Coleridge's plagiarism, his cross-dressing, his invention of new selves, and his retention of an unchanging inner person.

The biographical re-creation played out in "A Tombless Epitaph" is a linguistic-psychic economy Coleridge transacts again and again in his life and work: in the prose-gloss metacommentary of *Ancient Mariner*; in the Milton–Wordsworth–Lucy Gray aliases of "Dejection: An Ode"; in the Wordsworth-great-poet–Coleridge-great-critic chiasmus in *Biographia Literaria*; in the role of Malta's public secretary and servant of empire rewriting Alexander Ball's white papers on British hegemony in the Mediterranean; in the preacher-editor-commentator transactive exchange with Archbishop Leighton in *Aids to Reflection*; in the glossolalia of holy poet, skeptical prefatorialist, and dream-born Abyssinian damsel of "Kubla Khan"; in the theorist-translator-disciple kinship with German philosophers; in the transposition of Friederika Brun's Alps into Coleridge's Borrowdales; in the master-pupil relationship with the next generation's reformers of the Church of England—and, above all, in the human-divine nexus Coleridge sought tirelessly in the last third of his life between I am and I AM. It is a symbiotic stratagem, reproduced in endless mundane ways, tropes, and literary constructs, by which Coleridge perpetually rearranged a kaleidoscope of personas to hold at bay the entropism of identity.

Coleridge and British Society

Donald H. Reiman

Teachers who do not devote a full semester to Coleridge often have time only to discuss his most notable poems and a few chapters of *Biographia Literaria*—perhaps those from volume 2 on Wordsworth's poetry. Yet much of Coleridge's thought went into his political and social prose, now available in *The Collected Works of Samuel Taylor Coleridge (CC)*—*Lectures 1795 on Politics and Religion (CC 1)*; his periodical *The Watchman (CC 2)*; his journalism in the *Morning Post* and the *Courier*, collected as *Essays on His Times (CC 3)*; his later periodical *The Friend (CC 4)*; his two *Lay Sermons (CC 6)*; and *On the Constitution of the Church and State (CC 10)*. Even in Coleridge's works that are commonly taught—especially *Biographia Literaria (CC 7)*—many of his attitudes and aims cannot be fully understood without reference to that social philosophy. How, then, can we expand the consciousness of students to see Coleridge, the social prophet, as well as the inspired poet, without slighting his major literary works?

I

We can begin by drawing a psychological profile of Coleridge from five revealing autobiographical letters that he wrote to Thomas Poole between February 1797 and February 1798 (rpt. in Schneider, *Selected Poetry and Prose*; H. J. Jackson, *Coleridge*).

These letters let us into the mind of Coleridge not only psychologically but sociologically. They reveal that Coleridge—the youngest child in a large family—believed from early childhood that all good things come from above; he tells how his whole family—his grandfather (a foundling), his father (sponsored by local "Gentlemen" in setting up a school), and his older brothers —were educated or rose in their professions through the patronage of those above them in society or else married wealthy women. Coleridge himself was rescued by Sir Stafford Northcote, the local baronet, when, after a quarrel with his rival brother Francis, young Sam spent a night outdoors in the cold, nearly dying of exposure. These real benefits conferred from above were reinforced by young Coleridge's dreams of four guardian angels at the four corners of his bed, protecting him from imagined demons and monsters.

Having been sponsored for Christ's Hospital after his father's death, Coleridge continued to rely on patronage for his wants. A man whom Coleridge bumped into on a London street (and who first accused him of trying to pick his pocket) was so won over by the boy from the Bluecoat School that he bought him a subscription to a circulating library in Cheapside (Gillman 17); the widowed Mrs. Evans, whose son Coleridge defended against hazing by older boys, became a second mother to him (and her eldest daughter, Mary, the object of his adolescent love); Coleridge's brother George, eight years his senior, settled in nearby Hackney after taking his degree and became (Coleridge said) his surrogate father. Coleridge's most notable success in securing patronage and protection from older or more powerful members of society during his adult years was the granting of an annuity of £150 from the brothers Thomas and Josiah Wedgwood in January 1798 that, until half was rescinded after the death of Tom Wedgwood, enabled him to live modestly without too much exertion.

In later years Coleridge drew on the strength of a number of older or richer men, often gentlemen of old Norman families (e.g., William Sotheby, John Hookham Frere, and Sir George Beaumont), whose approval and support he craved to counterbalance the attacks on him by his middle-class contemporaries and by such younger writers as Hazlitt. Though in his later years his dependence shifted to men in the rising middle classes, such as John James Morgan and Dr. James Gillman, Coleridge repeated his practice of seeking patronage and protection from those with greater power and status within the social nexus, a pattern that can be read as a "Stephen Daedalus–like search for a substitute father" (Lefebure 75) or as an ingrained part of his political philosophy based on his family's traditions and his own experiences. Coleridge even seems to have been willing to compromise his independence and to pay lip service to the virtues of men (and women) whose abilities and sometimes whose characters he did not truly respect as the price of their approval, financial support, and protection. (For a detailed analysis of the effects of Coleridge's dependence on *Biographia Literaria*, see chapter 3 in Reiman, *Intervals*.)

II

When introducing students to the social and political issues of the Romantic period, the teacher should, I think, emphasize that the sense of social-class divisions was much stronger in England in that time than it is today (as it remains much stronger in Britain now than in the United States or Canada). Besides the novels of Jane Austen, a good work from which to illustrate the attitude is Dickens's *Great Expectations*. Through much of that novel, Pip assumes that the benefactor who has given him his expectations is Miss Havisham, because as a "lady" she is entitled to raise someone below her up the class ladder. (The confusion of feelings between Joe the blacksmith and Pip after his elevation shows the width of the gulf produced by the move from one social class to another.) Pip is horrified to learn that his patron is Magwitch, not simply because the man is a convict, but because—since the benefaction resulted from Pip's own act of kindness to the outcast—Pip has become responsible for his own elevation, instead of receiving the blessing from a social "better" who was entitled to raise him. The extent to which Coleridge respected the legitimacy of such social barriers is evident from his reaction to the story of "the Beauty of Buttermere" in the *Morning Post*,

October-November 1802, where he bases the worthiness of Mary Robinson to marry the brother of a lord in part on rumors that she may be the illegitimate daughter of a gentleman (for the texts, see *CC* 3.1: 357–58, 374–76, 390–91, 403–16; for analysis, see "The Beauty of Buttermere as Fact and Romantic Symbol" in Reiman, *Romantic Texts* 216–47).

Coleridge himself, grandson of a foundling, might have fantasized a true Freudian "family romance" in which he was really of noble descent. Clearly, he accepted the social mode in which status was bequeathed by someone higher in the chain of social being, an attitude that was natural to the son of a clergyman-teacher whose family had for three generations been patronized by local squires and that was so ingrained in his character and so clear in his writings as to provide a viable point of entry into the psychology of much of his poetry and prose. Once the teacher has outlined these parameters, brief student reports on one excerpt or more from his social and political prose or on special topics pursued through the excellent indexes to relevant volumes of the *Collected Coleridge* (kept available on a course reserve shelf) could help students encounter the key issues of Coleridge's times that form one staple of his writings from 1795 through 1830.

Coleridge's lectures delivered in 1795 at Bristol, his most "radical" publications, already reflect his recognition of a de facto social hierarchy and his unwillingness to subvert it. In the "Introductory Address" to *Conciones ad Populum,* Coleridge—in keeping with the elitist attitude reflected in its learned Latin title and the Greek and Latin epigraphs to its two lectures— recognizes the distance between the educated classes and the common people:

> Society as at present constituted does not resemble a chain that ascends in a continuity of Links.—There are three ranks possessing an inter-course with each other: these are well comprised in the superscription of a Perfumer's advertisement, which I lately saw—"the Nobility, Gentry, and People of Dress." But alas! between the Parlour and the Kitchen, the Tap and the Coffee-Room—there is a gulph that may not be passed. He would appear to me to have adopted the best as well as the most benevolent mode of diffusing Truth, who uniting the zeal of the Methodist with the views of the Philosopher, should be *personally* among the Poor, and teach them their *Duties* in order that he may render them susceptible of their *Rights.*

Taking aim at Godwin's ideal of perfectibility and his dream of universal disinterestedness, Coleridge continues:

> Yet by what means can the lower Classes be made to learn their Duties, and urged to practise them? . . . In that barbarous tumult of inimical Interests, which the present state of Society exhibits, *Religion* appears

to offer the only means universally *efficient*. The perfectness of future Men is indeed a benevolent tenet, and may operate on a few Visionaries, whose studious habits supply them with employment, and seclude them from temptation. But a distant prospect, which we are never to reach, will seldom quicken our footsteps, however lovely it may appear; and a Blessing, which not ourselves but *posterity* are destined to enjoy, will scarcely influence the actions of *any*—still less of the ignorant, the prejudiced, and the selfish.

(*CC* 1: 43–44)

In the same manner, Coleridge begins "On the Present War"—the second part of *Conciones ad Populum*—with a denial that he is attempting to rouse the common people: "We should be bold in the avowal of *political* Truth among only those whose minds are susceptible of reasoning: and never to the multitude, who ignorant and needy must necessarily act from the impulse of inflamed Passions" (*CC* 1: 51). Even if he disclaims rabble-rousing partly to forestall governmental persecution, his ingrained attitude is clear from his spontaneous quips to silence hecklers. When asked why, if he were so public-spirited, he charged admission to his lectures, Coleridge replied, "For a reason which I am sorry in the present instance has not been quite successful—to keep out blackguards" (*CC* 1: xxxi). When we analyze the early lectures closely, we find that Coleridge's chief complaints are directed not against the hereditary aristocracy and gentry but at the rich among the middle classes who wish to tear down the old order without allowing the poor to benefit from the change. These he characterizes as the "third class of the friends of Freedom" who

pursue the interests of Freedom steadily, but with narrow and self-centered views: they anticipate with exultation the abolition of privileged orders. . . . Whatever is above them they are most willing to drag down; but every proposed alteration, that would elevate the ranks of our poorer brethren, they regard with suspicious jealousy, as the dreams of the visionary; as if there were any thing in the superiority of Lord to Gentleman, so mortifying in the barrier, so fatal to happiness in the consequences, as the more real distinction of master and servant, of rich man and of poor. Wherein am I made worse by my ennobled neighbour? Do the childish titles of Aristocracy detract from my domestic comforts, or prevent my intellectual acquisitions? But those institutions of Society which should condemn me to the necessity of twelve hours daily toil, would make me a *soul* slave, and sink the *rational* being in the mere animal.

(*CC* 1: 39–40)

Much of the "Introductory Address" of *Conciones ad Populum* reappears in the revised version of *The Friend* (1818; *CC* 4.1: 326–38), and Coleridge expresses similar attitudes throughout his mature prose. Not only does he oppose "the abolition of the privileged orders," but he directs his own efforts as a writer to reaching them, so that they in turn can influence the lower orders of society. In his political journalism in the *Morning Post* (1798–1803) and the *Courier* (1804–05, 1809–18), gathered in the *Collected Coleridge* 3, his social philosophy is mirrored in his comments on daily political events in postrevolutionary and Napoleonic France. On 14 December 1808, Coleridge in a letter to Humphry Davy contrasts his forthcoming periodical the *Friend* with William Cobbett's more widely circulated *Political Register*. "I do not write in this work for the *Multitude*; but for those, who by Rank, or Fortune, or official Situation, or Talents and Habits of Reflection, are to *influence* the Multitude" (*CL* 3: 143); and Barbara Rooke's detailed analysis of the subscribers to the *Friend* (1809–10) shows that Coleridge had found the influential audience he sought, for those subscribers included not only leading publishers, writers, and intellectuals in Edinburgh, London, and other major centers but also nobles, bishops, and heads of colleges, as well as leading physicians, lawyers, bankers, and industrialists (many in these latter groups being Quakers, who naturally liked the periodical's name).

Coleridge himself selected his audience partly by his liberal use of the classical languages and learned allusions. The very titles of *Conciones ad Populum* and *Biographia Literaria* proclaim that they are addressed to those who have the advantage of a Latin grammar-school education. *The Statesman's Manual*—the first of Coleridge's two "Lay Sermons" of 1816–17—states at the end of its long subtitle that it is "Addressed to the Higher Classes of Society" (although, Coleridge writes to George Frere in December 1816, he directed that it be labeled as "addressed to the Learned and Reflecting of all Ranks and Professions, especially among the Higher Class" [*CL* 4: 695]), while *A Lay Sermon* (1817) is said on the title page to be "Addressed to the Higher and Middle Classes, on the Existing Distresses and Discontents." Yet however unsanguine Coleridge might be about the capacity of the working classes to understand his diffuse rhetoric and esoteric learning, he does not believe in trying to keep them in the dark. Rather, he welcomes an age of greater education for all. As he writes in *The Statesman's Manual*, one error is

> to think, that as the Peace of Nations has been disturbed by the diffusion of a false light, it may be reestablished by excluding the people from all knowledge and all prospect of amelioration. O! never, never! . . . The Powers, that awaken and foster the spirit of curiosity, are to be found in every village: Books are in every hovel. . . . Here as in so

many other cases, the inconveniences that have arisen from a thing's having become too general, are best removed by making it universal.
(*CC* 6: 39–40)

Until improved education can bridge the gulf between the enlightened and the benighted classes, Coleridge urges Britain's leaders to govern under the just idea of the traditional English common law and do their Christian duty by protecting and guiding the less fortunate. Thus the first subtitle to *The Statesman's Manual* reads: *The Bible the Best Guide to Political Skill and Foresight.* In that work, he asserts that it is "a moral duty for such as possess the opportunities of books, leisure and education" to study the history of the past in the Bible, "the records of which are as much distinguished from all other history by their especial claims to divine authority, as the facts themselves were from all other facts by especial manifestation of divine interference" (*CC* 6: 9).

III

During the agitation for political reform and Catholic Emancipation in the 1820s, Coleridge developed his ideas on the place of the Anglican Established Church in English civil polity. The result was his treatise *On the Constitution of the Church and State* (1830), now available both in *Collected Coleridge* and in an Everyman edition edited by John Barrell. As Barrell notes in his introduction, Coleridge's final book brings together "almost all his varied interests—in political theory, theology, education, and historiography" and is,

> with Burke's *Reflections on the Revolution in France*, one of the few classic works of conservative thought in English, and one which unites two remarkable traditions of political theory: that of Hooker and such early seventeenth-century eulogists of English Common Law as Sir Edward Coke and Sir John Davies, and that of the Romantic conservatism of Herder and his followers in Germany.

> (viii)

Teachers and students turning to this "classic . . . of conservative thought" will soon discover, however, that the "conservatism" or "Toryism" that Coleridge represents has little affinity for twentieth-century American conservatism or British Toryism. In Coleridge's era, the "liberals" and "radicals" were the financial and commercial interests, influenced by the secular, laissez-faire political and economic theories of Adam Smith, Thomas Robert Malthus, and David Ricardo and seconded by the value system of Benthamite Utilitarians. Coleridge, on the contrary, believed that a national interest of all the people had priority over the rights of private ownership of property, and he advocated a government-supported "clerisy" to maintain traditional humanistic learning and values against the radical proposals to make education secular and technical. After utilitarian interests came to power in both the British and American educational and governmental bureaucracies, the two groups reversed their stand on the value of governmental interference in private lives. Most "conservatives" today on both sides of the Atlantic would have little sympathy with Coleridge's ideal that the clerisy—including both those in universities and primary and secondary school teachers and parish clergymen scattered throughout the nation—form a third estate, mediating between the interests of conservative "permanence" represented in Coleridge's day by the landed interests and "the mercantile, the manufacturing, the distributive, and the professional" classes that Coleridge identified as the groups favoring progress and individuality.

Coleridge believed that the two houses of Parliament represented both landed and commercial-professional interests (with the rural members of the Commons forming a tertium quid between the interests of the House of Lords and the urbanized part of the Commons) and that the greater part of the *private* wealth of the nation (the *"Propriety"*) was also divided among those represented by the forces controlling Parliament. He saw the need for the clerisy (whom he compares with the tribe of Levi in Hebrew history) to be supported by a portion of the nation's wealth set aside for that public purpose (the *"Nationality"*)—in England through the Established Church and the endowments of schools and colleges and (we can extrapolate) in the United States by moneys provided by the government or donated by individuals to tax-exempt institutions—which would enable those in the clerisy to preserve and disseminate the cultural heritage of the past, as well as to add to it through research, study, and reflection. Reducing the role of the king to that of a symbol of national unity and chief of the executive branch, Coleridge writes that the balanced political forces of permanence and change in the legislature, held together by the executive, "depend on a continuing and progressive civilization. But civilization is itself but a mixed good, if not far more a corrupting influence . . . where this civilization is not grounded in *cultivation*, in the harmonious development of those qualities and faculties that characterise our *humanity*. We must be men in order to be citizens" (*CC* 10: 42–43).

Early in this century in America, the chief enculturating institution roughly parallel to Coleridge's idea of a clerisy was the public educational system (before it fell into the hands of the utilitarians). Teachers unabashedly taught both natives and immigrants the language, history, and ideals of the nation (including its Judeo-Christian religious heritage), with a final emphasis on "the American dream," only the possessors of which were thought to participate fully in American society. In Coleridge's somewhat different social setting (in which, as Cobbett and other spokesmen for reform pointed out, some were taught to respond like automatons to their "betters"), Coleridge emphasized the more fundamental cultivation of *humanity*—the subject of Anya Taylor's *Coleridge's Defense of the Human*—qualities that, when possessed by an individual, enable him or her to function as a free, comprehending, and voluntary member of the society, rather than as an unwilling slave or uncomprehending beast.

IV

Coleridge's psychology of dependence, which helped to shape his social ideals, also emerges in both the subject matter and forms of his poems. The most notable characteristic of the implied speakers or chief protagonists in the poems is their voluntary passivity, signaled by a substitution of emotions for actions and by repeated appeals to others for help. (The latter characteristic both provides a rationale for some of Coleridge's ubiquitous plagiarisms and distinguishes Coleridgean protagonists from the almost equally passive protagonists of Scott's Waverley novels.) In many of Coleridge's best-known poems the speaker is a passive witness whose emotional response to some scene or vision preempts any action he or she might take (as in comparable poems by other Romantics). Not only does Coleridge's nostalgic "Sonnet: To the River Otter" (1793; *PW* 48) end with the retrogressive wish "Ah! that once more I were a careless Child!" but the anticipatory sonnet "Pantisocracy" (1794) also finds the emigrant speaker passively watching abstractions perform:

> I seek the cottag'd dell
> Where virtue calm with careless step may stray,
> And dancing to the moonlight roundelay,
> The wizard Passions weave an holy spell.
> Eyes that have ach'd with Sorrow! Ye shall weep
> Tears of doubt-mingled joy. . . .
>
> (*PW* 69)

"The Eolian Harp" (1795) is, naturally, filled with minor images of passivity that reinforce the title trope: "many idle flitting phantasies, / Traverse my indolent and passive brain" (*PW* 101–02), but the speaker's major "action" even in Coleridge's ostensibly active companion poem "Reflections on Having Left a Place of Retirement" (1795) is to climb a hill to gaze out on a natural panorama and then to declare, in one of the *least* passive passages in Coleridge's poetry, "I therefore *go*, and *join* head, heart, and hand, / Active and firm, to fight the bloodless fight / Of Science, Freedom, and the

Truth in Christ" (*PW* 107–08; italics added). (To demonstrate how relatively passive even these lines are, the teacher need only compare them with Blake's comparable vow in the preface to *Milton*: "I will not cease from Mental Fight, / Nor shall my Sword sleep in my hand: / Till we have built Jerusalem, / In Englands green & pleasant Land.") In Coleridge's other Conversation poems, the speakers' chief actions are feeling, wishing, and praying.

Turning to Coleridge's three masterpieces, *The Rime of the Ancient Mariner*, *Christabel*, and "Kubla Khan," we find that in the last of these, Kubla (perhaps figuring the human imagination) "did decree" a pleasure dome and a park "with walls and towers was girdled round" (by whom?). All the rest of the action results from the river (which "ran"), forcing a fountain, and so on. The speaker then, totally passive and receptive, recalls a vision he once saw and wishes but is unable to "revive" it within himself; were he able to do so, he would find such delight as to appear weird to other people, who would fear and ostracize him. "Kubla Khan" is complete in both form, as demonstrated brilliantly by Alan C. Purves, and meaning, as S. K. Heninger, Jr., first convinced me. Coleridge's fear that the poem reveals too much about his psyche explains why (as Heninger suggests) he pretended that it was a meaningless fragment. One of those revelations is of Coleridge's repressed sexuality—figured as subterranean upwellings from a "deep romantic chasm," perhaps "haunted / By woman wailing for her demon-lover!" (*PW* 297)—a conscious repression now evident from numerous entries in Coleridge's *Notebooks*. Another revelation is how much Coleridge feared separation from others, a fear made meaningful by his account of his family history and his early years, particularly his role as the favorite of his father (who died suddenly) and his sense of alienation from his mother, who (he felt) favored his next older brother, Francis. "Kubla Khan" and the Conversation poems reflect Coleridge's anxieties that generated the need for his social philosophy, in which the religious guardians of the clerisy replicated his father's role in Coleridge's early life, mediating between the landed "Permanence" of his Devonshire childhood and the "Progressive" elements of the middle-class children with whom he grew up at Christ's Hospital in London.

Christabel presents an archetypal Coleridgean situation, in which a passive young woman surrenders her will to an older one and where even Geraldine seems relatively passive, partially controlled by supernatural forces beyond her power (as when Christabel must help her enter the castle). In the relationship between Christabel and Geraldine in part 1 and that developing between Sir Leoline and Geraldine in part 2, the poet both hints at and represses strong sexual components, which are related to death in the prefiguring story of the death of Christabel's mother during childbirth and underscored by the sex-driven separation that threatens Christabel again when she becomes aware of her father's attraction to Geraldine. The ideal of feudal chivalric order, earlier disrupted by the quarrel between Sir Leoline and Sir Roland de Vaux, has more recently been shattered by the knights who have (allegedly) raped Geraldine. Still, loyal Bard Bracy may represent an incipient power of humanity and traditional values—the poetic local representative of the clerisy—who can help return the community to its proper order.

The Rime of the Ancient Mariner does not stress sexuality; rather, as I have argued (*Intervals* 114–17, 150), it exhibits Coleridge's existential angst and guilt in one of their earliest embodiments—his rivalry with his brother Francis, which Coleridge connected both with their father's death (on the night he returned from putting Francis on a ship bound for India) and with Francis's early death in India a few years later. After killing the albatross (an action suggested by Wordsworth), the Mariner "does not act, but is continually acted upon" (Wordsworth, note in *Lyrical Ballads*, 2nd ed., 1800, 1: 214). The "guardian angels" that Coleridge as a boy had imagined standing at the four corners of his bed, protecting him from "armies of ugly things," appear in the *Ancient Mariner* as the Polar Spirits that both exact penalties from the sinful wanderer and protect him from the early death suffered by his brother sailors. These spirits also represent the religiously sanctified hierarchical society that protected Coleridge from the results of his own weaknesses, as do also the Hermit who rows out to meet and shrive the Mariner on his return and the "goodly kirk" that accepts him as part of its community of prayer.

V

To sum up: Coleridge extolled a neofeudal ideal of a hierarchical society in which the authority of Christian religious principles and the awareness of mutual interdependence—a balance characteristic of Ottery St. Mary and Christ's Hospital—curb the natural selfishness of individuals and the self-aggrandizing tendencies of classes and institutions.[1] Behind his emotional commitment to this perspective was his experience as the youngest son in a large family that had received support from the local gentry for three generations.

Coleridge's social thought remains relevant because the basic structures of Western society have not changed since his time, though different social elements now wield power within them. Modern social debates still pit a Judeo-Christian humanism, representing traditional Western moral and so-cial values, against a "scientific," or mathematically calculated, view of so-ciety based on polls and statistical averages, deriving ultimately from Bentham's "hedonic calculus." Coleridge's ideals center on the full development, within a stable social matrix, of persons who accept both moral freedom and its concomitant responsibility, who value the intellectual and material inheritance from the past, and who feel morally obligated to transmit to posterity sane moral values, the rich cultural heritage, and a safe and healthy environment.

NOTE

[1]Although Erdman has not yet published his anthology of Coleridge's political prose, teachers raising the social issues will find the most useful primary texts in Heather Jackson's Oxford Authors anthology, the paperback edition of the *Collected Coleridge* text of *Biographia*, and Barrell's edition of *On the Constitution of the Church and State*. Gettmann, Barfield, Calleo, Crawford, Prickett, Preyer, and Woodring have written books helpful to students analyzing Coleridge's social thought.

TEACHING THE PROSE AND LITERARY CRITICISM

On Tracking Coleridge: The Student as Sleuth

Laurence S. Lockridge

Attempting to produce a large yield of devotees of Coleridge's prose among today's undergraduate students is work without hope. As Huck Finn says of *Pilgrim's Progress*, "The statements was interesting, but tough." Even seasoned graduate students in Romantics often express little inclination to make their way through *The Friend* and *Aids to Reflection*. We should not delude ourselves about the pleasures of these texts in the collective mind of those not tolerant of labyrinthine hypotaxis, linguistic play, encyclopedic allusiveness, metaphysical speculativeness, and discontinuous exposition. Rather than assign large hunks of Coleridge's prose to whole classrooms—with the inevitable mutinous grumbling—I assign the usual anthology pieces, but I attempt to identify a smaller group of students who might be inclined to embark on an adventure of the soul amid what appears at first glance to be literary flotsam and jetsam.

In my essay "Explaining Coleridge's Explanation," addressed to critics and scholars doing basic research in the field, I discuss the opportunities in three major approaches to Coleridge—designated, after a suggestion by Richard Haven (7–8), as genetic, historical, and structural. Here I draw some corollaries on how Coleridge's prose might be taught to advanced undergraduates, with the understanding that, at whatever stage we engage with him, we all remain *students* of Coleridge. Many have drowned in that honied head, and it may even be a teacher's responsibility to raise a cautionary flag to a student who is undertaking, say, a senior thesis on Coleridge and Hegel without the necessary perambulatory gear.

Recent discussions of Coleridge—for instance, Jerome Christensen's *Coleridge's Blessed Machine of Language* and Jean-Pierre Mileur's *Vision and Revision: Coleridge's Art of Immanence*—cast good light on how Coleridge is always writing as commentator, positioning himself in the margins of innumerable texts, from the Bible to his own, with a rich intertextual and hermeneutical play of mind. Certainly these discussions teach ways of reading him, whether or not we read *Biographia Literaria* from cover to cover. But I think that with the pragmatics of the classroom in mind—syllabi, paper topics, tangible classroom discussion, and the effort to get a few students truly interested in Coleridge's prose—a somewhat different approach is needed. The one I suggest here is based on the pleasures of sleuthing.

The current emphasis on how a writer writes should not always overshadow what a writer says. Coleridge's prose invites interpretive structuring of the subdivisions of an encyclopedic mind—Coleridge on logic, learning, ethics, or language; on politics, literary theory, natural philosophy, or psychology; on history, prosody, exegesis, the Enlightenment, or Shakespeare. Most critics who write monographs on Coleridge first round up—with good reason—the pertinent texts on such and such a topic. One might object that we should read an author "whole" and that we should not pass along Hazlitt's notion that Coleridge's is a "tangential" mind. But one could also argue that discontinuous exposition justifies discontinuous reading. A proven discovery procedure is to read Coleridge with an eye to an interest or hunch, or what he calls an "initiative." When the monographs and papers on selected topics are all in, we can then await some grand synthesis. Meantime, beyond the editing of primary texts, the major task confronting Coleridge studies is to glean and structure his commentary, to determine what he thought on a variety of matters and why.

The teaching of Coleridge can foster this same kind of inquiry. Instructors can provide assistance to new students of Coleridge in two ways: they can set a list of relatively fresh topics, and they can offer rather precise bibliographical assistance from the beginning. On the first point, one can observe that even the critical literature reflects an unnecessary recycling of already tired topics—unnecessary in view of the new texts that editors are making available, not to mention the wealth of new critical approaches. Instead of generating yet another exploration of primary and secondary imagination in "Kubla Khan," lesbianism in *Christabel*, and original sin in *Ancient Mariner*—where we watch students rediscover the wheel while our own eyes glaze over—why not presume to suggest some topics that might advance critical discussion? Identifying such areas of inquiry for students is routinely expected of instructors in the sciences. One can inform the student that there is rich commentary tucked away in the *Notebooks, Letters,* and *Marginalia,* as well as in often ignored texts such as *The Friend* and *Essays on His Times.* If the topic is thematic, the student should be prepared, with regard to those texts now lacking a subject index, to sleuth through them. For an undergraduate colloquium on Coleridge and Wordsworth, I prepared an optional bibliography with rather copious references to the *Notebooks* and *Letters* on various topics—Coleridge as psychologist, as linguist, as literary theorist, as moralist, as religious thinker, as social critic, and so forth. This bibliography helped a small number of students get investigations under way on a variety of topics dealing with Coleridge's prose and led them into some relatively uncharted texts. Simply by calling attention to a previously overlooked or underdiscussed text, one may convey to students that they can quickly find themselves on the perimeter of critical exploration.

The three interpretive categories—genetic, historical, and structural—cut across particular topics and divisions by subject matter. In the genetic approach, critics view writing as in part a biographical or psychological resultant. They may seek links between the Coleridgean situation and Coleridgean ideas. Or they may focus on Coleridge's own treatment of origins —his psychogenetic explorations of literature, the passions, the act of thinking, disease, and so on. We are now at a stage in the profession when the author can be invited back to the text, even though we may no longer speak of an originating consciousness still present somewhere behind it. The author may now be only the textual representation of an authorial function, but for most of us the author is at least more than a name function at the head of the text. Coleridge has left a large number of texts permeated with the language of self-awareness, of self-positioning relative to the reader, of outright autobiographical narration. These texts give the impression that it is *he* who is thinking in the very act of writing. His prose as well as his poetry has the circumstances of composition and his embattled self-concept as writer deeply inscribed therein. Such writings are among his most vivid and inventive. That students respond strongly to biographical discussion of Coleridge is not some critical naïveté on their part; rather, such discussion helps bring to light a narrative causality that links one text with another and that provides a context for seemingly disparate or contradictory texts. As I discovered in Coleridge's reflections on duty, to anchor a set of miscellaneous texts in the narrative contexts of his life can make sense of a seeming muddle; ideas become dramatic when they are lived, when they are extensions of a life beset, in this case, by anguish and contradiction. Students are quick to note that *Ancient Mariner* proves prophetic of Coleridge's life in many ways. But he lives his ideas (or self-consciously fails to live up to them) as well as his poems.

In my colloquium on Coleridge and Wordsworth, following discussions given over mainly to the poetry, I introduced the topic "Coleridge on Coleridge." In addition to recommending the autobiographical letters to Thomas Poole and chapter 1 of *Biographia Literaria*, I suggested that some students read selections from the *Notebooks* and *Letters*, for which I supplied a fairly extensive list of references. I also recommended accounts of Coleridge by his contemporaries—Wordsworth (as seen in *The Prelude*), De Quincey, Lamb, Hazlitt, and Carlyle—as well as essays by F. J. A. Hort, John Stuart Mill, and Pater. Yes, I actually recommended that interested students do some work in the library! One student discussed "Coleridge as psychologist," dealing with Coleridge's psychogenetic analysis of personality, language, and education. This grounding in biography, autobiography, and psychogenetic inquiry encouraged a few students—arrested by the spectacle of struggle in a brilliant cultural figure who comes to life, as it were, in the homey details of letters and notebooks—to undertake additional readings in critical theory, ethics, politics, and religion.

By "historical" interpretation I refer here to placing Coleridge in intellectual history, whether with regard to influences on him, his overt commentary on other intellectual figures, or his influence on others. The pertinent question heard most often by teachers of Coleridge concerns plagiarism: students ask whether one standard operates for members of the literary pantheon and another for themselves. Why can Coleridge be exonerated of plagiarism, as some Coleridge critics still believe he can be, where they would simply fail the course? Had *Biographia Literaria* been submitted as a doctoral dissertation, would not the degree have been denied on discovery of the Schellingian material in chapter 12? My answer to such questions is yes—Coleridge would fail our undergraduate courses and even be dismissed from school (it would not be the first time he would have had to leave off a course of study); and yes, the PhD would be denied, with the Judicial Committee's lament that someone so brilliant should have erred so needlessly. It is doubtful that such a committee would entertain briefs that what appeared to be plagiarism was actually a mosaic of intense intellectual semiosis, or perhaps the symptomatology of some dark metaphysical pathology. Rather than enter the ranks of those defending Coleridge, I present him as an extraordinary cultural figure who is of great intrinsic interest even because instructively flawed and invite students to ponder the implications of this phenomenon in his life and work. Whether they ultimately decide that "plagiarism," with its moral opprobrium, is the apt term is up to them.

Beyond this, in keeping with the idea that the instructor should help point the way through the bibliographical morass, I think we should assign those texts or portions of texts that are clearly not plagiarized. The genetic emphases just spoken of help here: Coleridge does not plagiarize the autobiographical letters to Poole or those vivid ruminations through the *Notebooks* about consciousness where he circles the direct matter of his own observation in time and space. Only occasionally can direct commentary on another's text, as in the emerging *Marginalia*, raise the question of plagiarism (as, of course, it was raised in the matter of his Hamlet interpretation). Even if one grants that many passages in the familiar texts Coleridge published in his lifetime were derived from unacknowledged German sources, one finds the corpus shrinking in this respect and expanding in others, as more and more texts in which his creative mind has not flagged become available. Though to proclaim that such and such a text is not lifted may involve a degree of question begging, the instructor should attempt to point the way to those texts where Coleridge is alive and well.

Students may realistically decide they are lacking the requisite learning to write on most aspects of Coleridge's prose with regard to issues in intellectual history. But his own pedagogy may triumph here. One can become relatively learned *by reading* Coleridge. If we do not turn to him for a "reliable" account of etymology or medieval philosophy or biology or Kant, we at least learn what the names, terms, and issues are and how one strong mind has confronted them. To study Coleridge is to unsettle facile generalizations concerning intellectual history, an important mission of any teacher in the humanities.

Whatever the contradictions and changes of mind in Coleridge's development, those who have gathered Coleridgean texts and who have thought their way through them usually discover a fair degree of coherence. What I here term "structural" criticism concerns structuring what Coleridge left without overt structure. It entails bringing together scattered texts that have one or another affinity. Chronological ordering—important as it is in many aspects of Coleridge studies—may prove secondary for the structural critic, who can profitably see texts written years apart as if they were turns in a running dialogue. More than consistency in doctrine, one is likely to find the continuity of an internal dialogue. But whatever one finds, a common experience of working with Coleridge is that on his own terms he begins to make sense. Students can be assured that they will come to see some method in his madness if they persist in their labors. With the rest of us, students should be encouraged to withhold judgment of "what Coleridge thought" until the process of gathering the relevant texts has been completed.

The undergraduate instructor of Coleridge should assume, therefore, a greater than usual role in pointing out directions—suggesting fresh topics for investigation and providing precise bibliographical information for interested students, who might otherwise be prematurely discouraged by discontinuous exposition, the lack of subject indexes in some major texts, the qualitative unevenness of Coleridge's writings, and the plagiarism issue. For distinguished undergraduates, these topics may eventually lead to senior theses. Having given this initial counsel, the instructor would of course encourage students to continue the sleuthing on their own, with the assurance that Coleridge will frequently pick up the thread of his own thought somewhere or other. He asks us to track him, if we can.

Appendix

The following is a list of bibliographical references, restricted here to Coleridge's *Notebooks* (CN) and *Collected Letters* (CL), taken from my syllabus for an undergraduate colloquium on Coleridge. These references would be supplemented by texts that already have subject indexes (as in the *Collected Coleridge*) or whose titles indicate their relevance to a particular topic. Kathleen Coburn's anthology *Inquiring Spirit* is structured by similar topics and could supplement these references, which are only a sampling.

Ancient Mariner: CN 2: 1993–2099

Christabel: CN 2: 2144; CN 3: 3720; CL 1: 545, 631–32; CL 4: 600–04

"Kubla Khan": Coleridge's dreams: CN 1: 848, 1250, 1649, 1726, 1998, 2055; CN 2: 2441, 2468, 2539; CN 3: 3912, 4046. His opium addiction: CL 1: 249–51; CL 2: 662–63, 730–33, 884, 1028–29; CL 3: 125–28, 476–77, 489–92, 502, 511; CL 4: 633–34; CL 6: 894–95, 898–99, 936; CN 2: 2189, 2990, 3078; CN 3: 3361, 3398

Coleridge on Coleridge: autobiographical letters to Thomas Poole: CL 1: 302–03, 310–12, 346–48, 352–55, 387–89. CL 1: 24–29, 49–52, 61–68, 125, 129–31, 145, 160, 207–10, 235–37, 259–60, 330–31, 403–05, 420, 459–60, 478–81, 490–91; CL 2: 713–15, 767, 782–84, 887–88, 928–30, 959, 1011, 1012–13; CL 3: 19–22, 28–32, 48–49, 51–53, 63–64, 130–31, 296–97, 394–96, 397–402, 403–08, 489–90, 498–99; CL 4: 626–27, 948, 966–71; CL 5: 22–31, 79–81, 249–52; CL 6: 713–15, 729–30, 769–70, 962–63, 973–74, 985–87, 989–90; CN 1: 161, 174, 834, 1248, 1463, 1517, 1577, 1597, 1601, 1609, 1644, 1646, 1651, 1669, 1681; CN 2: 2064(9), 2367, 2368, 2398, 2441, 2453, 2486, 2517, 2527, 2623, 2647, 2703, 2704, 2726, 2860, 2861, 2866, 2944, 2975, 2998, 3045, 3148, 3215; CN 3: 3232, 3303, 3304, 3324, 3359, 3442, 3767, 3881, 3996, 3998, 3999, 4006, 4082, 4166, 4243, 4400

The literary critic: CN 1: 276; CN 2: 2407, 2516, 2598, 2728, 2826; CN 3: 3242, 3246, 3247, 3449, 3823, 3952, 3965, 3970, 4034, 4035, 4096, 4190, 4313; CL 1: 116, 133–38, 277–81, 290–92, 293–94, 320–21, 325, 441–45, 450–53, 584; CL 2: 713–15, 809–12, 863–64, 1080–83; CL 3: 67–68, 290–96; CL 4: 572–76, 833–34, 835–38; CL 5: 33–36, 93–95, 353–54; CL 6: 849–50

The critical theorist: CN 1: 383, 632, 1505, 1554, 2011, 2086 [fol. 40ᵛ]; CN 2: 2274, 2355, 2599; CN 3: 3311, 3325, 3328, 3573, 3584, 3611, 3615, 3744, 3827, 4066, 4176, 4232, 4250, 4397, 4503; CL 1: 557; CL 2: 830–31; CL 3: 352, 355–61; CL 5: 228, 496–97; CL 6: 811–13

Coleridge on language: CN 1: 866, 957, 1387, 1835; CN 2: 1848, 2431, 2784, 3027, 3217; CN 3: 3504, 3549, 3789, 3954, 4237, 4247, 4309; CL 1: 625–26; CL 6: 816–18

The psychologist: CN 1: 886, 894, 902, 921, 923, 924, 925, 1050, 1078, 1356, 1388,

1421, 1637, 1668, 1770, 1771, 1822, 1826, 1827, 2018; *CN* 2: 2357, 2399, 2414, 2458; *CN* 3: 3280, 3301, 3322, 3372, 3474, 3547, 3708, 3994, 4036, 4059, 4068, 4151, 4409, 4410; *CL* 1: 53–54; *CL* 2: 832, 1046; *CL* 3: 91–92, 529–30; *CL* 6: 933–34

The educator: *CN* 1: 1400; *CN* 2: 3023; *CN* 3: 3782, 3950; *CL* 1: 361; *CL* 2: 673; *CL* 3: 1–3, 9–11; *CL* 5: 97–98, 113–15, 219–21, 229–33, 296–98, 515–18; *CL* 6: 628–35, 797

The moralist: **Judgment:** *CN* 1: 74, 624, 1605, 1606, 1816; *CN* 2: 2471, 2830; *CN* 3: 3419, 3991; *CL* 2: 1014. **Moral agency:** *CN* 1: 1072, 1602; *CN* 2: 2343, 2361; *CN* 3: 4012; *CL* 1: 470–71; *CL* 3: 477, 489; *CL* 4: 553. **Will and evil:** *CN* 2: 2382, 2468; *CL* 3: 463; *CL* 5: 239. **Nature, the fall, sexuality:** *CN* 2: 706, 2398, 2495, 2543; *CN* 3: 3404, 4169; *CL* 1: 213. **Principles:** *CN* 2: 2627; *CN* 3: 3293, 3774; *CL* 1: 163–73. **Persecution:** *CL* 1: 364–67; *CL* 3: 316; *CL* 5: 177–78, 182; *CN* 1: 1815. **Duty and inclination:** *CN* 1: 1705, 1710, 1833; *CN* 2: 2398, 2531, 2537, 3231; *CL* 1: 132, 145, 149; *CL* 2: 768; *CL* 3: 489; *CL* 4: 791–92. **The self:** *CN* 1: 979; *CN* 2: 2000, 2509; *CN* 3: 3593; *CL* 5: 228–33, 515–18; *CL* 6: 551. **Love:** *CN* 1: 985; *CN* 2: 3146, 3148; *CN* 3: 3514, 3989; *CL* 3: 303–05. **Critique of British ethics:** *CN* 1: 1609; *CN* 2: 2058; *CN* 3: 3556, 3558, 3938, 4292, 4422

The political theorist: *CL* 1: 83–94, 97–100, 103–04, 121–23, 125–28, 163–73, 198–200, 212–216, 306–07; *CL* 2: 719–21, 998–1003; *CL* 3: 537–38; *CN* 3: 3835, 3845, 3850

The philosopher: *CN* 1: 556, 573, 626, 1313, 1758, 1759; *CN* 2: 2026, 2546, 3156, 3158, 3159; *CN* 3: 3295, 3320, 3517, 3575, 3587, 3588, 3592, 3605, 3628, 3632, 3670, 3756, 3758, 3768, 3824, 3825, 3869, 3935, 3962, 4012, 4057, 4058, 4060, 4109, 4251, 4358, 4408, 4445, 4449; *CL* 1: 538; *CL* 2: 670–703, 947–49; *CL* 3: 35; *CL* 4: 548–49, 589–90, 847–48; *CL* 5: 13–15, 399–400, 421–22; *CL* 6: 593–601

The theologian: *CN* 1: 129, 1247, 1619, 1622, 1680; *CN* 2: 2151, 2448, 2540, 2744; *CN* 3: 3256, 3510, 3550, 3581, 3701, 3743, 3765, 3787, 3817, 3820, 3847, 3857, 3871, 3872, 3885, 3888, 3889, 3892, 3894, 3973, 4005, 4007, 4047, 4088, 4173, 4341, 4401; *CL* 1: 255–56, 624–25; *CL* 2: 820–24, 1188–90, 1193–99; *CL* 3: 152–54, 481–86; *CL* 4: 676–77; *CL* 5 and 6 passim

Linguistic Approaches to Teaching Coleridge

James C. McKusick

Coleridge's career as an intellectual figure spans several decades and encompasses major works in several discrete fields, including poetry, criticism, philosophy, and theology. An advanced undergraduate course on Coleridge must also come to grips with his more personal and private writings—his letters, marginalia, fragmentary essays, and most notably his lifetime production of bescribbled "fly-catchers." The incredible variety of Coleridge's achievement and the incomplete or provisional state of most of his writings pose an enormous problem for teachers of his work. In my own courses on Coleridge, I often find myself grappling with the difficulty of creating a synthesis, of seeing the big picture in his scattered and fragmentary work. In immediate practical terms, my students are eager to know how the *Biographia* relates to the *Lyrical Ballads*; how the Conversation poems relate to the *Notebooks*; how the early political writings relate to *The Friend*; and whether Coleridge's writings amount to more than just a hodgepodge of incommensurable parts.

At the same time, I find myself resisting the factitious unity imposed on Coleridge's writings by scholars in the New Critical tradition, especially by those who regard his prose works as a belated commentary on the *Lyrical Ballads* and who see the doctrine of secondary imagination as his essential contribution to Romantic aesthetics. This view of Coleridge, most persuasively expressed in Robert Penn Warren's classic essay on *Ancient Mariner*, has many advocates among my students, many of whom seem to have been indoctrinated by the demotic version of Romantic symbolism still ubiquitous in undergraduate survey courses, even among teachers who claim allegiance to more advanced theoretical views. It is all too easy to fall back on New Critical methods of close reading, and on the aesthetic formalism they entail, in classroom discussions of Romantic poetry.

How can we go beyond formalism in our teaching of Coleridge? Clearly our students must learn to situate his individual works within the larger historical context of their production. One of the most important and least understood historical determinants of Coleridge's textual practice is the new conception of language that emerged in England during the Romantic period. Coleridge himself was largely responsible for promulgating this fundamental shift in linguistic understanding, most overtly in such works as *Lyrical Ballads* and the *Biographia*, but also in a number of works that are less familiar to our students. In teaching Coleridge, I encourage my students to reexamine all his writings from the perspective of his lifelong engagement with linguistic theory. Coleridge's articulation of a distinctively Romantic conception of language, gradually formulated and modified throughout his career, provides a unifying principle in his poetry, criticism, and philosophy.

Several useful strategies have emerged from my experience in teaching

Coleridge's poetry and prose from this perspective. I have found that the *Notebooks* furnish the best introduction to Coleridge's linguistic practice. At the beginning of my advanced undergraduate course on Coleridge, I assign the entire first volume of the *Notebooks*, with the understanding that it should be read with an eye to its verbal texture, its odd juxtapositions and seminal conjunctions, and an ear for the many voices that ventriloquize in its scrappy transcriptions from other works. I encourage my students to focus on the moments when Coleridge examines the nature and origin of language, as, for example, in an entry (dating perhaps from the mid-1790s) that combines etymological speculation with observations of infant language: "Smile from subrisus. B and M both labials / hence Infants first utter a, Ba, pa, ma, milk" (*CN* 1: 4, corrected from Add. ms. 47496, fol. 1ᵛ, in British Library). What is the implied relation between etymology and the acquisition of language? Evidently both provide evidence concerning the ultimate origin of language; infants can tell us something about the *Ursprache*. Several later entries examine infant language from this point of view. Coleridge notes that "[c]hildren in making new Words always do it analogously" (1: 867), implying a general principle of analogy in the formation of language. Later he describes how the young Hartley Coleridge used stones to signify "fire" in a scene of aboriginal naming (1: 914). All these entries bear witness to Coleridge's fascination with infant language, regarded as a source of information about the prehistoric origin of language and, more generally, the origin of human consciousness. The careful study of these notebook passages adds a new linguistic dimension to the well-known Romantic topos of the wise infant and offers a more plausible justification for Coleridge's rather doting portrayal of Hartley in "The Nightingale" or Wordsworth's paean to the "blessed babe" in *The Prelude* (2.232).

Students are often curious to know just what is new and different about Coleridge's approach to the problem of linguistic origin. Coleridge is clearly in sympathy with the post-Lockean tradition of linguistic speculation in England and France, especially in the work of Berkeley, Monboddo, Condillac, and de Brosses; he also evinces some strong affinities with the major figures of the German Enlightenment, such as Lessing, Herder, Michaelis, and Humboldt. Students desiring a fuller discussion of the history of linguistic speculation in the Enlightenment and the Romantic period should be referred to two seminal works by Hans Aarsleff: *The Study of Language in England* and *From Locke to Saussure*. These works describe the enormous fascination exerted by the question of the origin of language: Did language arise from arbitrary signs (as Locke supposed), or were the first human words connected in some natural way with their referents? Coleridge addressed this question in a variety of ways throughout his career, and he evidently intended to write a treatise on the subject of linguistic origin. In a notebook entry of 1803 he indicates his plans to write a "philosophical Romance to explain the whole growth of Language" (*CN* 1: 1646). Although he never got around to writing this treatise, he was constantly gathering materials for it in his notebooks, which became a storehouse of information on etymology, language acquisition, and comparative linguistics.

The notebooks provide a significant historical and intellectual context for Coleridge's poetry, particularly for his revolutionary linguistic practice in the Conversation poems. I assign these poems in conjunction with the notebooks, in the hope that they will prove mutually illuminating. Here again, I encourage my students to focus on the verbal texture of these poems, to examine their abrupt shifts in tone and subject matter and their frequent use of quotation and allusion. Coleridge's theoretical understanding of language, as expressed in the notebooks and elsewhere, can furnish the basis for a detailed analysis of the phonetic, lexical, and syntactic features of these poems. Why are they called "Conversation" poems? Does the term imply that they are written in the everyday language of conversation? Or do we find deviations from ordinary usage? I entertain these questions in class discussion while bringing to bear a variety of stylistic concepts generated by our reading of the notebooks. In particular, I seek to establish a distinction between "ordinary language," a term that Coleridge often mentions with contempt (*CL* 2: 699), and "natural language," a term that meets with his highest approbation (*CC* 7.1: 22). The Conversation poems, in my view, clearly deviate from the norms of spoken discourse, especially in those elevated moments that verge upon the "lovely shapes and sounds intelligible / Of that eternal language, which thy God / Utters" ("Frost at Midnight" 59–61). This "eternal language" can only be regarded as "natural" by virtue of its immediacy to the feelings of the human heart and the objects of the natural world.

My teaching strategy at this point in the course is to air a number of conflicting views concerning the essential stylistic features of natural language. I find it instructive to require each student to bring a specimen of natural language to class. The student must be prepared to explain what is "natural" about it. Specimens tend to include various types of vernacular discourse, samples of literary language, and a few anomalous responses, such as non-English languages, animal noises, baby talk, and picture writing. All these responses raise typically Coleridgean questions about the relation of speech to writing, the propriety of slang and colloquial expressions, the origin of language, and the arbitrariness of the signifier.

Our classroom debate over the stylistic features of natural language establishes a theoretical context for our discussion of Coleridge's critique of Wordsworth's Preface to *Lyrical Ballads*. As I argue in *Coleridge's Philosophy of Language* (100–18), the entire controversy between Wordsworth and Coleridge arises from their very different conceptions of natural language. For Wordsworth, "natural language" is synonymous with "ordinary language" because only in everyday conversation can the referents of words be determined sufficiently to make communication possible. The process of communication, in his view, requires the presence of unchanging natural objects to provide objective standards of usage. For Coleridge, however, "the best part of human language, properly so called, is derived from reflection on the acts of the mind itself" (*CC* 7.2: 54). If there is any shared linguistic structure, in Coleridge's view, it will be formed through the process of education, by which the mind's innate faculties are "educed" and made available to conscious reflection. Only in this way can the "voluntary appropriation of fixed symbols to internal acts" (2: 54) become intelligible to readers of poetry. Ordinary conversation, being unreflective, is not particularly conducive to the communication of ideas. Coleridge regards the words of ordinary language as mere *"arbitrary marks* of thought, our smooth market-coin of intercourse with the image and superscription worn out by currency" (2: 122). Coleridge's predilection for individual forms of expression stands in strong opposition to Wordsworth's dream of a common language.

Coleridge's Mystery poems may be examined in the linguistic context established by the *Biographia* and the notebooks. In the *Biographia*, Coleridge claims that the poet should not simply copy "the sort and order of words which he hears in the market, wake, high-road, or plough-field" (*CC* 7.2: 81) but should exercise creative powers by coining new words or reviving ancient usages. The notebooks exemplify this radical linguistic doctrine in their odd textual juxtapositions and their wild deviations from ordinary English usage. *Ancient Mariner*, with its strange words and its intrusive, hypnotic narrator, may be regarded as an extension of this linguistic experiment. My students examine the version of this poem first published in *Lyrical Ballads* (1798), with its deliberately archaic diction and spelling. As John Livingston Lowes points out in *The Road to Xanadu* (296–310), this version of the poem is more than just a fake antique ballad on the model of Percy's *Reliques* and Chatterton's "Rowley" poems. Lowes demonstrates that Coleridge combines three fairly distinct types of archaic usage: first, the traditional ballad lexicon (*pheere, eldritch, beforne, I ween, sterte, een, countrée, withouten, cauld*); second, the diction of Chaucer and Spenser (*ne, uprist, I wist, yspread, yeven, n'old, eftsones, lavrock, jargoning, minstralsy*); and, third, seafaring terminology (*swound, weft, clifts, biscuit-worms, fire-flags*). All three types of archaic usage are severely curtailed in the 1800 version of the poem, perhaps in response to a reviewer in the *British Critic* (Oct. 1799) who denounced the poem's "antiquated words," citing *swound* and *weft* as flagrant examples of nonsensical diction. Coleridge omitted both these words in 1800, along with most of the other words listed above. In class, my students argue the merits and demerits of Coleridge's 1800 modernization and his later addition of a marginal gloss in *Sibylline Leaves* (1817). Lowes and a host of subsequent commentators have seen Coleridge's revision of *Ancient Mariner* as a definite improvement, and my students tend to accept this established opinion. I am inclined to agree instead with critics like William Empson who prefer the poem's original version, not for its consistent adherence to any single type of usage, but precisely for its multi-faceted syncretic quality, which bespeaks the author's desire to reassemble the surviving fragments of archaic language into an older, more natural mode of poetic discourse. The "natural" here is equated with the primeval origin of human consciousness and social values.

A similar criterion of linguistic naturalness seems to be at work in "Kubla Khan." The realm of the emperor is a world of beginnings, where Alph, the sacred river, bursts from a mysterious cleft in the rock, where walls and towers rise silently from the earth at a single word of command. The magical powers of language result from the very priority or firstness of the names by which the objects in this landscape are known. The proper name *Alph* suggests an etymological relation to *alpha* or *aleph*, the first letter of the alphabet and thus a figure for absolute linguistic origins. The name *Abora* is more complex in its associations, but they all have to do with the idea of firstness. *Abora* suggests *Amara*, the exotic pleasure garden mentioned in *Paradise Lost* (4.281). The word *Abora* may also allude to the aborigines, or first inhabitants of Italy; moreover, according to John Beer (*Coleridge the Visionary* 256), the word *Abor* is a name for the sun in some ancient my-thologies. In addition, *Bethabara* is the name of the place where Christ was baptized; Coleridge probably noticed this word in Joseph Cottle's poem "John the Baptist" (1796). The name *Abora* thus adds a whiff of ancient pagan ritual and a hint of Christian revelation to the scene of poetic inspiration portrayed in the poem's last section. It ties together a web of intralinguistic associations that evoke absolute scenes of origin.

In pursuing our analysis of Coleridge's poetic language, we have come to regard his quest for linguistic naturalness as motivated by an underlying nostalgia for the alleged transparency of primitive language, the immediacy of relation between the linguistic sign and its referent. Coleridge's distaste for ordinary language is motivated by a corresponding reaction against the defacement of words in the tawdry transactions of everyday life. If words are mere arbitrary signs, then they cannot possibly be misused, because any enunciation, no matter how deviant, can be assimilated to existing usage. But if words have a single natural or proper signification, then any change of their meaning threatens the entire delicate fabric of the English language. Coleridge's early journalism and political lectures complement the linguistic texture of his poetry by engaging in a systematic critique of the contemporary abuse of words, especially in the windy rhetoric of parliamentary politics. In seeking to establish the historical determinants of Coleridge's linguistic theory, I find it helpful to assign readings from the 1795 *Lectures on Politics and Religion* (*CC* 1) and the first volume of *Essays on His Times* (*CC* 3). I encourage my students to examine the relation between Coleridge's radical politics and his quest for the radical origins of the English language.

In the 1795 lectures, Coleridge repeatedly criticizes the abuse of language perpetrated by his "aristocratic" opponents; he gives several examples of names arbitrarily imposed on objects or events for nefarious purposes. The aristocratic appeal to "Church and Constitution" (CC 1: 38) only serves as a smoke screen for irreligious and unlawful purposes; and the dubious equation of "Illumination and Sedition" (52) stifles any criticism of the established political order. The hated aristocrats rely on slogans and catchwords that acquire "almost a mechanical power" over the minds of the common people (53). Coleridge deplores the plight of his friend and fellow radical John Horne Tooke, who was put on trial for sedition because of his writings in defense of liberty (19). Horne Tooke, a renowned linguist and etymologist, experienced firsthand the tyranny exerted by the political establishment in its power to alter and misconstrue the meaning of words. Only by attending carefully to the meaning of words can we resist the insidious rhetoric of the politicians; otherwise we may be "hurried away by names of which we have not sifted the meaning" (33). The ringleader of this abuse of language, according to Coleridge, is William Pitt, whose false eloquence masks the utter vacuity of his discourse. Pitt's speeches consist of "words on words, finely arranged, and so dexterously consequent, that the whole bears the semblance of argument, and still keeps awake a sense of surprise—but when all is done, nothing rememberable has been said; no one philosophical remark, no one image, not even a pointed aphorism" (CC 3.1: 224). Such rhetorical deception threatens the entire structure of language with a collapse of meaning, a descent into darkness.

In this context *The Friend* takes on a renewed immediacy and interest for my students. They are enabled to see it not simply as a miscellaneous collection of essays but as a coherent and many-faceted attempt to remedy the contemporary abuse of language by reestablishing the proper meaning of words. Coleridge declares the purpose of his periodical in an eloquent defense of his "metaphysics," which he uses "to expose the folly and legerdemain of those who have thus abused the blessed machine of language" (CC 4.1: 108). He proceeds to make a series of precise verbal distinctions, showing that the often abstruse terminology of politics, economics, ethics, and religion can be demystified by careful linguistic analysis. The *Essays on the Principles of Method* furnish a more general statement of the analytic method employed throughout *The Friend*. This method consists in the incremental elaboration of linguistic structures, either in relation to abstract ideas or to "the truths which have their signatures in nature" (CC 4.1: 492). In either case, the progress of human understanding requires the precise conformity of words with the concepts they signify.

Coleridge's method of linguistic analysis requires him to distinguish between words that are closely related in meaning and often regarded as synonymous in ordinary usage. This is his technique of "desynonymization," a term he invented in 1803 to denote the act of distinguishing between apparent synonyms (*CN* 1: 1336). In the *Biographia* he describes the contribution of this process to the historical evolution of language, arguing that "in all societies there exists an instinct of growth, a certain collective, unconscious good sense working progressively to desynonymize those words originally of the same meaning" (*CC* 7.1: 82). He suggests that this gradual process of differentiation can account for the entire formation of a lexicon, from a few simple sounds to an immense nomenclature. Coleridge's critical and philosophical vocabulary derives largely from his habit of desynonymizing. Several of his most crucial distinctions—between fancy and imagination, genius and talent, symbol and allegory, copy and imitation—result from this technique of linguistic analysis. As a class project, I ask my students to collect examples of Coleridge's practice of desynonymization from their reading in the *Biographia*, the *Notebooks*, and *The Friend*. In class we share our findings and assess their significance. Students are surprised to discover just how large a role these distinctions play in the formation of Coleridge's critical discourse.

The constitutive role of desynonymization in Coleridge's intellectual development raises a larger set of questions concerning the relation between language and thought. Is language merely the dress of thought, the means by which we express our knowledge of things? Or does language actually determine the process of thought by circumscribing the range of possible concepts? Coleridge addresses the problem of linguistic relativity in the *Logic* (*CC* 13), a work that languished in undeserved obscurity until its first publication in 1981. The *Logic* is the most coherent and systematic expression of Coleridge's philosophy of language, and it contains the fullest articulation of his views on the origin and acquisition of language, the relation between grammar and logic, and the role of language in thought. More than just a paraphrase of Kant's *Critique of Pure Reason*, it enacts a "linguistic turn" on Kant's philosophy. The *Logic* argues that epistemological questions cannot be resolved without a prior analysis of linguistic structures, since language itself constitutes the only possible medium of intellectual inquiry. Coleridge seeks to rewrite Kant's philosophy in such a way as to reveal its dependence on lexical and grammatical categories that, as innate modes of conception, determine our perception of reality. The activity of thought, in this view, is wholly constituted by the activity of language.

My students come to grips with Coleridge's mature philosophy of language through reading and classroom discussion of selections from the *Logic*, particularly the sketch of linguistic evolution in the introductory chapters, the analysis of logical acts in part 1, and the discussion of categories in part 2. Considered in relation to Coleridge's earlier works, the *Logic* offers a provisional resolution of several issues concerning the role of language in the formation of human consciousness and social values. In this way it provides a logical conclusion to our reading of Coleridge's poetry and prose.

As teachers of Coleridge, we must challenge our students to discover new ways of understanding the unity of his thought while doing justice to the variety and complexity of his writings. Too often his poetry is regarded as his only significant achievement, and his prose works are reduced to the status of mere footnotes or afterthoughts. We can develop a more adequate way of teaching his work by attending more carefully to its medium, the evolving historical structure of language, and by examining how Coleridge's conception of that medium affected his textual practice. By teaching Coleridge's writings through the perspective afforded by his lifelong engagement with the problems of language, I have found a coherent focus for my efforts to convey the enormous scope of his intellectual achievement.

Truth and Pleasure in Wordsworth's Preface and Coleridge's *Biographia Literaria*

Don H. Bialostosky

In undergraduate courses on British Romantic literature and on the history of literary criticism, Coleridge's *Biographia Literaria* inevitably comes up in connection with Wordsworth's Preface to *Lyrical Ballads*. Coleridge, of course, presents his inquiry into poetic principles as provoked by his encounter with Wordsworth's poetry, and he defines his principles in contradistinction to what he takes to be Wordsworth's poetic principles. Coleridge also presents himself as a philosopher-critic who can explain and judge Wordsworth's poetic practice better than the poet himself can, and he has succeeded with many generations of academics and their students in placing himself between them and Wordsworth's poems. Whether the course at hand is primarily concerned with poetic theory or practice, it is impossible to treat one of these texts without reference to the other.

In either kind of course, the complexity of both texts makes it difficult to locate a point at which, as Coleridge puts it, "all lines of difference converge as to their source and centre" (*CC* 7.2: 45). I have elsewhere shown that Coleridge himself offers several conflicting accounts of the point at which those lines converge ("Coleridge's Interpretation"), and we may even expect, in the light of sophisticated recent readings of the *Biographia*, that the search for a center is a misguided logocentric preoccupation. But logocentric preoccupations are hard to escape, and pedagogical responsibilities require us to focus our students' attention somewhere. One topic that has proved useful to me in focusing important differences between the two thinkers is that of the relation between pleasure and truth.

In my course entitled The History of Literary Criticism, this topic comes up as a reprise of issues originally opened between Plato's *Republic* and Aristotle's *Poetics*. Plato's privileging of philosophy over poetry and of philosophers committed to truth over ordinary people corrupted by pleasure is answered by Aristotle's linking of poetry with learning that is pleasant for philosophers and ordinary people alike. Plato's position is reaffirmed and reformulated by Francis Bacon and his Enlightenment followers in terms of science (rather than philosophy) versus poetry—terms that both Wordsworth and Coleridge appropriate and revise.

In my course on the Romantic period, I begin with selections from Edmund Burke's *Sublime and the Beautiful* that stand in for the Enlightenment and provide what Mikhail Bakhtin would call a "dialogizing background" for the Romantic writers. In Burke's main argument, the opposition between truth and pleasure appears as a narrative of the necessary diminution of pleasure as judgment matures. In all but his concluding section, "On Words," which anticipates Romantic departures from his main argument, Burke presents the experience of aesthetic pleasure as naive and illusory, while the knowledge of judgment is mature, accurate, and incompatible with any pleasure except the one that "consists in a sort of conscious pride and superiority, which arises from thinking rightly" (25). Blake's contrast between "the Poetic or Prophetic character" and the "Philosophic and Experimental" in "There is No Natural Religion" and "All Religions Are One" poses the first challenge to Burke's account of these matters; Wordsworth's and Coleridge's differences over truth and pleasure offer further alternatives.

Wordsworth introduces the topic of truth and pleasure in the Preface of 1802 in the passage that opens with his coy and exaggerated allusion to Aristotle's supposed declaration that "[p]oetry is the most philosophic of all writing" (Brett and Jones 257). Aristotle, of course, had said only that poetry is more philosophic than history, and Wordsworth's further exaltation of poetry over even philosophic writing itself is one of the many statements we can learn to hear with Coleridge's sensitive ears as a challenge to his own claim to philosophic authority. Wordsworth goes on to declare that Aristotle is correct about poetry: "its object is truth" pursued by the poet "under one restriction only, namely that of giving immediate pleasure to a human Being possessed of that information which may be expected from him . . . as a Man" (257–58).

This restriction, Wordsworth goes on, is not, however, to be "considered as a degradation of the Poet's art," because the poet's commitment to give immediate pleasure is grounded in "the grand elementary principle of pleasure," a fundamental truth that underlies not only the poet's participation in the pleasures of other people but also the scientist's isolation in specialized pursuits of knowledge. Both the poet and the scientist are motivated, on Wordsworth's account, by a common principle of pleasure, and both of them are dedicated to discovering the truth. Poets, however, restrict themselves to celebrating the truth of the pleasure they share with all human beings, whereas the scientist avidly pursues the uncommon truths of "those particular parts of nature which are the objects of his studies." They differ, then, neither in the ends they pursue (truth) nor in the pleasurable interests with which they pursue them but rather in the relative commonality of their objects and the communicability of their findings. Scientists have more specialized interests than poets and they address themselves to other scientists rather than to "all human beings," but they are not, as, for example, Bacon would have it, heroes of truth who achieve knowledge only by denying their pleasures, while poets seduce themselves and others away from knowledge by indulging pleasures contrary to truth. Bacon and the tradition he fostered thus oppose the scientist to the poet on the premise that "so differing a harmony there is between the spirit of man and the spirit of nature" (133), but Wordsworth denies this premise and asserts that "the mind of man is

naturally the mirror of the fairest and most interesting qualities of nature"
(Brett and Jones 258–59).

The widely neglected passage in which Wordsworth develops this line of
thought requires careful unpacking. It is not easy to sort out the antecedents
of "he" and "him" in the sentences where Wordsworth answers the question
"What then does the Poet?" or to clarify the sense in which the poet takes
on the task of popularizing or familiarizing the scientist's discoveries. The
reading is difficult partly because its grammar is obscure but also because
the thought Wordsworth is articulating goes counter to widely accepted
oppositions between pleasure and truth, the scientist and the poet, and the
human mind and the natural world. Students can recognize that the argument here belongs to the ongoing "two cultures" debate, often symbolized
by the two ends of campus at which the science laboratories and the humanities building stand, and they can be engaged, through their own experience of experimental inquiry, to test Wordsworth's claim that the
knowledge of the scientist is pleasure, just as they can examine whether
human beings they know, contemplating the infinite complexity of pain and
pleasure in their ordinary experience, tend to interpret that experience in
ways that give them pleasure. Do scientists take a pleasurable interest in
science or do they pursue their inquiries in a spirit of disciplined self-denial?
Do the interests that scientists take in their work necessarily distort their
knowledge? Do people tend to rationalize their confused experiences of
pleasure and pain? Why would a poet want to celebrate their tendency to
do so? What is gained and lost by contemplating scientists and poets on this
common footing of pleasurable motivation *and* commitment to truth?

Having opened these questions in response to Wordsworth's Preface, one
can turn to Coleridge's reassertion of the oppositions between poetry and
science, pleasure and truth, mind and nature, without taking them for granted
as cultural givens. Coleridge draws on these distinctions in the second step
of his definition of a poem in chapter 14. Having first distinguished prose
from composition in meter and rhyme, he writes:

> A difference of object and contents supplies an additional ground of
> distinction. The immediate purpose may be the communication of
> truths; either of truth absolute and demonstrable, as in works of science;
> or of facts experienced and recorded, as in history. Pleasure, and that
> of the highest and most permanent kind, may *result* from the *attain-
> ment* of the end; but it is not itself the immediate end. In other works
> the communication of pleasure may be the immediate purpose; and
> though the truth, either moral or intellectual, ought to be the *ultimate*
> end, yet this will distinguish the character of the author, not the class
> to which the work belongs. Blest indeed is that state of society, in

which the immediate purpose would be baffled by the perversion of
the proper ultimate end; in which no charm of diction or imagery could
exempt the Bathyllus even of an Anacreon, or the Alexis of Virgil, from
disgust or aversion!

(2: 12–13)

Coleridge here distinguishes between history and science, which aim at
truth, though they may give pleasure, and poetry, which aims at pleasure,
though it ought ultimately to aim at truth. Coleridge allows that a high-
minded poet may aim at moral or intellectual truth as well as at pleasure,
but this aim characterizes the author rather than the art of poetry itself,
which, under the present "state of society," is capable of giving poetic pleasure in works that treat immoral subjects (the subject in question in Coleridge's examples, we may note, is male homosexuality).

Coleridge further clarifies his view of these matters in chapter 22 in his
objection to Wordsworth's choice of characters. There he attributes to
Wordsworth's high-mindedness Wordsworth's decision to ascribe high moral
and intellectual virtues to a figure like his Pedlar, but Coleridge nevertheless
objects,

> because the object in view, as an *immediate* object, belongs to the
> moral philosopher, and would be pursued, not only more appropri-
> ately, but, . . . with far greater probability of success, in sermons and
> moral essays, than in an elevated poem. It seems, indeed, to destroy
> the main fundamental distinction, not only between a *poem* and *prose*,
> but even between philosophy and works of fiction, inasmuch as it
> proposes *truth* for its immediate object, instead of *pleasure*. Now till
> that blessed time shall come, when truth itself shall be pleasure, and
> both shall be so united as to be indistinguishable in words only, not
> in feeling, it will remain the poet's office to proceed upon that state
> of association which actually exists as *general*, instead of attempting
> first to *make* it what it ought to be, and then to let the pleasure follow.
>
> (2: 130–31)

The present "state of society" we discover here stands in opposition to a
future "blessed time" in which truth and pleasure, philosophy and poetry
may be united. Under present fallen conditions poets go beyond their office
in writing as if that blessed time were already here or were achievable
through pretending it were here. The quixotic poet who defies "that state
of association, which actually exists as *general*" not only produces incon-
gruous poetic effects but also threatens "the main fundamental distinction"
between philosophy and poetry. Such a poet behaves as if the world were

not fallen and as if there were no essential difference between the aims of poetry and philosophy.

Coleridge's insistence on the fall and his reassertion of a fundamental distinction between poetry and philosophy can lead us to ask in what sense he can nevertheless praise Wordsworth, later in the chapter, as capable of producing "the FIRST GENUINE PHILOSOPHIC POEM" (2: 156) and to wonder how the poet he envisions can at once accept this radical division in *"real life"* (2: 130), while struggling always "to idealize and unify" in poetry (1: 304). What is the difference between what Coleridge takes to be "real" and what Wordsworth takes to be "real"? How does Coleridge's account of imagination's re-creation of the real differ from Burke's view of imagination's rearrangement of the real and Blake's view of imagination's creation of the real? Why does Wordsworth's Preface not need a concept of imagination to account for what the poet does? How do Coleridge's and Wordsworth's differences over the postulate of a fallen "present state of society" affect their views of rustic language and rustic characters? How does Coleridge's view of the hierarchy of truth and pleasure connect with his presentation of himself as a philosopher and of Wordsworth as a poet? What is Coleridge's personal stake in maintaining "the main fundamental distinction" between philosophy and poetry? What is his religious stake in this distinction? What, to place this whole issue in the somewhat grandiose context of deconstruction, is the stake of Western culture itself in maintaining this distinction?

These questions point in a number of directions that class discussion might take from the topic and the passages I have focused on. In the one or two class hours available for this discussion in either of the courses I have taught, one can hope at most to construe the passages, align them with one another, recall their connection with issues raised in earlier classes, and open the lines of inquiry such questions introduce. In either course, I might well reintroduce the passages in a question on a midterm or final examination to ask students to recall who said them where and to explain what the passages say, how they bear on one another, and how they address the larger issues raised by the course.

To focus on the topic of pleasure and truth is to engage Wordsworth and Coleridge where their fundamental convictions about the human mind, the world, and the vocations of philosophy and poetry are at variance. It would be sophomoric to ask sophomores to choose between Coleridge's conviction of a fallen world and Wordsworth's belief in a world essentially adapted to the human mind, or between the claims of philosophy and science, on the one hand, and of poetry, on the other, to tell us the truths that matter about ourselves and the world. But students can be asked to recognize the high stakes in the differences between these men and to discover how their fundamental choices on these serious matters inform the poems they write and the judgments they announce on poetic subjects, language, and meter. Scholars are still debating the theoretical differences and the mediations between theory and practice in the work of both these writers; I would be satisfied if undergraduates arrived at the point where they recognized that these questions are indeed debatable and that they are important.

Building Domes in Air: "Kubla Khan" in the Introductory Literary Criticism Class

James Holt McGavran, Jr.

As an undergraduate a generation ago, I learned that Samuel Taylor Coleridge's interrupted dream fragment "Kubla Khan" should be enjoyed aloud for its verbal music but that no meaning could be assigned to its haunting patterns of imagery. Today I make Xanadu's rich, strange indeterminacy work for me in the classroom by using "Kubla Khan" to illustrate the wide variety of critical methods that form the substance of a sophomore-level course, Approaches to Literature, which the University of North Carolina at Charlotte requires of its English majors. I assign "Kubla Khan" near the beginning of the term, to outline general critical concerns. As I teach each new critical approach, I refer to the poem as a first example before assigning other texts. Finally, "Kubla Khan" serves as a focus for review at the end of the course.

Very useful in opening class discussions of literary criticism is the diagram on the orientation of critical theories (see fig. 1) in M. H. Abrams's *Mirror and the Lamp*. All theories of art, Abrams argues, must consider four major elements (capitalized in fig. 1); an individual theory may be classified according to its most prominent element.

Our discussion begins after an oral reading of "Kubla Khan" and some in-class journal writing to focus students' responses; as it proceeds, I align these responses with the four points of Abrams's diagram. Comments from students completely baffled or even repulsed by the poem, from those who freely associate with their personal experience, or from those few who think they know what designs Coleridge may have had on them fall under Abrams's AUDIENCE and pragmatic theories; although they do not yet know it, the students are producing reader-response criticism, which I have encouraged by assigning the journal and by welcoming their reactions to virtually every-

UNIVERSE
mimetic theories

WORK
objective theories

ARTIST
expressive theories

AUDIENCE
pragmatic theories

Figure 1.

Source: Abrams, *The Mirror and the Lamp* 6–29.

thing we study. Class discussion of the UNIVERSE the poem mirrors may center on oriental exoticism and mystery; these I see as a reflection of Coleridge's vast knowledge of the world of books, specifically his sources in Samuel Purchas and John Milton. Alternatively, students may comment on oriental despotism and brutality; suggestions of slavery and of future conflict in the Khan's commanding decree and the "ancestral voices prophesying war" may generate a historical or sociological reading of the poem. Students influenced by Coleridge's comments in his 1816 preface and by the phantasmagorical images and echoes in his poetic language see "Kubla Khan" as a dream whose universe is the mind of the dreamer; this perspective takes us from the mirror to the lamp, and to the Romantic-expressive theory of art Abrams derived largely from Coleridge: the work of art radiates the inner life of the ARTIST. As Coleridge writes in the *Biographia Literaria*, "What is poetry? is so nearly the same question with, what is a poet? that the answer to the one is involved in the solution of the other" (*CC* 7.2: 12). Those who already know Coleridge may mention biographical matters such as his friendship with William and Dorothy Wordsworth, his marriage to Sara Fricker, or his use of laudanum; this awareness lays a groundwork for psychological and feminist readings of the poem. Finally, students used to formalistic approaches illustrate Abrams's objective theories of art by focusing on the WORK itself; they note patterns of antithetical images—male and female, birth and death, sun and ice—or the three-paragraph structure of the poem (1–11, 12–36, 37–54) whereby Coleridge implies what he called in the *Biographia* a "balance or reconciliation of opposite or discordant qualities" (2: 16); thus the Khan's decree and the woman's wail may perhaps be synthesized or transcended in the final attempt of the first-person speaker to "build that dome in air."

After this encounter with Abrams, Coleridge, and "Kubla Khan," I proceed to the study of specific critical approaches, using Bonnie Klomp Stevens and Larry L. Stewart's fine *Guide to Literary Criticism and Research* as my textbook, and using "Kubla Khan" as a first text for illustrations. I begin where I left off—with formalism (Stevens and Stewart 13–21). Close reading is the best preparation for the approaches that follow in the course; moreover, students already know this approach from high school or from my review of the elements of poetry (Brooks and Warren), fiction, and drama at the beginning of the term. They need little prompting, therefore, to discuss imagery, structure, and paradox in "Kubla Khan." Immediately striking are the pairs of contrasting images in the central section of the poem: the "woman wailing" and "her demon-lover," "the sacred river" and the "lifeless ocean," "the fountain and the caves," the sun and ice. Some students sense a moment of stasis when "[t]he shadow of the dome of pleasure / Floated midway on the waves"—as if the opposites were for a moment perfectly balanced or unified; others tend to find only dissolution and frustration, a mockery of harmony or even of sense. Students may note that the first section of the poem seems the clearest and most straightforward, both syntactically and imagistically; the Khan builds the pleasure dome; a diction of control ("decree") and enclosure ("girdled round," "enfolding") dominates. The final section, coming after the order of the first section and the turbulence of the central section, implies a possible resolution of the conflict between the first two—or at least a new beginning. But many questions arise about exactly what occurs and how: What does it mean to "build that dome in air"? What is there to beware of in visions of paradise? Who is the "damsel with a dulcimer"? How, if at all, is she connected to the wailing woman? Who is the speaking "I"? How, if at all, is he connected to the Khan? Questions like these demonstrate the usefulness of the New Critics' exclusive focus on the poem as artifact; we could not have formulated them without careful close reading. Simultaneously, however, we may feel we cannot articulate the secrets of a text as passionate and elusive as "Kubla Khan" without speculating beyond it into history and psychology.

Next we study traditional historical approaches to literature such as textual scholarship, source study (Stevens and Stewart 56–60), and the history of ideas (Stevens and Stewart 43–50; see also 63–67, "Moral and Religious Studies"). Once again, "Kubla Khan" serves as a useful first example; and once again, new interpretive possibilities occur, but new questions arise as well. Textual evidence, here the use of the Crewe manuscript, gives the lie to Coleridge's suggestion in his 1816 preface that "Kubla Khan" was the interrupted, unedited transcription of a dream "without any sensation or consciousness of effort" (*PW* 296). As Norman Fruman shows, revisions Coleridge made between the time of the Crewe manuscript and the published text of 1816 improve both the sense and the dreamlike verbal music of the earlier version (338–43). But textual scholarship fails to answer such questions as why Coleridge misrepresented his work in the preface and what he really expected readers to find in it. With regard to source study, the seventeenth-century travel book *Purchas His Pilgrimage* clearly provided Coleridge a historical setting and occasion for his dream-vision; the physical remoteness and exoticism of Xamdu/Xanadu entrance readers and listeners today almost as much as they did in the pre–*National Geographic*, pre–TV-news days of Purchas and Coleridge. But Coleridge's second major source, Milton's description of Eden in book 4 of *Paradise Lost*, demonstrates the close relation of source study to the history of ideas. On the one hand, to recognize the Miltonic echoes is to confront the concept of a paradise spiritual as well as physical and the vast distance in time, space, and experience between us and that innocent state. On the other hand, for Coleridge to re-create Milton's prelapsarian Eden in Xanadu's "deep romantic chasm" is to recast Eve as the wailing woman and, even more strangely, to suggest that either Satan *or* Adam could play "demon lover." To bring purity and perfection so close to riot and dissolution is to suggest a revolution in traditional Western Christian thinking about the gap between spiritual and physical realities. Revolution on the political level, moreover, constitutes another historical-philosophical theme of the poem. Like most of his contemporaries, Coleridge was much influenced by the French Revolution; in "Kubla Khan" revolution may be implied in the "ancestral voices prophesying war" and also in the first-person speaker's desire to "build that dome in air"—thus making the power and glory of Xanadu accessible to all people, not just the Khan himself. New historicists among the students who want to learn more about the historical Khubilai Khan may consult Morris Rossabi's biography; those interested in pursuing Coleridge's reading history may read John Livingston Lowes's *Road to Xanadu*.

I next present Marxist criticism as a revisionary development of traditional historical criticism (Stevens and Stewart 68–75). As an illustration of specific Marxist concepts such as infrastructure, superstructure, and class conflict, "Kubla Khan" again is both useful and ambiguous. The historical Khan's grandeur and art rested on his absolute control of the means of production within his realm; he commanded the slave labor that put in place the walls and towers of his pleasure dome, the superstructure of his ideology and art. A true revolution of the proletariat could not occur with a populace so totally controlled from above; war could only originate in a foreign invasion led by a ruler as powerful as the Khan or in a coup organized by other members of the ruling class: thus the Khan's "ancestral voices" could speak and wage war through his kindred. The dreamer may be the only revolutionary in the poem, as we have seen; alternatively, as Jerome McGann suggests, he may express the repressed desire of the conservative Coleridge, terrified by the French Revolution and Napoleon, to identify with the Khan as a tyrant of the imagination (*Romantic Ideology* 102–03). Still more problematical is the applicability to "Kubla Khan," a dream-vision, of the basic dictum of Marx and Engels, "Life determines consciousness" (Eagleton 6). Granted, to have a dream there must be a dreamer, who must exist in a given set of economic and social circumstances. Nevertheless, in the poem the power of the dream is so strongly felt, by both dreamer and reader, as to call into question the primacy of material existence over consciousness and "Romantic ideology." Interestingly, Lowes cites one Arabic chronicle, unknown to Coleridge, where the Khan himself is said to have fashioned his palace after one he saw in a dream (326).

Revolution on the psychosexual level is implied in the seismic upheaval of the "deep romantic chasm" as it rises in counterassertion to the controlling, defining efforts of the Khan. With its extraordinary powers of suggestiveness, "Kubla Khan" is an ideal text for the study of psychological approaches to literature (Stevens and Stewart 87–93). The three sections of the poem illustrate Sigmund Freud's tripartite division of the psyche (*Introductory*

Lectures 82–112): First is the superego, the morality principle, embodied in the Khan's attempts to impose order and limits upon nature, society, and the self. Next is the id, the pleasure principle, the desire voiced by the "woman wailing for her demon-lover" against the restrictions of the super-ego. Finally, the "I" of the last eighteen lines becomes Freud's ego, the reality principle that attempts to establish and maintain identity throughout the conflict of superego and id. "Kubla Khan" also illustrates Freud's ideas about the artist as a neurotic daydreamer who tries to make child's play out of personal frustrations (*On Creativity* 44–54). We now may recall in more detail such aspects of Coleridge's life as his self-deprecating awe of William Wordsworth's poetic powers, his unhappy marriage to Sara Fricker, and his growing addiction to laudanum ("Biographical Studies," Stevens and Stewart 51–55); thus students may see psychobiographical significance in the great powers of the Khan, the howls of the wailing woman and the Abyssinian maid's "symphony and song," and the final references to "honey-dew" and "the milk of Paradise." Freudian insights fail to establish, however, whether "Kubla Khan" is to be read as neurotic escapism or rather as the attempt of an essentially healthy psyche to restore and assert itself.

Jungian psychology and mythic and archetypal criticism (Stevens and Stewart 82–87) bring a positive emphasis on psychic integration that opposes the Freudian emphasis on pathology and diagnosis. Major aspects of myth criticism, too, can be illustrated concisely with "Kubla Khan." Most compelling are Coleridge's anticipations of Jung's archetypes of the psyche: the shadow and the anima (Jung 3–7, 8–10, 11–22). If the "I" of the third section of the poem is the Jungian persona or public self struggling toward individuation, then the audaciously powerful Khan becomes that persona's shadow self, his key to what lies repressed in his personal unconscious; similarly, the wailing woman and the singing maid may represent aspects of his anima, his potential access to the still more deeply buried collective unconscious. The poem is rich in archetypal images for identification and discussion: the walls and towers of the pleasure dome, the chasm and the fountain of Xanadu, the sacred river of life, the sunless sea of the unconscious, the "flashing eyes" and "floating hair" that may recall either Plato's Ion or, more ominously, the dismembered Orpheus. Still more central to the poem, and to Northrop Frye's systematization of archetypes, seasons, and literary genres ("Genre Studies," Stevens and Stewart 25), are the various garden images (Frye, *Educated Imagination* 53, 55) in Coleridge's vision of paradise: the Khan's measured, protected pleasure grounds; the fecund chaos, thrilling and menacing, of the chasm; and the speaker's reconstructed garden of the "dome in air," at once more ethereal and more openly accessible.

I turn to feminist criticism (Stevens and Stewart 75–82) late in the course because feminist approaches are eclectic, drawing on textual, historical, and psychological methods that I prefer to teach separately first. Yet, as this essay has demonstrated, it is neither possible nor desirable to keep questions of gender entirely in abeyance in our earlier discussions of "Kubla Khan." Whether discussed now or earlier, specific feminist issues in the poem include the following: Do the Abyssinian maid and the wailing woman conform to the angel/monster, madonna/whore dichotomy central to Sandra Gilbert and Susan Gubar's arguments in *The Madwoman in the Attic?* Are the Khan and the "I" opposites, the former an extreme embodiment of male chauvinism and the latter, the poem's speaker, a more balanced, androgynous being (Heilbrun) transformed by the music of the Abyssinian maid? Do the Khan's attempts to dominate his empire parallel the attempts by Romantic writers, in Alan Richardson's argument, to "colonize the feminine" in order to achieve either psychic or textual androgyny or both? Does the syntactical contrast between the tightly structured statements of the poem's first section, describing the Khan's acts (esp. 1–9), and the fragmented phrases of the second section, describing the chasm and the woman's inarticulate wailing (esp. 12–16), point to differences between men's and women's relations to, and use of, language (Vlasopolos)? Is language itself, like the other structures and institutions of Western society, masculinist in bias? If so, how can the Abyssinian maid's song help the speaker? Virginia Woolf speaks evocatively but somewhat obliquely of women's sentences in *A Room of One's Own* (79–81, 95), and subsequent feminist theorists from Gilbert and Gubar to Luce Irigaray (*This Sex* 205–18) have examined these problems. Once again, "Kubla Khan" rewards study but eludes any simple, doctrinaire answers.

I give less detail in outlining the usefulness of "Kubla Khan" for discussions of reader-response and poststructuralist criticism. The subjectivity demanded by the many unanswered questions in Coleridge's text—and by the application of other critical approaches, as we have seen—makes relevant all varieties of rhetorical criticism (Stevens and Stewart 27–33), from Stanley Fish's "affective stylistics" to David Bleich's "readings and feelings." And, given the evidence of the Crewe manuscript, the 1816 preface to "Kubla Khan" makes Coleridge a complex real-life example of Wayne Booth's "unreliable narrator" (211). Further, this entire dome-building project has also been an exercise in de/re/construction (Stevens and Stewart 39–42), in its attempt to account for the poem's many gaps or mysteries by using various structures of critical thought. To paraphrase Catherine Belsey, I have tried to locate the points of contradiction not just within the poem but in the critical approaches as well—the points at which both break free of their own constraints (104; qtd. in Stevens and Stewart 40). For these reasons, some teachers may prefer to save "Kubla Khan" for a preexamination review at the end of the term rather than to refer to it throughout the course. In any case the magnificence, pain, and mystery of "Kubla Khan"—the poem critics once considered unapproachable—continue to flourish unexhausted, regardless of what critical architecture we raise in Xanadu's gardens.

TEACHING THE CONVERSATION POEMS

Trembling into Thought: Approaching Coleridge through "The Eolian Harp"

John A. Hodgson

An introduction to Coleridge does not always go as easily as it comes. Usually a fascinating or (depending on the auditor's viewpoint) overbearing conversationalist, as acquaintances from Charles Lamb and Dorothy Wordsworth to Carlyle and Emerson all witness, he was only rarely a casual one. ("Have you ever heard me preach, Charles?" he once asked Lamb. "N-n-never heard you d-d-do anything else, C-c-coleridge," came the reply.) That he could be off-puttingly daunting he well knew: in the "very judicious letter" from a fictitious friend that provides his excuse for breaking off the ponderous and abstruse opening of *Biographia Literaria*'s chapter 13, he describes the experience of reading himself as an exercise in bafflement and unsettling disorientation, an encounter with a "tale *obscure* of high and passionate thoughts / To *a strange* music chaunted!" (*CC* 7.1: 304, 302). A similar self-recognition, at once proud and apologetic, informs his identification with the Cumaean sibyl (in 1817 he finally publishes his collected poetry as *Sibylline Leaves*), another author whose writings are deep, fragmentary, and obscure. These traits can be barriers to acquaintance; and, as it is our business as teachers to appreciate, they can make some approaches to Coleridge much more difficult than others.

More manageable and coherent than "Religious Musings," more original and sustained than the poet's earlier, derivative effusions and lyrics, "The

Eolian Harp" is a natural and convenient starting point for an undergraduate's approach to Coleridge. The poem richly anticipates the characteristic works, issues, and tensions to follow—the tendencies toward both philosophical speculation and doctrinal faith, the introspective insights and blindnesses, the interpersonal sympathies and antipathies, the voice ambivalently colloquial and abstruse, domestic and exotic. "The Eolian Harp" introduces Coleridge fairly and powerfully. Though not what students will finally call an "easy" work, it is a work they can ease into; as Coleridge's complexity becomes gradually more apparent to them here, they become increasingly ready to address it.

As background to a discussion of the poem, it is helpful for students to know at the outset that lines 26–33 are a later addition to the poem (Coleridge did not insert them until 1817) and that "pensive Sara" was Coleridge's fiancée at the time of the poem's composition. They will also need to know, of course, what an aeolian (the more usual spelling) harp is and does. (The one-sentence explanation their text probably supplies is hardly sufficient. The eleventh-edition *Encyclopaedia Britannica* entry is helpful; the current *Britannica* and *World Book Encyclopedia* both include a small illustration.) And some students may need to be told, incidentally, that the "cot" Coleridge refers to at the beginning and end of the poem is not a bed but a cottage.

In preliminary guidance, I simply urge my students to follow Coleridge's central, aeolian-harp figure carefully through the poem, paying particular attention to its applications and implications; and that is what we do together in class. Such an approach leads clearly and directly to the poem's major issues and effects and teaches lessons about how to read Coleridge that will be directly applicable to his later works.

"The Eolian Harp" builds to, and turns on, the central conceit of lines 44–48, and it is with this that I begin the class discussion:

> And what if all of animated nature
> Be but organic Harps diversely fram'd,
> That tremble into thought, as o'er them sweeps
> Plastic and vast, one intellectual breeze,
> At once the Soul of each, and God of all?

The complex figure represents the climax of Coleridge's speculations in the poem; and his immediately following retreat before the "mild reproof" of Sara's "more serious eye" constitutes the major development of the poem's plot. Here, then, at this crux where the philosophical and romantic strands of the poem threaten to twist apart, we can the more readily see them separately and appreciate what has been holding them together.

Coleridge's central conceit is a great analogy: as the wind awakens the harp, so God inspires and animates all the myriad creatures and aspects of the natural world. The analogy—vaguely Neoplatonic, vaguely pantheistic —is not unchristian (Dekker 114–20; Piper, *Singing* 32–34). But it is unorthodoxly speculative, even freethinking, for all its piety; and as such, it provokes resistance from the orthodox, fideistic Sara, to whom such metaphysical musings seem ambivalently "vain"—useless, but also proud (cf. Wheeler 85). The metaphorical is also a theological extravagance: the rhetorical flights of unbridled philosophy strain against the militant meekness of Sara's orthodoxy.

It might seem at this climactic point, then, that the poem's central tension opposes the self-indulgent freedom of Coleridge's metaphysical conceit to the resistance of Sara's more conventional self-restraint: his aeolian-harp metaphor stands rebuked by her plain-dealing orthodoxy. Just so, as a sort of philosophical standoff between young lovers of different persuasions or temperaments, students can easily read the disagreement. But in fact Coleridge's conceit here does not simply constitute one side of this tension but also encompasses the whole: the tension also strains *within* the conceit. This kind of complication is typically Coleridgean and will later inform such diverse works as "Kubla Khan," where dreaming alternatively opposes interruption (the person from Porlock) or subsumes it (the tumult of the river, the ancestral voices prophesying war); "Reflections on Having Left a Place of Retirement," "A Poem Which Affects Not to Be Poetry," according to its original subtitle; "Dejection," a passionate expression of an inexpressible, "unimpassioned grief," a poem about Coleridge's inability to write poetry; *The Statesman's Manual*, where Coleridge ultimately celebrates symbol's superiority to allegory by allegorizing it (*CC* 6: 30–31); and *Biographia Literaria*, where he figures the imagination in terms of his image for the fancy, an echo (*CC* 7.1: 304; cf. *CC* 6: 30). Students who receive a heuristic jolt on discovering this complication for themselves in "The Eolian Harp," as most quickly do, are subsequently more sensitive to the cruxes of those later texts.

This heuristic jolt comes from recalling how the aeolian harp first figures in Coleridge's poem, as an emblem of coquettish courtship. A light breeze brings forth soft harmonies from the aeolian harp set in the cottage window:

> . . . by the desultory breeze caress'd,
> Like some coy maid half yielding to her lover,
> It pours such sweet upbraiding, as must needs
> Tempt to repeat the wrong!

Here the harp corresponds to the coy maid, and so to Sara; the caressing wind, to her lover, and so to Coleridge; the harp's harmonies, to the maid's sweet upbraidings, and so to Sara's response to Coleridge's mild musings (implicitly, his poem thus far). Sara, we infer from the figure, mildly protests Coleridge's idling, flattering speculations, but in a way that coyly encourages them. Viewed in this context, Sara's reproof to Coleridge at the end of the poem seems not a rejection of Coleridge's metaphysical conceit but an extension of it: her firmer, no longer coy upbraiding of his now more daring speculations suggests the harp's harsher response to a stronger, bolder (cf. 18) wind. Like the harp before the wind, Sara responds harmoniously to his desultory musings but dissonantly to his more forceful and daring meditations. These implications, moreover, are entirely and significantly consistent with aeolian harping; for the harp produces various harmonies in light breezes, but "with the increased pressure of the wind, the dissonances of the 11th and 13th overtones are heard in shrill discords" (*Britannica*). Sara's resistance to Coleridge's conceit yet makes a part of that conceit and represents, as Albert S. Gérard suggests, "something in Coleridge himself" (46). Like so many later disturbings of Coleridgean conceits—the stone cast into the mirror of the stream, the person on business from Porlock (both in the preface to "Kubla Khan"), the judicious friend of *Biographia Literaria*'s chapter 13 (see Brisman 30–33)—the disruption is part of the whole.

If we now hope, after all, to find Coleridge's aeolian-harp figure consistently accommodating the plot of his poem, the intervening developments of the figure in lines 17–25 and 34–43 (in the poem's original version these were adjacent passages) will quickly give us pause. For here, as the sweep of Coleridge's speculations gradually builds toward the climax of lines 44–48, the correspondences of his central figure begin to waver and shift. Originally suggestive of the maid's responses or Sara's, the harp's harmonies now come to evoke more generally the exotic world of unrestrained fancy, "footless and wild" (the phrase will be starkly countered by Sara's closing remonstrance to "walk humbly"); and eventually Coleridge acknowledges this fancy as particularly his own. Such thoughts of "witchery of sound," "twilight Elfins," "Fairy-Land," "honey-dropping flowers," "birds of Paradise" anticipate the exoticisms of the famous Mystery poems to come (the spellbindings and sweet-singing spirits of *The Rime of the Ancient Mariner*, the visions and charms of *Christabel*, the wishful poet of "Kubla Khan" who "on honey-dew hath fed, / And drunk the milk of Paradise"). But they also recall the sentimental fancies of Coleridge's earlier, less memorable lyrics. Now, at this stage of the class discussion, I introduce some samples of those earlier poems for the class's consideration.

Poems on Various Subjects, the 1796 volume in which "The Eolian Harp" (then titled simply "Effusion XXXV") first appeared, also contains such verses as "Songs of the Pixies," wherein the pixies their "soothing witcheries shed" on a youthful poet, crowning him with "faery garlands"; "Kisses," describing

Cupid's chemical creation of kisses from a mixture including "Nectar and Ambrosia" and "the magic dews which Evening brings, / Brush'd from the Idalian star by faery wings"; and "Lines: On an Autumnal Evening," with its prayer to the "Spirits of Love" to "hither wing your way, / Like far-off music, voyaging the breeze!" These syrupy excerpts typify the thoughts that Coleridge now in "The Eolian Harp" identifies as "idle flitting phantasies, / Travers[ing] my indolent and passive brain." And it is in the context of these "wild and various" phantasies—it is, indeed, as merely one more of them, only the latest of many—that Coleridge's climactic figure ("And what if all of animated nature / Be but organic Harps diversely fram'd . . .") presents itself to Sara (cf. Magnuson, " 'Eolian' " 4–10). Seen in this light, her reproof is not to "serenely brilliant" philosophy—"(such should Wisdom be)"—but to intellectual indolence and vagary, all "swell and flutter" and "glitter" (cf. Matlak 105).

This new perspective on "The Eolian Harp" finds particular reinforcement in another of those sentimental exercises in the 1796 volume, an effusion later entitled "The Kiss," as an in-class recitation of the poem (it is only 28 lines long) instantly demonstrates. In this poem the speaker begs a kiss from his beloved: the zephyr, he argues, inhales sweetness and vigor from the rose's "nectar-breathing kisses" without harming it, while she, as he sighs back her perfume in dew, bashfully "darts a blush of deeper Red," implicitly the more beautiful for her boon. The conceit, however romantic, shows affinities as a flight of fancy to the climactic figure of "The Eolian Harp." And the kinship of the two poems becomes sharply apparent in the conclusion of "The Kiss," where the lady faintly refuses to grant the speaker's request:

> In tender accents, faint and low,
> Well-pleas'd I hear the whisper'd "No!"
> The whispered "No"—how little meant!
> Sweet Falsehood that endears Consent!
> For on those lovely lips the while
> Dawns the soft relenting smile,
> And tempts with feign'd dissuasion coy
> The gentle violence of Joy.

Here again is the "coy maid half yielding to her lover" whose sweet rejection of him "tempts to repeat the wrong!"

We have seen how, in the context of Coleridge's metaphysical, implicitly imaginative perspective, Sara's final rebuke seems not a rejection of his aeolian-harp conceit but an extension of it. What we are now alternatively seeing is that, in the context of Coleridge's sentimental, implicitly fanciful perspective, his aeolian-harp conceit seems not an exception to his desultory and random phantasizing but an extension of it.

Thus "The Eolian Harp" suggests different, even contrary, ways of reading itself—a challenging but fruitful topic for class discussion. The poem's self-interpretive ambivalence proceeds from a fundamental ambivalence in the harpist wind. Are the harmonies of "this subject lute" evoked by a figuratively external, independent wind, a Godly, "intellectual breeze," coherent and sustained, or are they instead responses to a figuratively internal, psychologically subjective exhalation, "bubbles" of "vain . . . babbl[e]"? The confusion becomes especially noticeable when Coleridge self-reflexively muses on his musing:

> Full many a thought uncall'd and undetain'd,
> And many idle flitting phantasies,
> Traverse my indolent and passive brain,
> As wild and various as the random gales
> That swell and flutter on this subject Lute!

The thoughts that play breezily on the lute of Coleridge's brain are also alternatively the thoughts that issue harmoniously from the lute. The traverse across the passive strings of the brain is also a crossing from infusion to effusion. Or is it only a blurring or confusing of the two?

Coleridge here verges on a philosophical and theological issue that he would engage throughout his life: the contest between pantheistic and transcendental philosophies, the metaphysician's quest after the grounds of existence and of knowledge. The tensions of "The Eolian Harp" suggest those of *Ancient Mariner*, where the Mariner's experience and his moral remain at odds, as do his integrative message and his alienating effect; of "The Nightingale" ("In nature there is nothing melancholy") as countered by "Dejection" (in nature there is nothing joyful, either: "we receive but what we give"); of chapter 12 of *Biographia Literaria* and the "Essays on Method" in *The Friend*, where Coleridge tells us not to "think of ourselves as separated beings, and place nature in antithesis to the mind," but to "possess ourselves, as one with the whole" and "know that existence is its own predicate" (*CC* 4.1: 520–21). In all those works he strives at great length to resolve these tensions; in "The Eolian Harp" the closing seven lines suggest a much quicker readiness to elide them, particularly in the 1796 version. In 1817, however, with his famous addition to the poem, Coleridge returns to confront this crux directly (much as he does in *Ancient Mariner* at just the same time when he adds its marginal gloss). Whether in doing so he improves his poem or mars it remains a matter of critical debate.

Certainly the newly inserted lines suggest a grand resolution of the poem's seeming inconsistencies:

> O! the one Life within us and abroad,
> Which meets all motion and becomes its soul,
> A light in sound, a sound-like power in light,
> Rhythm in all thought, and joyance every where. . . .

Suddenly, the straightforwardly interpretive questions that the poem has provoked—whether these inspirational breezes are Godly and intellectual or merely subjective and fanciful, whether Coleridge's thoughts correspond to aeolian wind or aeolian music, whether the harp's sounds figure Coleridge's words or Sara's—yield a single, sustained answer: both, both, both. In such a world all life, all things are mutually stimulative and responsive. When that which "meets all motion . . . becomes its soul," distinctions between the mind as passive or as active become meaningless; when "the breeze warbles, and the mute still air / Is Music slumbering on her instrument," wind and music, "air" and "air" (Wheeler [78] notes the pun) are one.

But this resolution, after all, may be more apparent than real—as the recanting close of the poem implies. And the problem is not merely one of Sara's stubborn antipathy to metaphysics; Coleridge's new extension of his aeolian-harp figure is itself subtly but importantly flawed. That this breeze "warbles," recalling the "Melodies" earlier likened to (not sung by) "birds of Paradise," is technically apt: the word can denote not merely song or birdsong but also both the quavering sound of the wind and the sweet sounding of a harp or other stringed instrument (see *OED*). But with his further insistence on the *Rhythm* "in all thought," like his following pun on *air* and personification of the still air as "Music slumbering," Coleridge begins to beg his poem's question. For an aeolian harp can produce harmony, but not music; its chords are arrhythmic. To attribute rhythm to thought is to abandon aeolian harping as a figure for thought; it is, in fact, surreptitiously to substitute poetry as that figure. Poetry intrudes to clinch philosophy's argument—yet inevitably the intrusion mars the argument.

Metaphysics weds, but imperfectly accords with, religious faith; poetry and philosophy struggle for ascendancy over each other; the author tries to have it both ways: already in "The Eolian Harp" we can recognize the Coleridge to come. Learning to read this one early work, we learn much about how to read his later ones.

Teaching the Coleridge-Wordsworth Dialogue

Paul Magnuson

The Romantic ideology of the individual imagination and the economics of publishing anthologies organized by individual authors have conspired to obscure the interesting fact that Romantic creativity was often collaborative and often found its outlet in joint publication. *Lyrical Ballads (1798)*, one of the most important single volumes in all English literature, was just such a joint publication, and *Ancient Mariner*, surely the most popular poem in the volume, was begun as an experiment in joint authorship. More than a few of its lines and several of the incidents originated with Wordsworth. The final poem in *Lyrical Ballads*, "Tintern Abbey," is closely modeled on Coleridge's "Frost at Midnight." The more one looks at the issues of collaboration and joint composition, the more it appears that many major poems were written in the circumstances of a poetic dialogue in which one poem answers, challenges, completes, revises, or transforms an earlier poem by the other author. In constructing course outlines we often acknowledge a dialogic aspect of Romantic creativity. Coleridge commented extensively on Wordsworth's poetry to praise Wordsworth and to assure readers that he, Coleridge, did not totally agree with Wordsworth. Blake also annotated Wordsworth's poetry, treating it with both humor and scorn. Yet we use these rudimentary dialogic exchanges to emphasize individuality. Coleridge suggests in chapter 14 of the *Biographia* a clear distinction between Wordsworth and himself. Wordsworth is the poet of nature; Coleridge, of the supernatural. The major Romantic poets share an interest in the human imagination and individual genius as well as in political freedom and human sympathy. Yet in the interests of rigorous examination and individual ideology, we use the evidence of dialogic creativity to illustrate the uniqueness of each author.

The evidence of dialogic creativity, however, should be used to illustrate the facts of dialogic creativity. I teach not only to preserve the individuality of each author but also to explore the similarities among authors, the joint possessions in their poetic and critical dialogue. For instance, by listening closely to the echoes and allusions of Wordsworth's "Ode: Intimations of Immortality" in Coleridge's "Dejection: An Ode" and in Wordsworth's "Resolution and Independence," students realize that the poems form a genuine dialogue on the loss of imagination. With the same purpose, a course could be organized by genre: some lyrical ballads, a few poems from Blake's *Songs of Innocence and of Experience*, and, perhaps, *Ancient Mariner*; the standard selection of Romantic odes; and a grouping of Romantic narrative poems. Such a structure may be a refreshing alternative to the course in which one reads Wordsworth for a few weeks, then Coleridge, then Blake, with the assumption that the individuality of the poet is best preserved by reading that poet alone. I prefer to present the dialogic groupings in two forms: the first is the dialogue of two poems of two authors, and the second, the dialogue within a single author's volume. Thus, focus is on the genesis of the poems, not the growth of the individual poet.

Chronological proximity often signals poetic dialogue. A significant responding poem may be written within weeks or months. Responding poems may be connected by quotation, allusion, or echo, by structure or by narrative order. In addition, there are repetitions both of significant figures of speech from poem to poem, such as the inspiring breeze, and of significant human figures. Tracing such similarities helps students align the canon and identify the sequences of works, but the vital issue for study is the differences among the poems. The responding poem identifies its origin in the earlier one by interpreting its predecessor, finding the theme or figure that provides a central motive and emotional power and then revising, reenvisioning, or replacing that figure or theme within another context. A dialogic reading of a joint canon cannot take place if each poem is a lifeless imitation of the earlier one, nor can it take place between poems that are completely different. For a dialogic reading to occur, traces of the original poem must appear in the later one, embedded in the structures and figures. The context of a poem in such a set of readings consists of the surrounding poems in the dialogue. The more one begins to see the connections among poems, the more obvious it becomes that an individual poem, whether a completed poem or a mere notebook fragment, is a fragment of a dialogue, a part of a whole that constitutes a Romantic discourse. The full significance of a fragment is seen only in its relation to other poems.

The construction of a set of poems for discussion, perhaps over several periods or classes of a week or so, may require special preparation by the instructor because of the need for early versions and drafts. It makes little sense to try to understand what Coleridge thought in 1798 by citing texts that he revised twenty years later. Some of the earlier drafts and versions are available in the newer anthologies, but, particularly with Coleridge, an instructor must make some effort to recover the early versions of "The Eolian Harp," "This Lime-tree Bower," "Frost at Midnight," and *Ancient Mariner*. Students who have worked their way through an analysis of "Frost at Midnight" discover that they must rethink their responses when they find out that in 1798 Coleridge returns from his excursion in memory and imagination to a "dead calm," not to a "deep calm."

One form of dialogic reading places an individual poem in the context of its first publication or in the contexts of its various publications, where its significance may be radically altered. "Frost at Midnight" is usually adequately discussed in the context of Coleridge's other Conversation poems as a Romantic lyric, an intensely personal meditation about the relation of the isolated human imagination to the surrounding world of nature and nature's language. The "numberless goings-on of life" suggest the workings of the natural forces of the frost. Not a word of politics anywhere, yet in the context of its first publication, the poem does have political significance. It was first published in 1798 with "Fears in Solitude" and "France: An Ode." Did Coleridge simply toss "Frost at Midnight" in with the others to make up a quarto pamphlet, or did he give some thought to the connections among the poems? The private, meditative voice of "Frost at Midnight" seems entirely out of place with the turgid public oratory of the other two poems. To be sure, there are sections of "Fears in Solitude" that resemble the nature poetry of "Frost at Midnight," but there is little of that in "France: An Ode." What is the political significance of "Frost at Midnight" in the context of these two poems? How is "Frost at Midnight" changed with their influence? Obviously the "numberless goings-on" include the turbulence of the events of the late winter and the spring of 1798, the fears of invasion. Political allegiances were being sharply drawn. In the Tory rhetoric of the day, the nation was being threatened with rebellion and atheism. The two went together. A republican was, quite simply, an atheist in the eyes of the church-and-king crowd. Thus a poem in praise of domestic virtues could not simply be a private poem. Like the other poems in the volume, it was a public, political defense. Does it constitute a coherent political argument along with the other poems, or is its self-defense merely tendentious or duplicitous? These questions would not arise unless one looked at "Frost at Midnight" in one of its original contexts.

I offer one more example of the placement of an individual poem in a volume, which alters both the poem's significance and the significance of the context. "The Eolian Harp," in 1796 called simply "Effusion xxxv," one of a series of effusions grouped as a sequence, was republished in Coleridge's (1797) *Poems*, where it was followed by "Reflections on Having Left a Place of Retirement." The two poems form a sequence in which the later poem turns abruptly from the pleasant domestic isolation of "The Eolian Harp" toward social and political involvement. The first line of "Reflections," "Low was our pretty Cot," doubles and turns on the final line of "The Eolian Harp," "Peace, and this Cot, and thee, heart-honour'd Maid!" The landscape is the same, but its figurative significance is altered; awkwardly emblematic of innocence, love, and wisdom in "The Eolian Harp," it is purged of such associations and naturalized with no emblematic quality in "Reflections." What does the change suggest about Coleridge's attitude toward both nature and language? What does it indicate about his certainty of being able to read the landscape? More important, "Reflections" explicitly rejects the isolation of domestic retirement because it reposes in "feelings all too delicate for use." If that rejection applies to "The Eolian Harp" as well as to the opening scene of "Reflections," the uneasy resolutions of the former become little more than a transitory utterance in an extended dialogue conducted in the volume. The final verse paragraph of "Reflections" changes the landscape of the setting to a dream image that both prefigures and postpones the paradise to come. How does this transformation of the landscape change a reading of the speculations on the "intellectual breeze" that informs "animated nature" in "The Eolian Harp"? Is the "intellectual breeze" only a dream image "too delicate for use"?

A second, perhaps more interesting, form of dialogic reading groups poems by Coleridge and Wordsworth in a common dialogue. Perhaps the most often read portion of their dialogue is the poetry of the spring of 1802. Coleridge's "Dejection: An Ode" becomes a richer experience by reading it in its many contexts. It belongs to the poetry of 1802, when Wordsworth wrote the four opening stanzas of the Immortality Ode. Coleridge's verse letter to Sara Hutchinson, the first version of "Dejection," follows the writing of the opening stanzas and clearly answers them. And just as clearly Wordsworth's "Resolution and Independence" answers Coleridge's verse letter. If one were to read these three poems as variations on the theme of loss, one would pose standard questions about the differences in their attitudes toward nature. What is the significance of Wordsworth's lament about the loss of sight and Coleridge's complaint about the failure of feeling? What is the significance of Coleridge's insistent claim that what we see in nature is the mind's construction, especially since Coleridge's first and clearest statement about the idea of the One Life comes a few months later in his letters (*CL* 2: 866)? Such questions often become documents in the poets' biographies, particularly with Coleridge's verse letter in evidence. What does the letter have to do with Coleridge's attitudes toward Wordsworth, toward sexuality, and toward his own insecurity and isolation? To see these poems in chronological sequence as a series of statements and counterstatements, however, is to raise specific questions about the kind of utterances they are. Why does Coleridge answer Wordsworth's Immortality Ode with a verse letter? Why does Wordsworth shift so suddenly in his opening stanzas from a private interior voice of loss to a public blessing in his "timely utterance"? What is the significance of Coleridge's struggle to utter a blessing in the verse letter? Is Wordsworth's "Resolution and Independence" an answer to his own loss or an answer to Coleridge's dejection? Inquiring about these poems as utterances in a dialogue also raises questions about literary speech acts, the ways in which such a dialogic reading accounts for the presence of auditors and contexts, the generation of poems, and the figures in the poems as tropes on those in earlier poems.

Another possibility for a dialogic sequence is Coleridge's Conversation poems—"The Eolian Harp," "Reflections on Having Left a Place of Retirement," "This Lime-tree Bower," and "Frost at Midnight"—read in the context of Wordsworth's use of them in "Tintern Abbey" and in the early drafts of *The Prelude*. A standard structural reading of Coleridge's poems concentrates on their structure, on the movement of the speaker's consciousness

from the concrete perceptions of nature and the natural world to the speculations on the one life and the return to the natural world. Each poem is
a variant of that paradigm. What is the relation between the mind and the
natural world? How does Coleridge read the text of nature? What qualities
of symbolism appear, and how does Coleridge vary them? I find it curious
that these questions are more appropriately asked of Wordsworth's poems.
Our tendency is to read Coleridge's poems with Wordsworth's eyes, from
a perspective conditioned by Wordsworth's concerns. Perhaps it is true that
Wordsworth's poetic and philosophic sensibility is shaped by Coleridge's
influence, but it is clear that his later poems, particularly "Tintern Abbey,"
are appropriations of Coleridge's poems and of the Romantic lyric and interpretations of it. Why not read Coleridge's poems as a sequence in order?
What changes occur as the sequence progresses? If "Tintern Abbey" is an
interpretation of "Frost at Midnight" because it duplicates its structure, how
does it read "Frost at Midnight"? What does Wordsworth identify as the
troublesome points in Coleridge's portraits of memory and self consciousness? What variations of the form of the lyric does Wordsworth create, and
why?

One of the best ways to assess the importance of Coleridge's poems is not
to read Coleridge by himself but to read other writers whom he influenced.
Teaching Coleridge may involve teaching other poets. It would be particularly worthwhile to continue the sequence of the Conversation poems and
"Tintern Abbey" to investigate the first work on *The Prelude* with Coleridge's
poems in mind. Is "Tintern Abbey" an adequate response to Coleridge's
poems? What does the early work on *The Prelude* reveal about Wordsworth's
confidence in the resolutions of "Tintern Abbey"? What is the balance of
doubt and confidence in that early work and to what extent does it reflect
Coleridge's uncertainties about the power of memory and imagination and
about imagination's ability to read the natural world? Answers to these questions are not easy to come by, but establishing the grounds on which they
can be asked alters students' perspectives on Romanticism and creativity.
To ponder whether Wordsworth or Coleridge holds this or that position in
opposition to the other may lead to a realization that their creativity and
consciousness are more a collaborative matter than an individual one.

The two groupings suggested so far seem rather obvious. Two other sequences that I propose for study need a good deal of argument and explication
to justify their being placed in a dialogic relation. The first sequence begins
with Wordsworth's drafting of the sailor's story in "Adventures on Salisbury
Plain" and includes *Ancient Mariner* and Wordsworth's "Discharged Soldier." If they are to be taught, most likely both Wordsworth poems and the
early version of *Ancient Mariner* will have to be duplicated for class, since
they do not usually appear in anthologies. "Adventures on Salisbury Plain"
and *Ancient Mariner* contain a similar narrative. A sailor or mariner is per-

secuted by unjust powerful forces, commits a crime for reasons that are never fully explained or clear, wanders aimlessly pursued by the unjust powers and a sense of guilt. In "Adventures on Salisbury Plain" and *Ancient Mariner* the psychological effect of the crime and the wandering is that of the destruction of personality and the dizzying submission to tormenting dreams. "Adventures on Salisbury Plain," along with "Salisbury Plain," which it revises, is explicitly a poem of political protest. The major issue is the injustice in the persecution of the sailor and the vagrant woman, for whom there is no charity. When Coleridge adopts the plot for *Ancient Mariner*, the late medieval setting seems to exclude the explicit references to contemporary events. Yet traces of Wordsworth's poem remain: persecution, injustice, and tyranny. In part *Ancient Mariner* is a poem of victimization, yet it is almost never read in its political context. The appropriate questions in a dialogic reading concern Coleridge's changes. Does his change of setting represent an evasion of political themes? Does his use of supernatural symbolism indicate a change of political views? (Does Blake's increasing reliance on visionary poetry indicate a change of political views?) Why does Coleridge seem to be more concerned with a psychological rather than a social explanation of guilt? Do Coleridge's changes in Wordsworth's narrative constitute a critique of Wordsworth's poems? Why does Coleridge let the Mariner become the narrator of his own tale? What, in this dialogic sequence, is the significance of the Mariner's "strange power of speech"? Finally, "The Discharged Soldier" is a commentary on both "Adventures on Salisbury Plain" and *Ancient Mariner*, even though Coleridge had not completed his poem when Wordsworth drafted "The Discharged Soldier." Both the Mariner and the soldier have returned, but they still wander, outcasts narrating their tales. Why does Wordsworth duplicate the physical appearances of Coleridge's Mariner? What is the significance of his naturalizing the tale that Coleridge presented as supernatural? If these poems do in fact form a sequence in which each poem is a revision of the previous one, then the figures of the sailor, the Mariner, and the soldier are not merely representative victims of injustice but allude to previous figures. What is their figurative significance if they are the signs of previous figures?

Finally, Wordsworth's "Ruined Cottage" and "Pedlar" (1799) and Coleridge's *Christabel* form a sequence. Margaret's story and Christabel's are strikingly similar. Each tells of a woman attached to a dwelling, the cottage or the castle, whose lover is away at war, who represents charity associated with the dwelling, who sinks into a form of passivity or despair, and who yet tries to find a sign of her lover by wandering from her home in reality or in imagination. Whereas *Ancient Mariner* and "Adventures on Salisbury Plain" are anatomies of fear, these poems are anatomies of despair. Why does Coleridge change the setting again from the contemporary world to a supernatural and medieval one? What does his use of gothic motifs do to transform Wordsworth's narrative? Does Coleridge's use of the supernatural call into question Wordsworth's calm confidence in the literal and in nature's language? What figurative value does the supernatural have? The narrator of Margaret's story claims he can read landscape that the young poet cannot read, yet in *Christabel* reading the landscape, like reading the figures, is a difficult matter. How do the issues of doubling, echoing, and duplicity comment on the simple assurance of the narrator of Margaret's tale that he can see things with a clear and sympathetic eye?

My recommendations for teaching Coleridge imply that it cannot be done fully by teaching only Coleridge. Reading individual authors, like reading individual poems, is a limiting procedure, a form of reduction, which institutes an exclusion of the wealth of reference and allusion within the poems. Dialogic reading also implies that one poem cannot stand for, or represent, the whole dialogue, because it must differ in important ways from the other utterances in the dialogue. Only the dialogue can represent itself.

Those who want to experiment with dialogic reading and to teach the early versions of poems in their original contexts will find ample information in the Cornell Wordsworth, a series of editions of the longer poems containing a wealth of scholarly information, and the *Collected Coleridge*. Also of great help are Mark Reed's volumes of *Wordsworth: The Chronology*, which include many references to Coleridge; E. H. Coleridge's edition of Coleridge's poetry; and the brief, but useful, checklists of works on the relationships of Coleridge and Wordsworth in Karl Kroeber's and Max Schulz's essays in Frank Jordan's *English Romantic Poets*. Most critical works on one author make reference to the other, but the books by Lucy Newlyn, Nicholas Roe, Gene Ruoff, and my own *Coleridge and Wordsworth* place equal attention on the two, contributing further to an understanding of their dialogue.

What Comes of "Dejection"?

John T. Ogden

"Dejection: An Ode" dramatizes the poet's fluctuating moods as he observes a beautiful evening scene, regrets the loss of his former joy, envisions mighty forms of destruction, and finally turns his thoughts to the joy of the lady he has been addressing. In teaching this poem, I try to help students see how much it tells us about Coleridge's notion of dejection, how it embodies that dejection through its poetic technique, and how in the course of the poem the poet carries himself beyond dejection. My questions may be modified to suit the class at hand. My condensed answers are not conclusive; rather, they suggest possibilities to pursue or issues to argue with.

What does the poem tell us about dejection? Apparently dejection is related to the "dull pain" that the poet mentions at the end of the first stanza and elaborates in the opening of the second stanza. Is dejection itself that pain and grief, or is it the force that stifles that grief, dejecting (casting down) the poet and preventing him from expressing the grief, from finding a "natural outlet" and hence "relief"? Or is it both the repression and the pain? The very evasiveness of the feeling characterizes it. What does a "grief without a pang" feel like? Dejection seems to be both a feeling and a condition that opposes feeling, as exemplified at the end of the second stanza: the beautiful scene arouses the poet's recognition of its beauty but no corresponding feeling of beauty.

Dejection is further variously represented in stanzas 3 and 6, implicitly in stanzas 4 and 5 (in contrast to joy), and in the images of stanza 7. But before moving into the middle of the poem, students might well take into account what happens at the beginning. How is the poet's dejection apparent in stanza 1? Indications of dejection may be found in the image of "the dull sobbing draft, that moans and rakes" and in the curt remark "[w]hich better far were mute," but not in the calm and nonchalant opening quatrain, or in the subsequent excited description of "the New-moon winter-bright" (in effect quite different from the epigraph), or in the agitated anticipation of the storm. The shifting moods are embodied in the meter, syntactical rhythms, and other sound effects, which reveal the "strong music in the soul" (line 60) that Coleridge uses throughout the poem and which approximate the larger movements of the poem.

How those larger movements occur deserves consideration. Each stanza begins with an idea or motif from the previous stanza and then proceeds to shift direction so as to contrast with the previous stanza. Stanza 2 expands "this dull pain" from the end of stanza 1 and shifts the tone to a somber lament. It concludes with a specific dissociation of sight and feeling that in stanza 3 becomes generalized to a failure of genial spirits. That failure to imbue outward forms with passion and life from within turns, in stanza 4, into a celebration of the glory that the poet has lost. Observing the poem's overall movement in this manner reveals its transitions and coherence. It also raises questions about what propels the poet's thoughts in the particular direction that they take.

Who is the Lady introduced in stanza 2 and addressed again in stanza 4? She remains insubstantial but becomes more fully represented in stanza 5. Why need she not ask "What this strong music in the soul may be"? She need not ask because she is pure in heart, so that she is given the joy the poet lacks. The Lady serves as a foil to the poet: as he idealizes the joyful marriage of mind and nature that is denied to him, he seems to move into a deeper grief. But what happens to the tone in these stanzas 4 and 5? Does the poet sound dejected? Coleridge seems to get caught up in the joy that he claims to have lost. The exclamatory mode, the repetition, the striking metaphors, and the imagery of radiating light and sound convey an exultation in which the poet, by articulating, seems to share both in his tone of voice and in the height of his poetic vision.

However, as he moves in stanza 6 to contrast his former joy with his present affliction, the poet still sees himself as excluded from that joy. Why can joy predominate over past distress but not over present afflictions? Is the poet's separation of thought from feeling comparable to the separation of seeing from feeling in stanza 2? Has he then imposed this condition on himself? These questions may expose logical inconsistencies in the poem, but the inconsistencies may be understood as the dramatic representation of the dejected poet, who views himself and his world in a way that reflects his state of dejection.

In stanza 7 the poet turns from his inward "viper thoughts" to the rising wind that he forecast at the beginning of the poem. Having anticipated that wind, and even more having longed for it—"oh! that even now the gust were swelling!" (15)—why has he not noticed it sooner? Presumably he has been too preoccupied with his own excited thoughts, but now the wind outdoes him in its sound, its emotion, and its poetic creation, as it plays a wild and various song on the aeolian lute. In what sense is the wind a "mighty Poet"? It makes music, raises passions, and shapes them into figures and stories. Is the wind then comparable to the poet speaking in the poem? We may see the wind as producing an exaggeration (or perhaps even a caricature?) of Coleridge's own lament.

But is Coleridge in his dejection not the opposite of this "mighty Poet"? Unlike the speaker, whose grief is stifled and whose afflictions are unnamed, the wind expresses feelings in specific forms and sharp images. And as "Actor" the wind delivers "tragic sounds" first of a massive defeat and then of pathetic grief and fear. In creating these roles, the wind transcends them. In contrast, the poet has not been acting a part but has been suffering from feelings and circumstances against which he sees no action he can take.

Has the poet not, however, created these very roles that he attributes to the wind? If it is the wind that tells such tragic tales, interpreting them still requires a creative mind. Consider how the poet's activity in stanza 7 relates to what he has said earlier in the poem. In listening to the wind and hearing it the way he does, Coleridge displays that very "shaping spirit of Imagination" (86) whose loss he has lamented. The howling wind sends the poet's soul abroad, as it has done in the past; it makes his "dull pain" "move and live," as he longed for at the beginning of the poem. The division of sight and feeling in stanza 2 is overcome in the synesthesia where sound creates a vision that contains powerful feelings.

If stanza 7 exhibits imagination, is that imagination not very different from the one that stanzas 4 and 5 present? Contrast the imagery and tone as well as the feeling of that earlier vision with the creative activity in stanza 7. Instead of beauty and joy, the poet finds horror and defeat. How are we to account for such different views of imagination? Consider the contrasting dramatic circumstances: in stanzas 4 and 5 Coleridge envisions an ideal of imagination in absolute purity, whereas in stanza 7 he is not speaking about imagination but is caught up in its power.

In stanza 8, how do we account for the complete shift in subject and tone? How is this final stanza related to the rest of the poem? Is the poet simply turning away from his troubles to the more comforting subject of wishing the Lady well? In wishing for her the utter joy of imagination, he displays a generosity of spirit and a conviviality that go far beyond his own dejection. What brings about this change? Stanza 7 has served as a purgation, bringing the poet out of the self-pity and dejection of stanza 6 into the benediction and contentment of stanza 8. Has he then overcome his dejection? Probably not—"small thoughts have I of sleep"; but his thoughts, feelings, and actions are no longer limited to that dejection.

His blessing is an act of giving. If, then, "we receive but what we give," should he not receive a blessing in return? And does he? He does not say so, but students should consider what the tone shows in the evenness of the meter, the regularity of the end-stopped lines, and the peacefulness of the imagery. He remains unaware of the blessing he has received because he is thinking of the Lady, not of himself.

A discussion of the poem might conclude with a comparison of two kinds of imagination—the ideal imagination of the Lady that the poet describes and the human imagination manifested in the poet's responses. The one is pure but naive, vulnerable, and solipsistic; the other may be turbulent and even painful, but it can confront distress and misery and transform them. Both shape and create, and both attain joy—the one naturally, the other through struggle. Readers will want to decide for themselves to what extent that struggle limits or heightens the concluding sense of joy.

Once "Dejection" is understood in its own integrity, students may gain further insight by examining it in relation to other writings by Coleridge and his contemporaries. I draw attention only to some of the fundamental points of comparison as starting points for further study.

Coleridge's verse letter to Sara Hutchinson (in the manuscript simply named "A Letter to ——— / April 4, 1802—Sunday Evening," but variously named by editors) is usually considered the original form of "Dejection: An Ode," though George Dekker argues that it is an offshoot from "Dejection" in a developing state (47–54). Are these two versions of the same poem, the published one removing the embarrassingly personal references and the informal language and structure of the unpublished one? If so, we could say that the manuscript assists us in understanding "Dejection" by identifying the Lady as Sara Hutchinson and the grief as Coleridge's problems in love—his unhappy marriage and the impossibility of fulfilling his love. While such biographical information explains the personal circumstances of the poem's composition, we may question whether the published version does not shift to a different emphasis and achieve a different outcome. In any event, the two poems or the two versions invite comparisons that sharpen our understanding of each (see Parrish, *Coleridge's "Dejection,"* for the original versions with photographic copies of the manuscripts).

"Dejection" was first published in the *Morning Post* on 4 October 1802, the wedding day of Wordsworth, to whom the poem in this version is addressed (using the pseudonym "Edmund"). Besides comparing this intermediate version with the earlier "Letter to [Sara]" and the later version published in *Sibylline Leaves*, students may consider the intricate interrelation of Coleridge's "Dejection" and Wordsworth's "Ode: Intimations of Immortality"—a relation identified by Fred Manning Smith and frequently explored, recently and extensively by Paul Magnuson (*Coleridge and Wordsworth*), and by Gene Ruoff.

Coleridge's Conversation poems display an evolution of style, form, and themes that leads directly to "Dejection." The same conversational tone and situation are there, though modified into a more formal structure. As in the Conversation poems, "Dejection" works through the interplay of scene and personal reflection, of present and past, and of the poet's experience vis-à-vis that of the person addressed. The alternating systolic and diastolic rhythms described by Albert Gérard are evident here (Coburn, *Coleridge: A Collection of Critical Essays* 78–87). Particular motifs may also be recognized. The instrument of "The Eolian Harp" is obviously central, though the harpist wind becomes more important (see John A. Hodgson's discussion in this volume). "A light in sound, a sound-like power in light" from that poem may be taken to characterize the paralleling of light and music in stanzas 4 and 5 of "Dejection."

In "The Nightingale" Coleridge criticizes the man who "made all gentle sounds tell back the tale / Of his own sorrow" (20–21) instead of "Surrendering his whole spirit" "to the influxes / Of shapes and sounds and shifting elements" (29, 27–28). Compare such responses with the poet's responses in "Dejection," stanzas 1, 2, and 7. "This Lime-tree Bower My Prison" also offers a situation for comparison. The poet regrets his confinement: he is unable to enjoy the "Beauties and feelings" (3) that his friends enjoy. Through imagination he overcomes his loss and gains another sort of delight and a faith in nature (59–67). The blessing that closes "Frost at Midnight" may be compared with the blessing that closes "Dejection."

Coleridge's Mystery poems also contain pertinent points of comparison. The ancient Mariner's despair is imaged in more dramatic forms but with effects of isolation and suffering similar to those of the poet's condition in "Dejection." Note in particular how the Mariner's granting of a blessing brings about his own redemption—not complete (he can never regain his lost innocence) but not devoid of joy. "Kubla Khan" has a conjunction of joy ("delight"), music, and creativity similar to that in stanzas 4 and 5 of "Dejection."

Coleridge's theory of imagination is represented in "Dejection," especially in the line "We receive but what we give" and in the imagery of issuing forth a light and sending forth a voice. Although these lines must be understood in their dramatic context, they do agree with Coleridge's remarks on imagination in *Biographia Literaria*. Imagination as "shaping spirit" receives fuller treatment as the "esemplastic power" in chapter 10 and following. At the end of chapter 13 Coleridge defines imagination as an act of creative perception that unifies and gives life. Note how these activities apply to stanza 2: the division of sight and feeling may show a lack of imagination, but the imagery suggests an unacknowledged working of imagination. The notion of imagination as the reconciler of opposites (at the end of chapter 14) may afford a way of understanding how stanzas 4 and 5 embody both joy and dejection.

"We receive but what we give" has been both compared and contrasted with Wordsworth's "thou must give, / Else never canst receive" (*The Prelude*, 1850, 12. 276–77). Both lines require a giving of the spirit; but what we receive, according to Coleridge, is what we give, whereas according to Wordsworth, the giving and receiving between us and the surrounding world are reciprocal. The difference is far-reaching in a comparison of the two poets.

Coleridge's theoretical musings in his notebooks suggest additional approaches to "Dejection":

> In looking at objects of Nature while I am thinking, as at yonder moon dim-glimmering thro' the dewy window-pane, I seem rather to be

seeking, as it were *asking*, a symbolical language for something within me that already and forever exists, than observing any thing new.

(CN 2: 2546)

In stanza 2 the poet fails to find such symbols, or so he claims: however, the moon's combining of new and old in fact symbolizes a fundamental concern of the poem. Reeve Parker (182) finds the key to the poem in another notebook entry: "Misery conjures up other Forms, & binds them into Tales and Events—activity is always Pleasure" (CN 1: 1601). Coleridge's critical writings offer numerous other possibilities for glossing his poetry.

Finally, "Dejection" may be examined in the broader context of Romantic poetry. For example, M. H. Abrams pairs it with odes of Wordsworth, Shelley, and Keats to illustrate "the Greater Romantic Lyric" ("Structure"). The interdependence of joy and sorrow, the contrast of innocence and experience, symbolic landscape, imagination, perception, and vision are some of the topics to explore in relating "Dejection" to other Romantic poems.[1]

NOTE

[1]An earlier form of this chapter was presented to the Linguistic Circle of Manitoba and North Dakota and abstracted in its *Proceedings* (28 [1988]: 30–31).

TEACHING THE MYSTERY POEMS

Vision and Revision in "Kubla Khan"

Norman Fruman

To all the other nearly miraculous qualities about "Kubla Khan," one can add that no other poem affords an instructor so broad a range of opportunities to lay before a class—at all levels of instruction—fundamental problems in literary criticism, the significance of textual variants, the sometimes peculiar relation of an author to how readers apprehend a poem, the potential tyranny of received opinion, and the ways in which knowledge—real or supposed —outside the text itself can profoundly influence how a text is understood. Nor does this list exhaust the learning possibilities this poem provides. Even a rudimentary understanding of "Kubla Khan" involves vastly more scholarly knowledge than the study of any other poetry since the Renaissance almost ever calls for.

The student comes to "Kubla Khan: Or, A Vision in a Dream. A Fragment," through its famous and riveting preface, which begins by declaring that the "fragment" is being published "at the request of a poet [unidentified] of great and deserved celebrity and . . . rather as a psychological curiosity, than on the ground of any supposed *poetic* merits." A very odd statement, surely, about one of the world's supremely famous and justly admired poems. But it is odd only to the rare person who actually pauses to reflect. The rest of us read on with a sense of gathering excitement:

> In the summer of the year 1797, the Author, then in ill health, had
> retired to a lonely farm-house between Porlock and Linton, on the
> Exmoor confines of Somerset and Devonshire.

It sounds like the beginning of a thriller, heavy with expectation. Clearly,
something extraordinary is about to be recounted. Why else the strange
particularity about the location of the "lonely farm-house"? An ill author, "a
vision in a dream," a "psychological curiosity"—all these precise details are
about an event that took place twenty years before (the poem was first
published in 1816), obviously an event worth remembering. Suspense builds
as we hurry on.

But wait. Just where are Porlock and Linton? Why would a sick man
journey to a lonely farmhouse rather than stay at home and be properly
attended to? No one, of course, thinks to ask such questions the first time
through the preface, and, as a matter of historical fact, few readers (until
the last generation) have ever questioned the strict veracity of the preface
—at least not in print. We, and our students, are normally trusting souls,
especially in the presence of nonfiction prose. If, however, one took the
trouble to hunt up a large-scale map of England to locate Porlock and Linton,
one would find that they are on the Bristol Channel in southwest England,
some twenty-five miles from Nether Stowey, where Coleridge was living
when "Kubla Khan" was written.

What difference does it make? You merely have to state these facts in
class to see puzzled expressions appear all over the room, particularly when
you say further that there was no public transportation between these locales
at the time and that Coleridge did not own a horse. He would have had to
walk this considerable distance, across some rough and lonely terrain. Certainly a peculiar thing for a man in ill health to do. Some student is sure to
suggest at this point, since the one thing just about everybody seems to
know about Coleridge is that he took opium, "Maybe he just wanted to be
alone to turn on."

> In consequence of a slight indisposition, an anodyne had been pre-
> scribed, from the effects of which he fell asleep in his chair at the
> moment that he was reading the following sentence, or words of the
> same substance, in "Purchas's Pilgrimage". . . .

In a lonely farmhouse, who was in a position to "prescribe" an "anodyne"
—a pain killer of some sort? And what was "Purchas's Pilgrimage"? Nobody,
of course, has any idea.

An important and disturbing lesson is now emerging. It is a simple one
but needs to be learned again and again. Unless the reader is attentive,

words, place-names, titles, and much else can simply glide smoothly over the mind and leave behind little more than vague impressions. Down the generations, inattention and credulity have characterized the way almost all readers have responded to the preface to "Kubla Khan."

In 1797 *Purchas His Pilgrimage* was a rare book, last printed in the early seventeenth century. The 1614 edition was a heavy folio of over a thousand pages, surely not the kind of reading even a Coleridge would be likely to slip into his knapsack at the beginning of a twenty-five-mile walk, in good or ill health. Nor was Coleridge likely to have found this scarce volume in a lonely farmhouse.

It is not necessary here to rehearse all the other improbabilities and dubieties in the preface. Once genuinely engaged in reading it, students raise many probing and skeptical questions, sometimes with unbecoming enthusiasm. They wonder especially about the mysterious "person on business from Porlock" who interrupts Coleridge in his "eager" writing of the miraculously given poem and detains him for "above an hour." Surely this was not an itinerant peddler just happening by, and Coleridge would hardly have arranged a business meeting under such conditions. And why did Coleridge say that he'd fallen asleep in his chair "at the moment he was reading the following sentence, *or words of the same substance*," from Purchas? Would a man so interested in psychological phenomena, particularly his own mental processes, have failed down the years to check his poem against the actual words in Purchas; and in presenting this tale to the world, would he not have taken the slight trouble to quote accurately? In fact, he quoted inaccurately, thus: "Here the Khan Kubla commanded a palace to be built, and a stately garden thereunto. And thus ten miles of fertile ground were inclosed with a wall." Purchas's words stand much closer to the poem, especially to the Crewe manuscript, which is in Coleridge's handwriting. Purchas wrote, "In Xamdu did Cublai Can build a stately Palace, encompassing sixteene miles of plaine ground with a wall, wherein are fertile Meddowes, pleasant Springs, delightfull Streames, and all sorts of beasts of chase and game, in the middest thereof a sumptuous house of pleasure." Where the received text reads:

> In Xanadu did Kubla Khan
> A stately pleasure-dome decree:
> Where Alph, the sacred river ran
> Through caverns measureless to man
> Down to a sunless sea.
> So twice *five* miles of fertile ground
> With walls and towers were *girdled* round. . . .
>   (Italics mine)

the Crewe manuscript has:

> In *Xannadú* did *Cubla* Khan
> A stately Pleasure-Dome decree:
> Where Alph, the sacred River, ran
> Thro' Caverns measureless to Man
> Down to a sunless Sea.
> So twice *six* miles of fertile ground
> With walls and towers were *compass'd* round. . . .
> (Italics mine)

"Six" and "compass'd" obviously derive from Purchas's "encompassing six-teene miles of plaine ground." So does the spelling of "Cubla" and the crucial word "pleasure." Yet more significant of conscious artistic processes is the spelling "Xannadú," with an accent over the *u* to control pronunciation (hardly the work of the dreaming unconscious). *Xanadu*, as the place is now known to us, owes its spelling to the published version of "Kubla Khan." In Purchas the name is spelled either *Xamdu* or *Xaindu*, neither of which provides the three syllables demanded by the iambic meter. *Xannadú* is an intermediate invention of Coleridge's, and since it would be an unfamiliar name to the reader, the poet provided the accent as an aid to rhythm.

Why the change from six miles to five miles? One can easily hear what is unsatisfactory about six by speaking the lines aloud:

> Down to a *s*unle*ss s*ea.
> *S*o twi*ce six* mile*s* . . .

Coleridge would have recognized the excessive sibilance of these lines the first time he recited them aloud, if not sooner. Changing to "five" not only reduces the hissing *s*'s but brings forward the long *i* sounds in "twice five miles" and in "fertile" later in the line, in the English pronunciation. The vast superiority of the sensuous "girdled round" over the coldly geometrical "compass'd round" can be fully appreciated only in the context of the whole sound cluster: "fertile ground . . . girdled round." All this, of course, was done with deliberate artistry, and certainly not "without any sensation or consciousness of effort."

The claim made for the marvelous origin of "Kubla Khan" was but one of many dubious statements Coleridge made about the composition of his poems; he repeatedly claimed to have written spontaneously, or in strange states of mind, or under unusual conditions. Many of these can be shown to be false, or so exaggerated as to amount to the same thing. For example, he published "Religious Musings" as "A Desultory Poem, Written on the Christmas Eve of 1794," but he had not written it in a single night. His letters show that he had worked very hard for two years on the four-hundred-line work: "It has cost me much labor in polishing, more than any poem I ever wrote," he declared to a friend (*CL* 1: 162). Confiding to a new acquaintance about the composition of his "Hymn before Sun-rise, in the Vale of Chamouni," he stated, "I involuntarily poured forth a Hymn" (*CL* 2: 864); we now know that the poem and its pious preface are heavily indebted to a poem about Chamouni at dawn by Frederika Brun, an obscure Danish-German poet, and that, moreover, Coleridge had never even been at Chamouni. While traveling in Germany in 1798 and 1799, he sent his wife and Thomas Poole poems that he said he had "written 'one wintry night in bed' " or "yesternight, . . . dittied" (*CL* 1: 488, 493), without mentioning that they were translations or paraphrases from German poems, some of which he had copied into his notebooks. These and many other such claims seem psychologically related to Coleridge's repeated publication of poems supposedly written during his "schoolboy" days but actually the productions of his maturity and even middle age.

When in 1934 the Crewe manuscript of "Kubla Khan" came to light, it ought to have become impossible for impartial scholars to accept the 1816 preface as literal truth, for a note on the manuscript, in Coleridge's handwriting, read, "This fragment, with a good deal more, not recoverable, composed in a sort of Reverie brought on by two grains of Opium, taken to check a dysentery, at a Farm House between Porlock & Linton, a quarter of a mile from Culbone Church, in the fall of the year, 1797." Now "a sort of Reverie" is a very far cry from the three-hour deep sleep of the 1816 preface, with its unconscious composition of a great poem. Moreover, the manuscript shows many variants from the published text (all of which richly repay study), although Coleridge claimed to be publishing precisely what had been written in the farmhouse, "without any sensation or consciousness of effort."

Although the beauty and power of "Kubla Khan" are neither augmented nor diminished by the circumstances of its composition, whatever they were, it would be absurd to argue that the poem's *meaning* is equally unaffected. The interpretation of dreams remains one of the most intensely debated subjects in the whole field of mental functioning. That this "dream" is in hauntingly beautiful verse and that the dreamer has been dead for over a century and a half render impossible any kind of *assured* interpretation of this poem as a dream.

With respect to the tyranny of received opinion, it is well to remember how fixed was the belief, until well after the Second World War, that "Kubla Khan" was uninterpretable. When I asked one of my professors in graduate school what the poem meant, he replied firmly, "It doesn't mean a thing."

Of the conclusion of the poem John Livingston Lowes wrote, "Nobody in his waking senses could have fabricated those amazing eighteen lines," and he declared confidently that the final lines "should banish doubt" about the strict veracity of the preface (363).

If, however, one approaches the poem without preconceptions and accepts that the poem is a fragment, as Coleridge asserted in the title of the poem, again in the preface, and yet again in the note appended to the only known manuscript, then the interpretative problems are not necessarily any more difficult than those in *Ancient Mariner* or *Christabel*. The most important preconception to get rid of, in some ways as pernicious as that about dream composition, is that the poem is "about the act of poetic creation in which the major images are symbolic," to quote the headnote of *English Romantic Writers* (Perkins 430). Once one accepts this now widespread interpretation, Procrustes's bed is readily available to accommodate the poem. Thus Kubla Khan in decreeing that a pleasure dome should be built becomes an artist. No matter that he merely gives an order; the interpretation requires that he be a *creator*. The sacred river disappearing underground is the creative process, or the unconscious, depending. . . . The ancestral voices prophesying war symbolize a threat to artistic autonomy, or the resistance of the old order to the new, or the decay inherent in all human effort, depending . . . . My objection to interpretations of this kind is not so much that they are unconvincing as that they are quite unnecessary. The poem *is* about the creative process, but in a peculiar and quite unsymbolic way. To see this, one must ignore the preface and read the poem as one would any other.

Nothing in the first eleven lines needs comment or interpretation. In themselves the lines, however beautiful, describe straightforwardly the pleasure dome, gardens, sacred river, and forests. The same is true of lines 12–28, except for the reference to a "woman wailing for her demon lover," who may or may not actually be on the premises. The syntax is obscure. The savage place is

> as holy and enchanted
> As e'er beneath a waning moon was haunted
> By woman wailing for her demon lover.

The interpretive difficulty here is readily accounted for if we accept that the poem is a fragment. In the light of the supernatural phenomena in *Ancient Mariner* and *Christabel*, there is nothing at all extraordinary in the presence of the wailing woman, if indeed she is meant actually to be present and is not brought in simply to intensify the simile. There is nothing obscure or strange in the description of the turbulent geyser that throws up rocks and powerful streams of water or in the description of the sacred river that sinks tumultuously underground. The ancestral voices Kubla hears amid this tumult, however, are clearly supernatural. What Coleridge would have made of those voices had he finished the poem it is futile to guess at. It seems reasonable to suppose, however, given the prophecy of the ancestral voices and the leisurely development of the first thirty lines, that a finished "Kubla Khan" would have been a narrative poem of at least several hundred lines, not the short lyric we now have.

That the last eighteen lines should ever have been taken as part of the dream rather than as a comment on it is simply astonishing:

> A damsel with a dulcimer
> In a vision *once I saw.* . . .
> Could I *revive* within me
> Her symphony and song. . . .
> (Italics mine)

Is this not clearly past tense? After all, in the preface Coleridge is confident that in the dream he "could not have composed less than from two to three hundred lines; if that indeed can be called composition in which all the images rose up before him as *things*, with a parallel production of the correspondent expressions. . . ." But here already, at lines 38–39, the poem is *remembering* an Abyssinian maid seen in some *past* vision, declaring at once that if the speaker could recover the frame of mind ("delight") that the maid's song induced in the past, he could now "build that dome in air," as well as the "caves of ice." Then everyone hearing his verses would see them, and he would be able to speak (i.e., write a poem) with such power that auditors would regard him as possessed and would weave a triple circle around him, either to show that he is a tabooed object or to protect themselves against one who has experienced something forbidden. That is why listeners must close their eyes "with holy dread," for he, the speaker, the poet, he with the flashing eyes and floating hair, has eaten and drunk of that which is meant not for mortals but only, presumably, for gods.

Approached in this way, the poem falls into two clearly demarked parts, which happens also to be how the manuscript of "Kubla Khan" is divided, with a single break just before the last eighteen lines. The break after line 11, as the poem has always been printed, results from an error perpetuated since the first printing of 1816, where line 11 is at the bottom of the page. Editors ever afterward have falsely assumed that a break was intended here, and thus the poem seems to divide into three parts.

If we accept that the poem has only two parts, then its structure falls naturally into thirty-six lines of an unfinished poem, whose real subject and plot we can only speculate about. Figuring in the plot are a pleasure-loving Asian potentate, the mysterious voices of ancestors declaring that war will come to disrupt what appears to be some kind of earthly paradise, and perhaps a woman and demonic lover. But whatever the plot, intense visual images dominate the experience of reading the poem—as they do in much of *Ancient Mariner*. The last eighteen lines, then, state what frame of mind would be necessary to complete the poem and what effect it would have on listeners. But, perhaps oddly, what the poet speaks of is not the Khan, or war, or a wailing woman, but the sunny pleasure dome, and the caves of ice (the latter detail not appearing till line 36).

Let us pause to consider this problem, for it is of a kind that can appear in almost any interpretation and is sometimes raised by students. If one assumes, as almost all New Critics did and many interpreters still do, that there is an "organic" reason for every detail in a work of art, one inevitably finds such reasons, however unconvincing they may be to anyone else. Surely it is better to accept that one can often think of no convincing reason why the artist chose this word or image rather than that word or image. Nevertheless, one can speculate, and speculation can be evaluated by the usual standards of evidence, coherence, and plausibility. It is often wise to begin analysis of intractable interpretive problems with technical considerations. It may simply be that the driving rhythm and resonant vowels of "that dome in air / That sunny dome, those caves of ice" were more compelling than any of the other possibilities that occurred to him. But it is also possible, perhaps even probable, that the startling contrast between the sunny dome and the caves of ice was a major germinating matrix of this alternately paradisical and threatening poem.

Here what may be an entirely personal association enters into my sense of the poem's meaning. I have long felt that the root subject of "Kubla Khan" is not the creative but the procreative process, that the poem is profoundly autobiographical and reflects Coleridge's unconscious sexual longings and fears. I dealt with this idea to some extent in my *Damaged Archangel*, but since then have found evidence suggesting that the strangely powerful images of the sunny dome and caves of ice may be connected with Coleridge's wife, Sara.

In a journal entry of 1801 (which has been tampered with and transcribed by another hand), Coleridge wrote of his wife's "coldness": "I have dressed perhaps washed with her, & no one with us—all as cold & calm as a deep Frost . . . Sara is uncommonly *cold* in her feelings of animal Love" (*CN* 1: 979). Sara Coleridge was also an uncommonly attractive woman. Even after the bitterness of their separation, he could write to her that he had never "known any woman for whom I had an equal personal fondness. . . . I had a PRIDE in you, & I never saw you at the top of our Hill, when I returned from a Walk, without a sort of pleasurable Feeling of Sight . . . which is some little akin to the delight in a beautiful Flower joined with the consciousness—'And it is in *my* garden' " (*CL* 3: 77).

"A beautiful flower" in a garden who is "uncommonly cold" within—a pleasure house with caves of ice? Such a connection may sound preposterous. But it may seem less so when one considers some of the many other images in the poem that admit of sexual symbolism: a pleasure dome (breast or Mount of Venus); a chasm that slants down a wooded hill, in which are deep caverns; a turbulent geyser that erupts in "swift, half-intermitted bursts" from an earth that breathes in "fast, thick pants," and so forth.

To deal with such material in undergraduate classes is to invite an end to all other interpretive approaches, for many students are so enthralled by the possibility that these connections are real that they want to discuss nothing else. What needs to be emphasized is that psychoanalytic interpretation requires genuine psychological knowledge, which is not gained casually, and that the attribution of unconscious meanings to the poet Coleridge's utterances calls for far more information about him than is contained in anthology headnotes. In any case, all such interpretations can only be tentative, based as they are on assumptions about mental functioning that are themselves highly problematic. The more students come to see that interpretation is not a free-for-all but is constrained by the text, by history, and by much else, the better.

To return, then, to our general discussion of "Kubla Khan": In the strictly limited sense just described, we do have a complete poem—a glorious fragment with a comment on what would be needed to complete it. The fragment and the unforgettable eighteen-line tailpiece create a unique unity, neither mechanical nor organic. Let us call it a "Coleridgean unity," in honor of the master of fragments.

If "Kubla Khan" was not "given" in a dream, what might its finished form have looked like? Coleridge had no gift for plotting. His one complete narrative poem, *Ancient Mariner*, is heavily indebted to Wordsworth, who suggested the shooting of the albatross in antarctic waters and the spectral persecution by the "tutelary spirits" of the region. The story of the unfinished "Three Graves" was also supplied by Wordsworth. *Christabel* is a fragment, and the two conclusions Coleridge gave many years later to his son Derwent and to his physician, James Gillman, seem hopelessly inadequate to the psychological and symbolic riches the poem implies. Still, what we have of *Christabel* contains a coherent plot line. One can easily imagine many endings to the story, and there are plenty of hints as to what future cantos might contain. But "Kubla Khan" is a fragment that contains hardly any clues to what plot might develop from it. Indeed, its very incoherence seems to me to lend some credence to Coleridge's preface.

The point of all this is to suggest that just as the poem's magnificent verbal fabric testifies to deliberate, conscious artistry—reinforced now by the evidence of the manuscript variants—so does the succession of intense and seemingly unrelated images, as far as plot is concerned, imply that the images

(Khan, pleasure dome, gardens, sacred river, threatening voices, wailing woman, demon lover, Abyssinian maid) occurred to Coleridge with some suddenness, in some state of mind (perhaps "a sort of reverie") akin to daydreaming, when one can experience streaming mental images not controlled by the conscious mind. Such a flow of images, whatever their meaning in Coleridge's unconscious, might well have struck him with immense emotional force. At the height of his annus mirabilis powers, Coleridge could have described these images in the thirty-six lines we now have—at which point the images or their connections grew too hazy to be fixed in words. The last eighteen lines, then, "complete" the poem in the way I have described.

The preface to "Kubla Khan" is not something one would willingly give up in toto. In view of the history of critical commentary on this poem, however, one ought also to be hesitant to support those who seize on any opportunity to declare that, after all, despite some exaggeration, Coleridge's claim about the composition of this poem is essentially true. For years after the composition of "Kubla Khan" he said nothing about it (so far as the voluminous record of letters and journals goes), even on appropriate occasions, as when dreams were being discussed. And on 3 November 1810, during the bitter breach with Wordsworth, he wrote in his journal:

> If ever there was a time & circumstance in my life in which I behaved perfectly well, it was in that of C. Lloyd's mad & immoral & frantic ingratitude to me . . . on his side a series of wicked calumnies and irritations—infamous lies to Southey and to poor dear Lamb—in short, conduct which was not that of a fiend, only because it was that of a madman—on my side, patience, gentleness & good for evil—yet this supernatural effort injured me—what I did not suffer to act on my mind, preyed on my body—it prevented my finishing the Christabel —& at the retirement between Linton & Porlock was the first occasion of my having recourse to Opium. . . .
>
> (*CN* 3: 4006)

Because of this note, many scholars, despite Coleridge's twice-repeated statement that "Kubla Khan" had been written in 1797, have dated it 1798, since the quarrel with Charles Lloyd was at its height in May of that year. And it is natural to regard this note, with its references to "the retirement between Linton & Porlock" and an opium experience, as corroborating the "Kubla Khan" preface. But this note would rather seem to undermine the preface, since it says not one word about "Kubla Khan," certainly a miraculous gift, while bemoaning the inability to finish *Christabel*.

If Coleridge was here writing to relieve his own turbulent feelings, and not strewing red herrings for posterity, the note testifies to the radical distortion he had already imposed on the past. His letters show that he had been taking opium *regularly* since his Cambridge days, sometimes against mental distress, and experimenting with different kinds of narcotics (with Thomas Wedgwood) before 1798.

Still, I think it not unreasonable to hypothesize that on some occasion, while under the influence of opium, Coleridge had a series of free-floating associations ("a sort of Reverie") that included fantasies of power (a great ruler) and sensual gratification (magnificent gardens and grounds with a house of pleasure therein) and an Abyssinian maid who sings of an earthly paradise on Mount Abora. The reverie also contained threats (ancestral voices prophesying war) and disquieting or ominous features of various kinds, including a "holy and enchanted" "romantic chasm," a sacred river sinking underground to a lifeless ocean, and a turbulent geyser of immense power.

In themselves there is nothing startling about such a series of images and free associations. What psychic integument linked them specifically for Coleridge can never, of course, be known, but the images seem to have a powerful emotional coherence if we assume that the (day)dreamer was projecting deeply felt desires for authority and erotic gratification, perhaps with forbidden partners (the woman wails for a demon lover; the Abyssinian maid, as a black female, would have been a forbidden sexual object). In full possession of his senses, Coleridge set down a description of his reverie, *without any plot in mind*. At line 36 he ran out of images that had any kind of linkage.

What to do? We all know how difficult it sometimes is to recall the seemingly chaotic pattern of associations that has taken us from one idea or image to others seemingly unrelated. Coleridge knew there was more to his reverie, but what he remembered was either unfit or too incoherent to express. But he did remember, vividly, the Abyssinian maid singing of paradise. How do we know that this is what Mount Abora signifies?

In the early part of this century Lane Cooper suggested that book 4 of *Paradise Lost*, with its roll call of false paradises, lay behind "Kubla Khan," especially the lines:

> Nor where *Abassin* kings thir issue Guard,
> *Mount Amara*, though this by some supposed
> True Paradise. . . .
>
> (280–82)

In the Crewe manuscript the *Abyssinian* maid sings not of Mount Abora but of Mount Amara or Amora, depending on whether Coleridge originally wrote *Amara* and then changed it by adding a thin stroke to the top of the middle *a* to make an *o*, or vice versa by retracing the *o* to make an *a*. (It seems to me almost inconceivable that he originally wrote Amora.) In either case, he had not yet thought of Mount Abora, a change that presents a fascinating lesson in the *art* of poetry, even inspired poetry:

> A Damsel with a *Dulcimer*
> In a Vision once I *saw*
> It was an Abyssinian Maid,
> And on her Dulcimer she played,
> Singing of Mount *Amara*.
>
> (Italics mine)

Thus the Crewe manuscript. My italics show the only unrhymed lines in the poem, for "Amara" does not rhyme with "saw" or "dulcimer," and if "Amara" was pronounced on the first syllable (on analogy, say, with the familiar Mount Ararat), the rhythm of the line would have been violently wrenched: "Singing of Mount Ámara." In sound and rhythm, therefore, "Amara" is clearly unsuitable. "Amora" sets up lovely assonantal harmonies with both "saw" and "dulcimer." The problem here, however, is that anybody remembering the lines from Milton (which Coleridge would no doubt have thought a distinct possibility) would have seen the change from "Amara" to "Amora" as arbitrary because forced by mere technical considerations. To go from "Amora" to "Abora" was but a single, superb step, sufficient also to obliterate the origin in Milton until the Crewe manuscript confirmed Cooper's hunch.

Although the magnificent technical elaboration of "Kubla Khan" was clearly accomplished by a fully conscious Coleridge, it is, I believe, not obligatory to abandon altogether the belief that the strange and haunting images of the poem really were *given*, in the crucial sense that they were neither consciously controlled by Coleridge nor intended as part of any kind of narrative. "Kubla Khan" is strikingly different from anything else in the Coleridge canon, or in English poetry for that matter. If Coleridge had intended the whole poem as a hoax, inventing seemingly incoherent images to support a dream origin, he would surely not have waited twenty years before giving the poem to the world.

On the one hand, then, "Kubla Khan" can—and I think should—be seen as an unfinished poem on which Coleridge has brilliantly imposed a unity by describing the ecstatic state of mind necessary to complete it, which decisively shifts the poem's focus from everything described in its first forty-one lines to the artist who experienced the "vision." As for the possible connections among the Khan, demon lover, Abyssinian maid, and so forth, one should be sobered by the realization that *some* kind of unity can be imposed on or discovered in (depending on your point of view) *any* sequence of images. This is what has made possible the carnival of interpretations not only of "Kubla Khan" but of numberless other works. "Kubla Khan" thus offers an especially rich opportunity to discuss what principles once governed— and perhaps still legitimately govern—plausibility, not to mention validity, in interpretation.

Forty Questions to Ask
of *Ancient Mariner*

Richard E. Matlak

Probably because of its unique defiance to definitive interpretation from any critical perspective, Coleridge's *Rime of the Ancient Mariner* has become, as Jerome J. McGann claims, "one of our culture's standard texts for introducing students to poetic interpretation" ("Meaning" 35). Those familiar with McGann's *Romantic Ideology* will not be surprised by his contention that the poem's history of indecisive interpretations has nevertheless, and surreptitiously, preserved its Christian ideology, but his argument for the mechanism of this effect is brilliant and instructive on the act of reading. He suggests that to interpret the poem on its own terms is to follow Coleridge's exegetical model of reading and narration, the exemplum of which is *Ancient Mariner*'s prose glossist. "Hence," McGann concludes, "the literary criticism of the 'Rime' has never been, in the proper sense, *critical* of the poem but has merely recapitulated, in new and various ways, and not always very consciously, what Coleridge himself had polemically maintained" in his religious writings (57). McGann may not be giving Coleridge the poet his due for radical openness and doubt, because of the way he, McGann, reads the poem; however, his warning against the model of interpretation implied by the gloss is pedagogically valid.

An equally important pedagogical point is the self-reflexiveness students may be limited to in their interpretations, if we cannot open them to a phenomenological awareness of the Mariner's historical consciousness. Again, McGann's position is instructive:

> Alien works may be, as we say, "interpreted." But we must understand that such exercises, carried out in relative historical ignorance, are not *critical* operations. Rather, they are vehicles for recapitulating and objectifying the reader's particular ideological commitments. . . . The importance of ancient or culturally removed works lies precisely in this fact: that they themselves, as culturally alienated products, confront present readers with ideological differentials that help to define the limits and special functions of those current ideological practices. Great works continue to have something to say because what they have to say is so peculiarly and specifically their own that we, who are different, can learn from them.

(54–55)

One does not have to be a new historicist to acknowledge an imperative to disrupt the intellectual and cultural complacency of our students so that they may see beyond themselves and their own historical moment. To this end,

Ancient Mariner, with its masterfully contrived confusions, can offer an important experience of cultural dissonance. For the poem seduces its reader to make immediate meaning with the Mariner and the crew according to established cognitive and cultural patterns, but a more deliberate reading introduces the reader to an apparent epistemological impasse: either assuming causality because there *is* pattern, as does *Ancient Mariner*'s glossist, or unwittingly imposing preestablished patterns on reality to produce causality, as do the Mariner and the crew. This dilemma perplexed Coleridge as well during the compositional period of *Ancient Mariner*. He wrote within days of completing the poem, "I have for some time past withdrawn myself almost totally from the consideration of *immediate* causes, which are infinitely complex & uncertain, to muse on fundamental & general causes—the 'causae causarum' " (10 Mar. 1798; *CL* 1: 397). Ridding the thought process of complexity does not necessarily get one closer to certainty, however. Coleridge later offered an example of distinction between immediate and general causes in an attack on associationist psychology: "I almost think, that Ideas *never* recall Ideas . . . any more than Leaves in a forest create each other's motion—The Breeze it is that runs thro' them / it is the Soul, the state of Feeling—" (7 Aug. 1803; *CL* 2: 961). It may be, however, that the prior idea of Coleridge's "Dejection" (1802)—"we receive but what we give, / And in *our* life alone does Nature live" (48–49)—recalling the idea of feeling as *causae causarum* of thought pattern, undermines the argument against associationism itself, leaving us where we began. But this is the nature of and, finally, the permanent fascination of this cognitive experience that has no true end. At least, it has no end for the Mariner and, as the history of interpretations on *Ancient Mariner* shows, it has no end for the interpreter of his tale.

A commitment to having students confront the underlying epistemological questions of *Ancient Mariner*—What constitutes evidence? What preestablished cognitive and cultural patterns have intervened in making that determination for the Mariner and for us as readers? What drives the quest to make meaning?—has made the poem an indispensable text in most of my literature courses, though I approach it differently depending on the course and level. In freshman courses, I find *Ancient Mariner* invites and rewards the writing of detailed position papers on the insoluble issue of the metaphysical nature of the Mariner's universe: Is it Christian or pagan, meaningful or absurd? Or is it both, and how and why? In the course Traditions of English Literature, a survey that stresses formal continuities within and among historical contexts, I illustrate Coleridge's imitation of medieval consciousness by comparing *Beowulf*'s balancing of *wyrd* (fate) and divine providence to justify the outcome of events with the Mariner's artful pastiche of corresponding pagan and Christian elements to account for his experience. In Romanticism courses, I lead students to see the poem as an early text in the Wordsworth-Coleridge debate over the issue of figuration in the mind's relation to the universe, with *Ancient Mariner* paired against Wordsworth's "Ruined Cottage." Regardless of the direction I take with the poem, however, class is far more fruitful when the students have prepared with the handout appended to this essay, "Guidance on Reading and Writing about *Ancient Mariner*."

"Guidance" is composed of my "problematic" introduction to the poem followed by a list of questions that arrest the reading process at forty stopping places. The purpose of stopping is not to rest but rather to force hesitations and some eddying against the poem's narrative rush to moral closure. Although the questions follow the development of the poem, they can also be grouped about its commonly recognized themes: intermittent speechlessness; the meaning and function of spontaneity; illusive metaphorical patterns (e.g., false rebirth); the use of Christian and pagan imagery; the relation of crime to punishment; gaps in the causal explanation for events; literal veracity; the tale as hallucinatory fabrication. The student's task is to identify the questions of a thematic grouping, to think through them individually and connectedly, and then, while remaining mindful of all the questions, to prepare an essay that responds to one. Though I will lead a directed discussion in the second class on *Ancient Mariner*, the first is devoted to what the students discovered (or did not) about the poem's defiance to closure. It is a difficult conceptual task, but irreplaceable for teaching the fundamentals and perplexities of interpretation, argumentation, and composition.

The assignment on "Guidance" does not guarantee conceptual awareness, but it can be an effective catalyst. Many of the students I teach, for example, are true mariners—superstitious and gullible to a point deserving of academic death—on the use of Christianity in the poem. They rush for Christian-sounding topics in composing essays from "Guidance" because they recognize the common symbols and presume Coleridge must be talking their language about a story they know, or think they know, very well. Most fall for the tricks, making the right associations for the wrong reasons. Still, at worst, they will have organized related questions and responded to them— even seriatim is useful—and they will have read the poem in a more focused way to account for the pattern "Guidance" has helped them perceive.

It may be useful to contrast this much of their cognitive task with two other approaches for encouraging careful reading: the promptings of traditional study questions such as can be found in Royal A. Gettmann's excellent *Handbook*, and the creation by students of their own lists of questions. Comprehensive study questions may risk giving too much away, if they provide the appropriately precise question for an assignment, because framing a question is surely one of the most important intellectual skills that we seek to develop in our students. Teaching the student to become an active reader who questions everything is, in my experience, the beginning of this process. For that reason, paradoxically, I do not ask students initially to create their own questions. Left to themselves, they are too timid to ask the "stupid" question, which by their definition is the obvious question about literal matters—or, to put it another way, the one that sounds so simple a respondent would be afraid to answer it for fear of being wrong. Thus the questions, Why does the Mariner shoot the albatross? and What does the albatross symbolize? (which are something like—and as safe as—Why does Hamlet hesitate?) will doubtless make every student-generated list. But the question, How can someone bless something unawares? with reference to the Mariner's blessing of the water snakes, will make few student lists. For the correct and simple answer, "You can't," only begins a line of questioning that students find perplexing and sometimes awkward to engage. "Guidance" tries to show them that there is a point to questioning everything, and class experience shows them how a collection of "simple" questions might lead them closer to properly framing the Big Question.

Students generally come to the first class, then, prepared to defend a thesis derived from the subset of "Guidance" questions they organized. An ideal response to the assignment, but one beyond the confidence of most undergraduates, would be to admit uncertainty and attempt to explain why even the literal questions, such as those in item 19, are almost too puzzling to answer independently, let alone in connection with a network of other responses: "Why does a spring of love gush from his heart? What does it mean that he blessed the water snakes 'unawares'? How can he be unaware when performing what is by definition an intentional act? How and why does his saint get involved in this act?" Students rarely submit themselves to such a relentless inquisition in dorm rooms and thus usually come to class with answers that sound plausible but unchallenged.

Because I find it pedagogically useful to visualize abstractions, I have developed a simple schema for making the point about frustrated patterns in *Ancient Mariner*, using the Christian motif as my primary example and "Guidance" as the prompt. I form a cross on the blackboard composed of dots that represent every Christian image, act, word, and so on that the students can supply from their essays or that "Guidance" suggests. These would of course include the albatross as Christian soul, the vespers nine, the crossbow, the allusions to Mary, saints, and so on, until the casting of dice for the fate of the crew and the Mariner, which becomes a significant transitional image on which the Christian pattern begins to founder. For if Coleridge's image suggests, as my students invariably argue, the casting of dice for Christ's garments at the foot of the cross, it also suggests, as Edward E. Bostetter has argued (*Romantic Ventriloquists* 113–17), that justice capriciously dispensed does not suggest a loving or just God. I then begin to solicit data that defy our Christian pattern, placing correspondent dots helter-skelter in the quadrants of the cross so as to obliterate its form and thereby represent the insufficiency of a solely Christian interpretation. The issue then focuses on the conscious or unconscious motivation of the Mariner for blending two belief systems in accounting for his experience. If the grafting of Christianity on pagan religions was a transitional stage in medieval culture, Coleridge has romanticized this epoch with a focus on the act of consciousness in creating meaning. Considering the specter ship as a probable hallucination (who else sees it?), we find the real question becomes—even as it answers itself—Why can't the Mariner attribute the death of the crew to the loving God of the moral? Thus, in a retrospective reconstruction of events, he brings in a second metaphysical system to account for the bad, even as he uses a Christian metaphysic to account for the good. And both systems are employed to dignify with cosmic significance a series of fairly inconsequential events: he shot an albatross one night during an ice jam; the superstitious crew vacillated about the morality of his act; when stuck at the equator in a still sea, they hung the bird about his neck; men began to die, probably of dehydration, until all perish except the Mariner; he sees and hears many things in states of delirium and unconsciousness; he returns with an understandable need to explain what seems to him his ironic survival; he thus makes meaning out of poignantly meaningless, that is, unrelated, events.

When I critique essays with reference to "Guidance" and permit revisions, all students get the point to some degree, and some move into the issue of meaning making with fervor. At times this development has its costs. One bright senior in particular lucidly saw the point in a research essay that remained incomplete until a year after the course ended, when he returned to the essay as his writing sample for a graduate program in history. He then argued cogently for thirty pages that "the punishment of the Mariner was not imposed by Fate in the service of Justice, but was rather self-imposed by his acceptance of Causation in the service of Guilt." Barring such exceptional insights, however, students generally say they find "Guidance" usefully vexing throughout all stages of the writing process—prewriting, composition, and revision—in this sense, if I may quote from another of Coleridge's great works, William Wordsworth: "That whatsoever point they gain, they still / Have something to pursue" (Wordsworth, *Prelude* 1805 2.340–41).

Appendix: Guidance on Reading and Writing about *Ancient Mariner*

The first step is to get a basic understanding of what's happening in the poem. Then, raise as many questions as you can. Forget about questions sounding stupid. There are far more stupid answers than stupid questions. Generally, the more basic a question is, the more essential it is that you have an answer for it. When I read the poem, I rarely, if ever, write my questions down, but I am constantly asking them in seeking to reach a better interpretation—which means an interpretation that accounts for more of the things going on in the poem—or to understand why I can't reach a better interpretation. Questions I have raised on *Ancient Mariner* are listed below. There is no reason to believe that this is an exhaustive list, but it is long enough! Trying to answer some of them has been maddening, but I am at least temporarily satisfied with my answers. Other answers I have reached are still unsatisfactory. But you, as I once did, now have to begin somewhere.

There is something about this poem, and one or two others of Coleridge, that makes it a wonderfully inconclusive reading experience. He writes a narrative that seems to hang together but that is an illusion at the level of causation, as when the mariners sit stuck in the ice, the albatross shows up, they feed it, and then the ice jam breaks and they sail on. We are likely to see in this course of events what they see—causation, rather than coincidence. The ice broke because they fed the albatross, which obviously was a supernatural visitor. But I doubt that evidence from the poem supports these assumptions. For the moment, I'm sure that the opposite can be shown, that the mariners' primitive attempt to read causation into things gets them into real trouble (see pt. 2, lines 91–102, and pt. 3, lines 195–219). Of course, the text doesn't say that the specter ship has come to revenge the Mariner's act and the mariners' general culpability. I'm filling that in because of my insatiable desire to see causation instead of absurdity. Can even the causal relation of the crime-and-punishment sequence be doubted? But enough of this or we'll get nowhere. Let's just say that the Mariner's narration provides things in ordered sequence, as a good narrative should; however, his attempt to show cause-effect is limited, probably by a Christian worldview. The general point is that whenever something happens in sequence, our cognitive reaction is to assume causal relation. But cause-effect in the Mariner's narration is as elusive and maybe illusive as his reasons for shooting the albatross are. Why does he do it?

In the following list, you will begin to notice that questions group themselves (in our minds) around topics (which exist in our minds). Whether one writes a paper that addresses a question below or a topic that would presume a more general question, one should have in mind a way of responding or not responding to related questions. I will return to this stage of the writing process after you read the poem closely with the following questions in hand:

PART 1

1. Why does the Mariner stop "one of three"—in other words, that particular Wedding Guest?
2. Why does the Mariner prevent a man from attending a wedding? Is a comment being made on a wedding celebration in comparison with some other experience? (Note: The wedding can't be ignored, because it forms the frame of the story and intrudes in the middle.)
3. What does moon-sun/night-day have to do with the story? What kinds of things happen under those planets or at those times of day?
4. Why do the mariners hail the bird as a Christian soul?
5. Why does the bird relate to the mariners?
6. Why does the Mariner shoot the albatross? Is his act premeditated? Is it caused in any way?

PART 2

7. Why do the mariners change their minds about the value of the bird?
8. Why the stasis and the death imagery?
9. What does the Mariner's not being able to speak signify? (Later, he will not be able to pray; then he will; then he won't; then he'll have to tell his story forever.)
10. Why does the crew hang the albatross around the Mariner's neck? What does the bird have to do with the cross? Why should it be related to the cross?

PART 3

11. What is the "spectre-bark"? Who is on it? Is it really there? How do you know? Who else sees it? How do you know?
12. What does the act of rolling dice to determine fate mean about the nature of justice in the Mariner's universe? Or, if you believe the scene is a hallucination, what does rolling dice mean about the nature of justice in the Mariner's mind?
13. What about this justice anyway? What have the mariners done to deserve their fate?
14. Why does the Mariner get the punishment he does?

PART 4

15. Why is the Mariner made to suffer in the particular way described? How is his suffering related to his shooting of the bird?
16. Why does he compare himself to the snakes he describes?
17. Why can't he pray? (Recall that earlier he couldn't speak.)
18. What causes his change of perception of the snakes?
19. Why does a spring of love gush from his heart? What does it mean that he blessed the water snakes "unawares"? How can he be unaware when performing what is by definition an intentional act? How and why does his saint get involved in this act?
20. Why can he now pray?
21. Why does the bird fall off his neck?
22. Why does it sink "like lead"?

PART 5

23. Why can the Mariner now sleep? Is he forgiven?
24. Why is the dryness removed with water?
25. Why does the Mariner feel like a ghost?
26. Why does the air burst into life?
27. Why do the men arise from the dead? Are they forgiven?
28. Why is there music imagery?
29. What does the spirit's loving the bird who loved the man have to do with anything?
30. Why will the Mariner do more penance? Does the continued penance mean more than that the spirit cannot be repaid for his loss?

PART 6

31. Why hasn't the curse died away?
32. Why can't the Mariner pray again? Did he ever change?
33. Why do the men die again? Did they ever change? Speaking of death and rebirth, where's the bird?
34. Why does the Mariner think the Hermit can shrive him? Does the Hermit do this?

PART 7

35. Why does the ship go down like lead? Recall, that's how the albatross's sinking was described. Are these events associated?
36. Why does the Mariner have to tell his tale before he is relieved? Or is *forgiven* the better word?
37. Why does the need to tell his tale return? Why does the need come on spontaneously ("at an uncertain hour")?
38. Why is it sweeter for the Mariner to pray with the congregation than to attend a wedding feast? (Please don't say he wasn't invited!)
39. Why is the Wedding Guest now sadder but wiser? What in fact has he learned?
40. If the moral is as beautifully simple as "He prayeth best who loveth well," what's this poor fellow doing wandering the earth unforgiven, forever? Why hasn't he been forgiven? Is he wrong about his moral if his life doesn't confirm it? Is he wrong about other things too?

Having been asked this mouthful of questions, and you could probably add more on some parts, what are you to do next? Well, you may notice that some questions readily relate to particular topics. You could gather all the questions that relate to Christian symbolism, for example, or death and rebirth, or speech, and consider them very closely to see how answering them leads, or doesn't lead, to interpretation. Or you could answer a single question, being mindful of related questions.

It's very good to have a question in mind when you read and write, because the answers to that question create your thesis and the evidence you use to answer it provide your support. Reading goes this way: you ask a question and then you search for evidence to answer that question. Writing is the formal result of that search: you develop a thesis, or answer to the question, and you present supporting evidence.

As an example, suppose I were interested in the questions related to speech. They are numbers 9, 17, 20, 32, 34, 36, 37, 38, and 40. I would read the poem again seeking to answer them, while looking out for other instances of speaking that might matter. A more focused question on speech might form to subsume a group of smaller questions, such as What is the function of prayer in *Ancient Mariner*? Other questions could also be generated on the topic of speech, but the general question will have to be answered so as to account for all the instances of prayer.

The Questions of *Christabel*

Mary Favret

During class discussion of Coleridge's *Christabel*, a student remarked (with some frustration) that there were questions about the poem that "you were just not supposed to ask." Her comment reminded me of another I once received when, in a paper, I dared challenge the authorial voice in *Frankenstein*: "When Felix the Cat jumps in the air and stays there, the intelligent child accepts the feat; the stupid child questions it." Underlying both these responses is Coleridge's push for "poetic faith," the "willing suspension of disbelief" that, especially in *Christabel*, leaves readers scratching their heads in perplexity and submitting, gratefully or begrudgingly, to the inscrutable genius of the poet. I prefer to approach works such as *Christabel* by validating the readers' questions and by using those questions to expose the machinery that creates "inscrutability." Like other works of the gothic genre, *Christabel* can be identified with the very art of questioning—the art of creating problems and recognizing mysteries. As readers, we should be allowed to pursue the subtle implications of that art.

Because *Christabel* can be a mystifying text for first-time readers, it is important for students to recognize how many questions they share: that is, how much of their confusion is generated not by their own lack of perception but rather by the poem and its narrator. Their confusion is not an accident, nor should it surrender quietly. I would like them to see how and why the poet would guide us to turn off our queries and suspend our disbelief. Consequently, my second goal in teaching the poem would have students understand the social and literary ends served by mystery, especially mystery that centers on the female body. Although *Christabel*, like a maddening sphinx, provides endless questions, its questions are not as singularly disjointed, or even as monstrous, as Coleridge may present them. Rather, they belong to a whole family of gothic conventions. More curious to my mind are the poet's attempts to distance himself from the tradition (a specifically female tradition) he exploits.

I approach the poem, therefore, in three stages. The first examines students' questions and asks students to consider how and why the poem promotes or frustrates those questions. The second considers the particular question of narrative obstruction in the poem and how that obstruction moves the focus from the realm of women, sexuality, and empirical reality, in part 1, to the realm of men, dreams, and language, in part 2. The interpretations that dominate part 2 impose an unsettling silence on the questions and gothic sensibility of part 1. The final stage—one usually reserved for the following class period—places *Christabel* alongside contemporary works by women writers, in an effort to promote new questions about Coleridge's definition of poetry and his use of gothic conventions to construct poetic faith.

Time allotted to this poem could expand or contract quite a bit, depending on the class's readiness to pose and explore questions themselves. I am inclined to give *Christabel* a lot of play, for two reasons. First, *Christabel* is not only a fortuitously questionable work but also one that attempts to dictate its own questions (an inclination we all may share). Second, the recognition and analysis of the questions we pose to literary texts appear to me crucial goals in the classroom. *Christabel* allows me to teach much more than Romantic or gothic poetry.

The first stage of enquiry depends on a list of questions, drawn up by the students before class and translated to the board for discussion. These questions can branch off into several directions, and it may be valuable to identify these different paths of inquiry. In preparation, I ask students to read through the entire poem before class and then to draw up a list of problems or questions the work presents to them. In terms specific and simple, they should practice addressing direct questions to the text: What do they want to find out about the poem? Within that list of questions, students should determine priorities: Which questions most deserve or require a response? From which part of the poem do they arise?

I have discovered odd patterns in the questions students pose. When written down and handed in (not spoken aloud), their questions tend toward issues of "symbolism" or significance:

> What does Geraldine (or Christabel) represent?
> What does the mother symbolize?
> What is the significance of [various forms of] nature in the poem?
> What does Bracy's dream mean?
> What does the conclusion to part 2 signify? (Why is it so confusing?)

or they tend toward conventions and the composition of the poem:

> How does this poem relate to the gothic/chivalric tradition?
> How does this poem differ from the standard poem of the day?
> Why didn't Coleridge finish *Christabel*?
> What is the purpose of the preface/the two conclusions?

or else they dwell on the unanswerable mysteries of the tale:

> What is Christabel's "shame" or "sin" [lines 296, 381]?
> What happens between Christabel and Geraldine? or What did they do?
> Is Christabel really good or evil?

It is interesting to compare these written questions with the questions students raise in class. Whereas the written ones rarely shy away from inquiries about the "mysterious" sexuality of the poem, the classroom questions center more on "safe" mysteries: Is Geraldine a witch? Why does the fire start up when Geraldine passes? Why must the sacristan "tell" five and forty beads each morning? In several undergraduate classes, I have found students hesitate to propose the question, "What did they do?" More significantly (I believe), they were reluctant to address the most explicit mystery of the tale: What does Christabel see when Geraldine undresses? Clearly, a forceful taboo was at work; this was the sort of question "you were just not supposed to ask," at least not in public.

Rather than confront the class directly with this marked discrepancy, I try to demonstrate how the poem suggests its own questions, while silencing others. Later, the students may see how female sexuality, especially lesbian sexuality, has been "created" as an unspeakable horror. But initially, to help them understand how their questions (the "acceptable" ones posed out loud) are manipulated by the text, we turn to the "explanatory" material that accompanies the poem. One student wondered, "Would Coleridge's audience have automatically known Geraldine was a witch? (I had to read the footnote.)" Others referred frequently to Christabel's carrying Geraldine over the threshold, an event the *Norton Anthology* glosses thus:

> [Geraldine] cannot cross the threshold by her own power because it has been blessed against evil spirits; this is the first of several indications that Geraldine is a malign being.
>
> (Abrams 2: 360)

Not surprisingly, this note directs the students' attention to questions about vaguely gothic superstitions. At the same time, it deflects attention away from the more familiar tradition (to them) of the wedding night, when the groom carries the bride into their new home. This reorientation occurs not only in the notes, however; it is a function of Coleridge's poem.

The author's preface performs a similar deflection: Coleridge dwells on issues of the genesis, composition, and publication of this fragment. He himself introduces the questions of *Christabel*'s incompletion—"But for this I have only my own indolence to blame"—and its originality. The poet anticipates questions for us; he even anticipates objections: "as far as the present poem is concerned, the celebrated poets whose writings I might be suspected of having imitated, either in particular passages, or in the tone and spirit of the whole, would be among the first to vindicate me from the charge." He pictures criticism in terms of poetic convention and metric form, rather than of content:

The meter of *Christabel* is not, properly speaking, irregular, though it may seem so from its being founded on a new principle. . . . Nevertheless, this occasional variation in the number of syllables is not introduced wantonly, or for the mere ends of convenience, but in correspondence with some transition in the nature of the imagery or passion.

Without too much discussion, the class can perceive that Coleridge's definitions of "irregularity," "wanton" behavior, and "passion" seem deliberately to ignore the tale his poem tells. His terms are often legitimated by textual notes to the poem; they seem quite "scholarly" (see Abrams, *Norton* 2: 356; Perkins 414; Heath 456).

Yet it may be worthwhile to point out to students that Coleridge's contemporaries were not as interested in his sources or his metrics as they were in his fantastic material. The relationship between the two women fascinated and repelled Coleridge's first readers, too. "If we consent to swallow an elf or fairy, we are soon expected not to strain at a witch; and if we open our throats to this imposition . . . we must gulp down broomstick and all," complained the *British Review* (E. H. Coleridge, *Christabel* 100). Contemporary reviews centered on the night the two women spend together—"the keystone that makes up the arch" of the poem, in William Hazlitt's words. Hazlitt found "something disgusting at the bottom of [Coleridge's] subject" (E. H. Coleridge, *Christabel* 76n). After hearing the poem recited, Percy Shelley reportedly had horrifying visions "of a woman who had eyes instead of nipples" (Rossetti 126).

The fears and fascination that draw us into the poem are standard gothic fare, which students should recognize. What is curious is the counterpoint between the spooky confusion emanating from the poem and the "literary" questions that surround the poem. This counterpoint should be visible to the class in the list of questions they propose, in the questions Coleridge anticipates, and in those anticipated by his narrator.

Having questioned the critical apparatus of the text, we can turn to the sphinx itself and discover that our confusion has, in part, been fabricated by explicit questions posed by the poem's narrator. (One student asked, "Why so many question marks and exclamation points?") From the outset, the class may have one overwhelming question: What's going on? Not even the voice of authority (the narrator) knows. The narrator's calculated queries and their deliberately evasive answers contribute to our anxiety as readers. By focusing on seemingly inconsequential narrative details, these exchanges simultaneously direct and curtail our participation in the story. Ask students to consider these lines:

Is the night chilly and dark?
The night is chilly, but not dark.
The thin gray cloud is spread on high,
It covers but not hides the sky.

(14–17)

The night is chill; the forest bare;
Is it the wind that moaneth bleak?
There is not wind enough in the air
To move the ringlet curl
From the lovely lady's cheek.

(43–47)

And what can ail the mastiff bitch?
Never till now she uttered yell
Beneath the eye of Christabel.
Perhaps it is the owlet's scritch. . . .

(149–52)

These questions heavy-handedly conjure up the gothic "atmospherics" of *Christabel*. Only a "constructed" reader, one suspicious of natural phenomena, would pose these questions or be satisfied with these answers. And yet these questions promote our sense of supernatural forces at work: question lists often include conjectures about the "symbolic" value of midnight, oak trees, owls, and mastiff bitches. From the beginning (" 'Tis the middle of night by the castle clock"), an insistence on measurable empirical evidence actually predicts mystery: it pushes us beyond empirical reality. By offering up these useless questions and answers, the narrator draws our allegiance away from natural causality and toward unnatural explanation.

The trick lies in making factual explanation and sensory description so disorienting and frustrating that the poem provokes our desire to know more. Ask students why these questions do not elicit the desired information. Often, the narrator begs a question with cumbersome specificity: "What makes her in the wood so late / A furlong from the castle gate?" The response provides no practical explanation: "And she in the midnight wood will pray / For the weal of her lover that's far away" (25–26; 29–30). The furlong is immaterial. Instead we respond by wondering why Christabel cannot pray at home, why she must pray at midnight, and why her lover is "far away." Nor should our wonder make us feel as if we have "missed" something: our confusion has been written into the poem. Students may want to verify this realization by checking to see if they have accumulated questions in response to the narrator's vainly factual answers.

Disquieting suspicion is a far cry from that "willing suspension of disbelief," but it permits Coleridge to guide his readers to another level of questioning. The text asks its own questions, which, in turn, supply us with new doubts and a sense of unease.

The questioning and oblique answering in part 1 of *Christabel* ultimately mock our desire to gather information, to determine causes, and to see physical evidence. They lead us to the speculative trap of the tale, the point at which the narrator perversely begs us to look, then blocks our vision: "Behold her bosom and half her side— / A sight to dream of, not to tell! / O shield her, shield sweet Christabel!" (252–54). At this time, the reader loses connection with Christabel, not only because of the spell of silence that now governs her, but also because the reader, unlike the heroine, *has* been "shielded."

This movement, from leading questions to narrative obstruction, brings us to the second step of our analysis. For now we can begin to question the power of the poet (and his narrator) to control our reading. The second part of the poem reinforces the notion that we cannot ask about what lies beneath Geraldine's robe, nor can we ask what two women might do together in bed at night. Although the narrator suggests one alternative—they "seem" to slumber "As a mother with her child" (301)—yet, as several students remarked, "You expect the worst," "It makes you imagine the most awful thing." These circumlocutions ("worst," "most awful," etc.) repeat the narrator's "shielding": lesbianism becomes "most awful" in the not-telling. This is a useful moment for the students to recognize how gothic doubts about epistemology can reinforce social taboos. Moreover, their own fears and curiosity (in this case, perhaps, homophobic or misogynistic) have been constructed for them and reinforced not only through what they have been told but in what they have been told not to question: sights "to dream of, not to tell."

If only the narrator and Christabel have seen the "sight to dream of" and if Christabel remains unable to tell her vision, then the narrator gains authority by default. His only rival must be Geraldine herself. How can we find out what she knows? Our sympathy for Geraldine has been sustained up to this point by that lady's plaintive words (see lines 73–103, 194–203, 226–34). However, in part 2, Geraldine is given even fewer lines than Christabel is (see lines 368–69). The attention paid to Christabel's spellbound tongue blinds us to the other woman's silencing. Our sympathy, already fragile, crumbles against the narrator's pejorative exclamations "Ah wel-a-day!" (269), "ah woe is me!" (292), "O sorrow and shame!" (296), "O Geraldine!" (303). These exclamations enlist our help in the narrator's dismissal of his rival.

The terms of inquiry have changed, and this change can probably be perceived if the class considers which of their questions arise from part 1 of

the poem and which from part 2. Part 2 generates fewer questions: with the
security of his big mystery, the "sight to dream of, not to tell," the narrator
ventures into the second part equipped with a privileged "vision," with
explanations and interpretations that silence our moral ambivalence. Note
the frequent "I wis" and "I ween," personal interjections that find no room
in part 1. Notice especially the scarcity of deliberate questioning in this
section. The one question directly posed receives a substantial response,
full of the narrator's confident moralizing:

> And when she told her father's name,
> Why waxed Sir Leoline so pale? . . .
> Alas! they had been friends in youth,
> But whispering tongues can poison truth. . . .
> And thus it chanced, as I divine,
> With Roland and Sir Leoline.
>
> (404–15)

Otherwise the questions are purely rhetorical; the narrator already has the
answers (see 327–30; 455–56; 327–29). Students can usually pinpoint these
questions and characterize them out loud. I generally do not have to remark
that these interrogations have the tone of admonitions rather than queries.
I do point out that the narrator has moved far away from his calculations of
time and weather and toward moral instruction.

Significantly, the poem closes on another rhetorical question, one that
has lost the very mark of doubt:

> And what, if in a world of sin
> (O sorrow and shame should this be true!)
> Such giddiness of heart and brain
> Comes seldom save from rage and pain,
> So talks as it's most used to do.
>
> (673–77)

This conclusion, like the poem itself, begins as an open-ended question—
"What if . . ."—but ends as a speculation that disguises its merely hypo-
thetical origin. The change epitomizes the deflecting movement of the entire
poem: from the narrator's initially inadequate statements to his final assertive
judgments.

At the same time, part 2 deflects the poem's concerns, from the story of
(specifically female) sexuality to (specifically male) poetic power. On the one
hand, we watch the spoken dialogue between women converted to sheer
body language: mute seizures, rolling eyes, hissing noises. On the other
hand, this conversion permits a new dialogue to surface: a "masculine"

exchange that gives priority to the realm of the poet. What had been a battle over Christabel's body and soul gives way to a battle over "whisperings," words, stories, and dreams. The context of the poem's—and the reader's—questions swings away from material information toward poetic interpretation.

Part 2 of the poem works to dismiss the questions of part 1, but it simultaneously raises questions regarding the language of dreams and power. Thus Christabel's story is retold in Bard Bracy's dream. His allegorical vision, with its moralizing conclusion, replaces the "gothic" atmosphere of the first half. The bard elaborates the shift in the narrator's transformed commentary. And the Baron's "half-listening" interpretation of the dream (a questionable interpretation) translates the midnight encounter into the history of male friendship and politics.

The maternal is rewritten by and subject to the paternal. We see this revision at the end of the poem: both Christabel and the narrator invoke the memory of her mother, in order to influence Sir Leoline. Whereas Christabel appeals to the living power of "my mother's soul" (the soul that had interfered in the bedroom scene in part 1), the narrator recalls the maternal body, emphatically dead:

> O by the pangs of her dear mother
> Think thou no evil of thy child!
> For her, and thee, and for no other,
> She prayed the moment ere she died:
> Prayed that the babe for whom she died,
> Might prove her dear Lord's joy and pride!
> That prayer her deadly pangs beguiled. . . .
> (626–32)

From the father's perspective, the wishes of a dead body seem easier to resist than those of an active soul. For Leoline, the question does not involve labor pains and childbearing; it involves his word and authority. His wrath ignores Christabel and directs itself to the bard: " 'Why Bracy! dost thou loiter here? / I bade thee hence!' The bard obeyed . . ." (651–52). This move typifies the course of the poem: the struggle no longer concerns the girl and the body, it concerns the poet and language.

By now we are ready for the third step, which considers the implications on the study of Coleridge's poetry of this shift from (female) bodies to (male) poetic authority and examines this shift specifically in terms of the gothic tradition. As previous comments imply, the poem seems to find incompatible the realm of the bodily, sensory, and female with the realm of the visionary, linguistic, and male. Admittedly, Bard Bracy, like Coleridge, positions himself to reconcile the two realms, but the poem leaves that reconciliation problematic: "Perhaps 'tis pretty to force together / Thoughts so all unlike each other" (665–66). Furthermore, the narrator creates a vehicle for poetic authority that privileges "vision" over "sight." And this privilege requires repudiation of female experience and expression. But the students may maintain some skepticism about this authority: isn't Geraldine (now silenced) really dictating the behavior of the baron and the fate of Christabel and of the bard?

With *Christabel*, Coleridge works to formulate our questions and create a context for our reading of Romantic poetry. In his effort to straddle the natural and the supernatural, the male and the female, the story and the dream, the poet must eventually give one precedence over the other. Poetry, he seems to imply, can reconcile irreconcilable differences and accommodate contradictions. But even as he instructs us in the "willing suspension of disbelief" in "shadows of the imagination," he reveals that the suspension depends on a suspicious attitude toward empirical reality. He leads us to assume that poetry is to prose as vision is to sight. Prose, then, is bound by the material world that the poem demonstrates to be inadequate and ineffective. Only the (male) poet has the power both to dream and to tell. But what of the silenced "witch"?

Hidden under these assumptions is the poet's quiet refusal to acknowledge the correspondence of prose writers, especially women writers, with his work. This correspondence will revise the questions he has posed for us. In the preface, Coleridge nearly bends over backwards to convince us of his "originality." Not every rill of inspiration, he warns the critic, flows "from a perforation in some other man's tank." A few, however, might flow from some woman's store.

Critics have complied by tracing connections to and from *Christabel*, Scott's *Lay of the Last Minstrel*, Byron's Turkish tales, Burns's "Tam o' Shanter," Keats's "Lamia," and Spenser's *Faerie Queene*. One thing Coleridge's admirers insist on, however, is the poem's distance from any prose tale or writer. Charles Lamb advised Coleridge in 1803 not to mix *Christabel* with the normal offerings of "Anthologic . . . Epistolary Miscellanies." It was crucial, according to Lamb, to keep this *Christabel* clear from other women: "Don't let that sweet maid come forth attended with Lady Holland's mob at her heels" (Nethercot 15). The taint of Geraldine thus extends to a score of women writers and gothic novelists (see E. H. Coleridge, Christabel 13).

Yet it is clear from contemporary reviews that *Christabel* was considered a sensational, even obscene, scandal and was read in the light of popular gothic tales and sentimental romances, in verse as well as in prose. (For examples, see E. H. Coleridge, Christabel 99–102; J. R. Jackson.) To make this point more vivid, I refer to an early scene in Maria Edgeworth's *Belinda* (written 1800–01), in which the magnificent Lady Delacour reveals her secret—a hideous, cancerous blight on her breast and side—to the lovely young Belinda. How does Edgeworth's unshielding treatment comment on Coleridge's "Romanticism"?

Similarly, one could juxtapose Radcliffe's "black veil" from *The Mysteries of Udolpho* with the veil drawn by the narrator of *Christabel*. Compared with the suspension of terror and the ultimate demystification Radcliffe attempts in that novel (the veil hides not the corpse of a murdered woman but a wax dummy, proscribed for penitential meditation), does the "sight to dream of, not to tell" deliver a new message about our fears?

Another work that reorients the questions of *Christabel* is the poem "The Witch," by Coleridge's niece, Mary Elizabeth Coleridge. Here the narrator *is* Geraldine, speaking in "the voice that women have, who plead for their heart's desire":

> "I have walked a great while over the snow
> And I am not tall nor strong.
> My clothes are wet, my teeth are set,
> And the way was hard and long.
> I have wandered over the fruitful earth,
> But I never came here before.
> Oh, lift me over the threshold, and let me in at the door. . . ."
>
> She came—and the quivering flame
> Sank and died in the fire.
>   (Gilbert and Gubar, *Norton* 1164)

Such works may provide answers to questions about Geraldine's mysteries and intentions that the poem *Christabel* only silently allows (see Gilbert and Gubar, *Madwoman* 306–08).

My goal in teaching this poem is not to resolve these concurrent problems—that of a (specifically female) sexual identity or that of a poetic ideal. Rather, I want readers to acknowledge the connections Coleridge makes and breaks between these two problems. Readers should understand how each problem tends to eclipse the other, as if no common ground could accommodate the two. At the same time, however, I want readers to resist that blinding eclipse and search for the common ground. The dynamics of the poem itself have created a critical heritage that deflects our attention from the prosaic and that looks askance at the female. We as teachers should look again at the implicit questions we and our students raise in discussing this poem. We might reexamine the context in which we have set the poem: Do we teach it alongside the works of Radcliffe or alongside those of Words-worth? And why is that distinction so significant? Even if we cite the well-known lineage between *Christabel* and Mary Shelley's *Frankenstein*, do we move beyond the issue of influence and consider the thematic correspondences that separate female sexuality from artistic creativity in these works? How often do we take the poem's "originality" for granted, without considering the popular literary context? When do we recognize that the power of the Romantic poet's literary mothers and sisters is not incompatible with the poet's own compelling word?

Teaching *Christabel*: Gender and Genre

Karen Swann

Originally intended for the second edition of the *Lyrical Ballads*, *Christabel* bears an obvious family resemblance to other Coleridge and Wordsworth poems of that period. Like Wordsworth's experimental ballads and like Coleridge's own *Ancient Mariner*, the poem is about the fluxes and refluxes of the mind when it is under the sway of strong passions. Most obviously, both authors are concerned with exploring the passions—often verging on the pathological—of dramatized fictional characters. But even a cursory reading of Wordsworth's 1800 Preface to the *Lyrical Ballads* reveals that he was also highly concerned with the psychology—even pathology—of the reading public, particularly with what he called its "thirst after outrageous stimulation," its taste for popular sensational literature (Owen 160). Coleridge shared that interest. Like Wordsworth's most self-reflexive ballads, *Christabel* provokes and invites its readers to reflect on their passions for certain kinds of narratives and thus challenges the public taste.

But *Christabel* takes up this project in a peculiar—and peculiarly Coleridgean—manner. If one of Wordsworth's favorite tasks in the *Lyrical Ballads* is to trace "the maternal passion through many of its more subtle windings" (Owen 158), Coleridge's aim in *Christabel* is to follow the winding path of the wandering mother, or hysteria; if Wordsworth increasingly conceives his experiments as exposing the untoward investments of speakers and readers in certain genres of fiction, Coleridge charts in *Christabel* a narrative passion that undoes literary categories and even the "genres" of gender and identity. The poem's unsettling reworking of the new genre of the experimental ballad may have prompted Wordsworth to drop *Christabel* from the 1800 *Lyrical Ballads* at the last moment, complaining of its "discordancy" with the rest of the collection (*CL* 1: 643); its unsettling treatment of the genre of sensational romance was perhaps to blame for the critics' happily scandalized response to the poem in 1816, when it was finally published.

When teaching *Christabel* in a Romantic poetry survey, I try both to place it in context—to suggest the ways in which it belongs with the *Lyrical Ballads* and makes "answer meet" to a contemporary literary scene—and to explore why it is controversial in both those arenas. By the time we come to the poem, my students have read the 1798 *Lyrical Ballads*, focusing particularly on those ballads that most provocatively engage popular poetry and the public taste—"Simon Lee," "The Thorn," "The Idiot Boy," "The Ancyent Marinere." (I assign Owen's edition so that they can experience the collaboration as a collaboration.) At the beginning of our classes on the *Lyrical Ballads*, I lecture briefly on the gothic and ballad revivals and invite students to read around in Percy's *Reliques of Ancient English Poetry*, which I have put on reserve for them. I also distribute some of Walter Taylor's translations of Gottfried Burger's popular gothic ballads, many of which served as sources for Wordsworth's poems; they read at least "The Lass of Fair Wone" and "Lenore" (Jacobus 277–88). They have discussed Wordsworth's 1800 Preface, giving particular attention to his attack on the public taste for sensationalism; from reading Burger's ballads and Wordsworth's send-ups of gothic convention, students generally have a good idea of what kind of fiction Wordsworth is attacking. For the *Christabel* assignment I sometimes hand out "Sir Cauline," a traditional ballad in Percy's *Reliques* that features a character named Christabel, the daughter of a possibly tyrannical father, whose lover is and is not "far away" for most of the poem (the ballad has been heavily "improved" by Percy). To give them a sense of what made the poem controversial, I distribute one or two reviews of it from 1816, the year it was finally published—Hazlitt's in the *Examiner* is a good choice since it's at once shrill and insightful about the poem's disturbing character (Reiman, *Romantics Reviewed* 2: 530–31); and I have with me Wordsworth's and Coleridge's reports about why *Christabel* was pulled from the 1800 *Lyrical Ballads*. (Katz and Kissane both provide good accounts of this episode; see also *CL* 1: 643.)

To open a discussion of *Christabel*'s generic status, I generally elicit responses about what kind of poem students think it is: Does it seem to belong in a recognizable class of fictions? (A good way to raise this question is to read the poem's first stanza and ask students what kind of story they are led to expect.) *Christabel* might seem to resemble some of the more lurid or perplexing selections in *Lyrical Ballads*—"The Thorn," perhaps, or *Ancient Mariner*. More immediately, though, it reminds us of other stories we know about a mysterious, morally ambiguous interloper—of Spenser's *Faerie Queene*, perhaps, with its Duessas and false Florimels, or of folktales and popular ballads, with their equivocal *revenants*. (Many students see in Geraldine a resemblance to the lover in "Sir Cauline," who returns to his Christabel in disguise.) Most immediately, however, it reminds us of Romantic and modern gothic romances, including Burger's "Lenore" (to which Geraldine's account of her midnight ride alludes), Shelley's *Frankenstein*, George Eliot's "Lifted Veil," and a whole range of modern horror stories.

Central to our generic placement of the poem is of course the character of Geraldine. I rather quickly move students into a discussion of the portents that Coleridge has strewn liberally through part 1 of the poem—the witching hour, the contracted moon, the moaning mastiff, the flickering flame, and so on. These portents both tell us that this poem is going to be gothic in our modern sense of the word (that is, more like "Lenore" than "Sir Cauline") and indicate that Geraldine is not what she says she is. Or, rather, they indicate that to the reader who knows how these signs are supposed to function: both Christabel and the narrator see and hear the same things we do but often either find the signs meaningless or interpret them differently.

The narrator, for example, speculates that Geraldine sinks at the threshold because of "pain" (129), while Christabel attributes Geraldine's peculiar behavior to the "wildering" effect of her "ghastly ride" (216–17). There is in fact no strictly logical reason why the brands in Sir Leoline's hall should not flare up when the two women pass, because they've just opened the door and admitted a draft: we only know these signs are meaningful because we've come across them before, in other contexts.

Our experience of genre, then, affects what signs we take to be significant. It also informs our capacity to interpret them. For merely to know that signs mean *something* is of course not to know *what* they mean. Students frequently disagree about Geraldine's character, echoing disagreements, I point out, that have historically divided the poem's critics, who have seen her variously as a witch, vampire, or some other embodiment of supernatural evil; as a victim herself of some "spell"; or as an ambassador of good come to test Christabel. Although, as far as I know, no readers of the poem have suggested the argument, she could even be what she says she is—a victim of ruffians and the daughter of Sir Roland de Vaux of Tryermaine. Judging from these differences of opinion, readers of *Christabel* make choices about which of Geraldine's statements to accept as true and which to dismiss as false and about how to interpret her often contradictory behavior. Insight into how we make these decisions can perhaps be gleaned by looking to Geraldine's interpreters within the poem—Christabel, Sir Leoline, Bard Bracy, and the narrators. When I first invite students to speculate about why their own reading of Geraldine diverges from, say, Christabel's—Why doesn't Christabel find it suspicious that Geraldine sinks at the threshold? —they often respond that Christabel is naive: she hasn't read enough of the right books. But one can equally argue that the characters in the poem make decisions about Geraldine according to certain narrative expectations. Christabel, for example, seems to respond to Geraldine as though she were a romance heroine, a damsel in distress; she simply takes straight the very story of violent abduction that we find overconventional and sees innocence in the dazzling whiteness we suspect is mere glitter. Sir Leoline, in contrast, responds to Geraldine through the conventions of chivalric romance, his thoughts centering on the trials of manly friendships, the tests of the tourney court, and the triumphal procession; while Bracy casts the whole drama in the terms of allegorical romance, an elliptical story about a snake and a dove. Each character, that is, interprets Geraldine according to certain narrative codes; like our own, the characters' interpretive choices are informed by their experiences of genre.

Christabel makes us aware of the operations of genre. Thus it can be seen to further the social agenda Wordsworth lays out in the 1800 Preface to the *Lyrical Ballads*, where he claims that these poems are attempts to "counteract" a debased public taste for the literature of sensation. Like many of the highly self-reflexive poems in the volume, *Christabel* invites analysis of the way its dramatized readers are swayed by desires fostered by literary conventions and forces its real readers to confront their own demands for sensational event. Coleridge's treatment of Geraldine's bosom, for example, can be seen to mock his public's desire for the kind of horrific or erotic spectacle it had come to expect from a gothic tale. In the text Coleridge published in 1816, the description of Geraldine's bosom, which climaxes a teasingly detailed account of her disrobing, invites the reader to look ("Behold! her bosom and half her side—") but then suppresses the sight ("A sight to dream of, not to tell!") (252–53). This is a revision of the manuscript version of the poem, which describes Geraldine's bosom thus: "Behold! her bosom and half her side—/ Are lean and old and foul of hue" (252n). In a review of the poem, Hazlitt, who had read *Christabel* in manuscript, chastizes its author for his perversity in suppressing the "keystone" of the whole poem and supplies the missing line. The modern reader might ask with Hazlitt what motivated Coleridge to change the text, particularly since the bosom is described as a "bosom old" (410) later in the poem; it doesn't remain all that ambiguous. One answer is that he intends to tempt and thwart our licentious investments in the body of Geraldine. His tactics, then, would resemble Wordsworth's in "Simon Lee" when he has his speaker refuse to provide the "gentle reader" with the expected "tale" and thus focuses on the reader's own demands for lurid or at least overtly dramatic fictional events.

This formulation of Coleridge's aims in *Christabel*, however, doesn't seem quite adequate to our sense of the poem. When I ask the class what effect the suppression of the line describing Geraldine's bosom has, some students find the effect overmelodramatic and hear the passage as an elaborate joke on the reader, but at least as many others feel that the suppression of the sight makes the poem more mysterious, more of a gothic tale. (The willfully obscured horrific "sight" was of course standard fare in gothic novels—Emily St. Aubert's experience with the mysterious sight behind the veil in *The Mysteries of Udolpho* is a notorious example.) Much more than "The Idiot Boy," which burlesques the midnight ride of Burger's "Lenore," *Christabel* seems at least uneasily aligned with the genre whose conventions it also invites us to reflect on. I try to get at this problematic alignment by asking students if there were moments in their reading when they could not decide what kind of response Coleridge wanted to elicit from his readers. Many can come up with details that strike them as just a bit off. Is the clockwork barking of the mastiff bitch, "Four for the quarters, and twelve for the hour; . . . / Sixteen short howls, not overloud" (10–12), supposed to be comic? (Reviewers protested that the passage was mere doggerel.) When the first narrative voice asks, "Is the night chilly and dark?" (14), is Coleridge drawing attention to the conventions of gothic atmosphere, and is the second voice's response, "The night is chilly but not dark" (15), making a joke of gothic gloom? Or are both voices attempting to express something they "cannot tell," in a way we experience as genuinely eery? What about tonal instabilities—for example, the coda to part 1, which recapitulates the plot of part 1 in a more sentimental, less sensational style? These slightly tinny moments are disconcerting, not so much because they assault our appetites and expectations in the manner of Wordsworth's mocking addresses to his "reader," but because we aren't sure how to take them. (In my experience of teaching the poem, it frequently happens that a passage one member of the class insists is comic is the very moment that had struck another as particularly ominous or moving; to yet another student the same lines seem simply bad, overconventional.) Our uncertainty about how to characterize Geraldine, then, is paralleled by our uncertainty about how to respond to the poem—by turns comic and effectively creepy, it seems to fit neither in the genre of the sensational tale nor with Wordsworth's send-ups of that genre. I point out here that *Christabel's* tonal shiftiness seemed most to scandalize *Christabel's* first reviewers; their shrill attacks often focused on Coleridge's "licentious" treatment not of Geraldine but of his poetic materials—his apparent blending together of affecting passages and doggerel, his apparent unconcern for the reader's desire to know with certainty what kind of poem this was (see, e.g., Reiman, *Romantics Reviewed* 1: 36, 2: 866).

So far this discussion has focused more on genre than gender. It began by addressing questions about Geraldine's moral status—Is she good? evil? demonic? holy? To get at why a feminine character becomes the focus of these interpretive dramas, I generally invite students to take a more psychological approach and think of this dazzling, seductive, and thoroughly ambiguous creature as a projection or fantasy. Most obviously, of course, she's *Christabel's* fantasy. The passage describing Geraldine's first appearance, with its ambiguous referents (when the verse says, "The lady sprang up suddenly" (37), we aren't sure which "lady" is being referred to), hints that Geraldine somehow splits off from Christabel, and throughout the poem verbal tags—"the lady," "answer meet," "sweet"—pass from lady to lady, suggesting the two women's affinity. And, indeed, a case can be made that the two ladies together act out the life that was already Christabel's: one lady "stole" (31) out of her father's castle and two reenter it "as if in stealth" (120), and by the end of the evening the lady whose uneasy dreams had sent her out into the woods to pray has simply resumed "fearfully dreaming" (295); if at the beginning of the poem one lady moves "in silence" (36) ("she nothing spoke" [31]), by the end of part 1 a second lady has merely rendered the inhibition of her speech explicit as an overmastering "spell."

Coleridge's and Wordsworth's expressed intention in the *Lyrical Ballads* was, as we have seen, to dramatize psychological states, the fluxes and refluxes of the mind when swayed by passion. What passions do Geraldine and Christabel together dramatize? Students generally come up with a rich array of responses to this question—Geraldine "answers" Christabel's desire for her "lover far away" or reflects her ambivalence about that lover or allows Christabel to do without a human (or masculine or both) lover; Geraldine acts out Christabel's desire for her father or her desire to subvert her father's oppressive laws; Geraldine somehow embodies Christabel's lost mother. Of all these possibilities, the last is the most explicitly invited by the text, but to many readers it feels the most elusive. At one moment the narrative expressly identifies Geraldine with Christabel's mother: she sleeps with Christabel "as a mother with her child" (301). A psychoanalytic reading of the poem could make sense of this identification by speculating that in her role as a mother substitute, Geraldine allows Christabel to act out preoedipal fantasies about a powerful and ambivalently valorized maternal figure or, later in the poem, vicariously to act out a desire to supplant the mother in her father's affections. These theories certainly seem borne out by the poem but don't account for why Geraldine at times should seem to be not simply identified with the mother but possessed by her: What accounts for her invasion by the mother at the end of part 1, where she cries with "altered" and "hollow" voice, "Off, wandering mother" (204–13)?

At this point I invite students to entertain "the mother" not as a reference to Christabel's mother but as a pun, and I propose that the mental state Coleridge dramatizes in *Christabel* is the disease of the wandering mother, or hysteria. Coleridge would have known popular, often fondly misogynistic and anti-Catholic, accounts of hysteria that cast its primary victims as virgins, particularly Catholic virgins tyrannized by the repressive morality of the Church and parental figures; these accounts understood the symptoms of the disease to be hallucinations or "visions," "stifled breath," and an inability to "tell" one's ailments. (My guess is that Coleridge probably derived his sense of the affliction from Burton's *Anatomy of Melancholy*, which includes an account of "Maids', Nuns', and Widows' Melancholy" [416–18; cited in Swann 535–38]; in class I sometimes distribute and read parts of Burton's chapter, which is not only provocative in relation to *Christabel* but amusing and fascinating in its own right.) Possibly, then, in *Christabel* Coleridge follows the "turns" of a peculiarly feminine "passion," traditionally thought to originate in repressed sexual desires, and to afflict those women who suffer most intensely in a "world of death," the order of patriarchal and church law.

Geraldine, however, is not just Christabel's "vision": she also appears to Sir Leoline and Bard Bracy, entering the castle when both men are sleeping, as if she were a creature of their dreams. It's possible to speculate—and my students and I do—about what desires Geraldine might answer that are particular to each character. But soon I remind the class of our earlier discussion, where it was suggested that Geraldine makes "answer meet" to narrative expectations and desires. Geraldine is a generally available "vision" or representation, accessible to the readers of the poem as well as to her readers in the poem; she is not so much one (pathological) woman's fantasy or even a feminine fantasy as she is a collective or cultural fantasy. Her effect on the baron, moreover, is almost identical to her effect on Christabel: she makes him speechless and wreaks confusion—precisely the effect she has had on readers of the poem from Coleridge's day to the present. If on the one hand, then, the poem invites us to see hysteria as a female affliction, on the other it hints that the mother's flights cross gender lines. It even suggests that "gender" may be a cultural construction—a ploy to contain the threat of "confusion" by displacing it onto a "vision" of a radically self-divided or radically ambiguous female body.

Coleridge's poem suggests that interpreters of Geraldine are also dreamers of Geraldine, hysterically authoring the figure they perceive. This discussion of *Christabel* would conclude by focusing on the readers within the poem who most obviously adopt an authorial role, the narrators. One can speculate that they, too, are hysterics, acting out a drama much like the one enacted by Geraldine and Christabel. Here again we do not know if we have one identity or two, or one divided speaking subject. Like the women they describe, the narrators are overmastered by "visions," here, their own fictions—they repeatedly shift tenses, as if tumbling from an authorial perspective into the story's present; or they become overwhelmed by suspense and blurt out warnings and advice to the poem's characters; or they revise earlier, gloomy assessments of events when those characters seem persuasively optimistic. And at times they "cannot tell" the story they seem desperately to want to narrate: "A sight to dream of, not to tell!"

The effect was and is to make the poem's readers somewhat hysterical. For the poem finally suggests that gender, a category we think of as essential, is in fact a genre, a socially constructed kind, and that genres are permeable and undecidable—at least if we judge from this poem, which by turns strikes us as a horrific gothic tale, an allegorical romance, a psychomachia, and an elaborate send-up of all those genres. Like many other lyrical ballads, then, but, I argue, more unnervingly, *Christabel* promises to make "answer meet" to all our desires, only to mock our appetites and baffle our expectations.

Teaching *Ancient Mariner* and *Christabel* to Students of Criminal Justice

Anya Taylor

> One does not use poetry for its major purposes, as a means of organizing oneself and the world, until one's world somehow gets out of hand.
> —Richard Wilbur

> What thou lovest well remains
> . . . .
> What thou lovest well shall not be reft from thee
> What thou lovest well is thy true heritage.
> —Ezra Pound

Coleridge's *Rime of the Ancient Mariner* and *Christabel* are favorite experiences for my hundreds of students at John Jay College of Criminal Justice, a four-year college in the City University of New York. The reasons for the popularity of these poems are several: the nature of the students; the accessibility of the narratives and of their poetic techniques; the mysterious cruxes in the poems that provoke discussion about life's questions; the complexity of crime, suffering, guilt, and family tension in the poems; the glimpses of Coleridge the person within the poems; the clarity of the poems as definitive Romantic documents; and the centrality of the poems to other writings in the required survey course of European masterpieces, which may cover a variety of works such as *Candide, Crime and Punishment, Hard Times*, and *The Metamorphosis*.

Like many students at professionally and technically oriented colleges in multiethnic cities, students at John Jay are hardworking, ambitious, Irish, black, Hispanic, and "other" men and women of all ages who are eager to enter the criminal justice system and "the system" generally and to make lives for their families better than the lives of those they see around them. Some of the students are already police, fire, and corrections officers advancing their careers. Life in New York, as lived in streets, projects, subways, and on the job, has surrounded them with knowledge of crime, viciousness, weakness, and heroic survival. Many have siblings or children in jail or out on the streets; some have family members dead from gangs or drugs. They wish to change the city.

Most of the students are innocent of literature (having survived city public schools) but have vigorous, jargon-free writing styles, transparent to experience. These styles are purged of errors and swelled with details in the writing classes. When they get to the literature classes, they are easily persuaded that language has power, purpose, and coherence, that it will help them to succeed and to persuade others to make something of themselves. The excitement of finding multivalent coherence in a work of literature and of arguing with critics (whose paragraphs have been mimeographed) is new to them: they are not so sophisticated as to imagine that fictions have no meanings. The interest in powerful language (which is sometimes their second language), the experience of suffering, and the faith in coherence may contribute to the students' enthusiastic response to Coleridge's poems and to Coleridge the person.

Ancient Mariner and *Christabel* are accessible to students in ways that Wordsworth's and Keats's poems are not. Though we as scholars and critics know of the narrative layerings in the poems that call our interpretations into doubt (see McGann, "Meaning"), students appreciate the clear sentences, the provocative and descriptive metaphors (as of the sun looking through the grate, in *Ancient Mariner* 177–80), and the rhythm and speed, especially of *Ancient Mariner*, which may sound to some of the younger students pleasingly like rap music. They can figure out what is happening and find evidence for their interpretations in the lucidly shaped stanzas with short visible lines. This accessibility builds confidence and rouses curiosity. What techniques does Coleridge use to increase and retard speed? The admiration of Coleridge's skill leads to an interest in meter, line length, enjambment, alliteration, assonance, end rhymes and internal rhymes, and the pauses in narrative provided by numerous expanding figures of speech. Practical exercises in scanning open up the area of strategy, which Coleridge himself played with in notebooks and experimental poems and described in the introductory note to *Christabel*. The meters of the magical spell alert them again to the power and energy of language (see Taylor, *Magic*). Particular metaphors are analyzed in discussion. For example, in *Ancient Mariner* what does the dryness of lines 111–61 and 244–47 mean and how does this metaphor gradually include multiple meanings and become a symbol of certain states of mind? How does this metaphor contrast with the dream of rain at the end and what patterns are thus established?

Once plot and poetic technique have been examined, we turn to various points in the poems where questions arise. Each of several students is assigned to write a brief paper on one of these difficult moments. Questions on *Ancient Mariner* address the reasons for the shooting of the albatross (with Coleridge's comments on Iago's "motiveless malignity" as a text for meditation [Raysor, *Shakesperian* 44]); the vacillations of the crew (a perplexing topic neglected in criticism: Does the crew make any reliable judgments? Is it dehumanized by its lack of individualism?); the specter ship (What fatality or hazard governs the Mariner's actions?); the spirits (What kind of a universe is this: how much is it ordered by higher and invisible powers, and are these benevolent or malevolent?); the water snakes; the Hermit; and the "sadder and wiser" Wedding Guest (Does the Mariner teach him what he would never dare find out for himself or does the Mariner turn him into a "thing," a means for his own release from agony, mesmerizing him as Geraldine does Christabel?). Work on *Christabel* also focuses on problems of individual guilt, responsibility, and suffering, but in addition it extends the questions to family dynamics. The class considers Christabel's collusion at the beginning; varied responses to Geraldine as evil, as natural power, as woman's self-assertion; the nature of the sexual encounter; the father's morbidity; the bard's potential role; the connections between the poem and the conclusion to part 2. Students read aloud several paragraphs they have written explaining how these moments can be understood.

These interpretations lead naturally to discussion of life issues. For example, if the Mariner has no reason to shoot, why does he do it? Where does human malignity come from? Does every human act require a transgression, a breaking of harmony, as Lockridge disturbingly argues (*Coleridge the Moralist* 53–77)? The poem's inscrutability on this issue is a necessary challenge to the social-science views of environmentally induced criminal behavior that the students hear over and over in their criminal justice and sociology classes. Both *Ancient Mariner* and *Christabel* explore the possibility that an uncaused will to violence or desire to break away from "virtue" exists in persons who might think themselves basically decent. Wicked outbursts cannot always be blamed on upbringing, neighborhood, class, or society. It is useful to remind students that opposed opinions on human malignity already existed and were being debated during the Romantic period. Coleridge is not alone in finding that human beings are sometimes freely and deliberately evil and that original sin operates in each individual life as a moment of origination. Against the view that human beings are victims of society, voiced at the time by Godwin and Bentham, Coleridge is joined by Hazlitt, who attacks Bentham ("Bentham," in *Spirit of the Age*), and even by De Quincey (in "A Vision of Sudden Death"), who writes that "in the world of dreams every one of us ratifies for himself the original transgression" (Dobrée 106). Coleridge's belief that there are such things as origins and fountains that are not just "perforation[s] made in some other man's tank" (preface, *Christabel*) applies not only to creativity in art (a way into "Kubla Khan" and stanza 4 of the Dejection Ode) but also to human action. (Godwin's *Caleb Williams* with its cruelly imprisoning power structure would be a productive reading in this connection, especially as Coleridge's poems may work to modify the thesis of the novel.) Of the many questionable moments in *Ancient Mariner* the interpretation of the Hermit is particularly troubled: Does his "cushion plump" and "little vesper bell" suggest that he is too sheltered from suffering to shrive the Mariner? If he shrives him, why does the Mariner continue to suffer? Does suffering heal or only lead to more suffering? How much healing can organized religion provide? How one interprets the Hermit colors the ending (Is it a naive return or an ironically stated piety?) and the meaning of the poem's universe (Is it benign and structured or chaotic and random, a universe so lonely "that God himself / Scarce seeméd there to be" [599–600]?). Questions about responsibility and malignity also trouble the many moments of *Christabel* that prompt arguments about ethics: How does a "child" get led astray? Is Christabel passive? Who is responsible for her transformation and degeneracy?

Such large issues interest students of criminal justice, particularly as they bear on free will, dependency, punishment, and failures of love and responsibility. (See *CC* 4.1: 195–96, for Coleridge's view that most people are dependent in some way but can nevertheless disentangle themselves enough to make free decisions.) Formalist critics might be shocked to hear students talking about *Christabel* as an intricate family tragedy where Geraldine's seduction and Sir Leoline's abandonment stir memories of their own almost universally unhappy childhoods and strengthen their plans to specialize in protecting or rehabilitating youthful victims. The sexual scene is not too remote from explicit news articles of the nineties, and the psychic corruption that results from it and from the wildflower wine is interesting to students of drug and alcohol abuse. Although students often become too simplistic and particular, the transfers of psychic power between Mariner and Wedding Guest and Christabel and Geraldine enrich their understanding of how one person can come to control another and what that feels like.

Students' interest in the poems leads them to wonder about Coleridge the person. They are particularly attracted by aspects of Coleridge's life that echo elements in their own lives: his large and sometimes hostile family; his unhappy childhood; his urban schooling; his incognito career in the army; his early and unsatisfactory marriage; his passion for Sara Hutchinson; his opium and alcohol addictions; his anxieties; his trouble with his children; his indolence and restlessness and flashes of joy; his frequent sense of failure; his betrayal by friends; his recuperation in his forties, when he got a second wind; his vociferous concern for the plight of poor working children and other public issues. Thomas McFarland's depiction ("Coleridge's Anxiety") of him as a hero of existence, fighting from his knees, informs my narration of his life. The students see many parallels in their own situations: if Coleridge could struggle out of his sorrows, so might they struggle from theirs.

Coleridge's poems can be placed usefully at the center of a study of Romanticism. For my college in particular, his centrality to issues of criminal justice makes him crucial. Quite a few of Wordsworth's poems can be read in relation to Coleridge's (see Magnuson in this volume; Taylor, "Wordsworth's Arguments against Magical Words," *Magic* 134–83). Keats's "La Belle Dame sans Merci" and "Lamia," Shelley's "Alastor," and Mary Shelley's *Frankenstein* serve as varied responses to *Christabel* and *Ancient Mariner*. Blake's "London" and "Mental Traveller" provide parallel explorations of how people allow themselves to be enmeshed by systems of their own making. The prose of Hazlitt, Lamb, and De Quincey, who learned their themes, whether they acknowledged it or not, from Coleridge, can be profitably juxtaposed to any exemplary sentence by Coleridge. Many of the motifs typical of Romanticism can be studied in microcosm: the journey; the frame story; the circle or spiral; ironic and multiple voices and interspersed songs; the exile, wanderer, deviant, storyteller, bard, as hero; themes of mesmerism, magic, and supernatural force; of a sympathetic and living nature; of the human fall from innocence; of human imagination; and of an active formative consciousness. Students find it more convincing to watch these motifs emerge from a particular text than to accept them as abstractions said to define a movement.

As Coleridge's poems irradiate Romanticism, so, too, they irradiate other works in a survey of European literature, 1740–1950, particularly if the course is unified by an exploration of the many sources of evil and the precariousness of human will and behavior. After the relentless parade of human malice and greed in Voltaire's *Candide*, Coleridge's poems come as a welcome deepening of the inquiry, a reopening of the possibility that even the most innocent hero or heroine can be implicated. Novels such as Dickens's *Hard Times* or *Great Expectations* and Brontë's *Wuthering Heights* also profit from a juxtaposition with these poems. Austen's *Pride and Prejudice* extends the discussion of free choice and self-creation. (This novel is another central text of the course and also a favorite, because it presents a community where choices of words and deeds matter and where poor girls can determine their own lives by learning to read other people anew, just what the students themselves are hoping to do.) One of the clearest examples of novels that can be illuminated by juxtaposition with Coleridge's *Ancient Mariner* is Dostoevsky's *Crime and Punishment*. A brief writing assignment asks for elements of similarity. Students have unearthed the following: the early act of killing; the incomprehensible motives; the long penance; the hauntings from alternate spiritual sources (Svidrigaylov and Sonya); the debilitating effect of utilitarian and self-aggrandizing theory divorced from feeling; the isolation of the criminal from the human community; the criminal's burden of willful self-destruction; the final uncertainty about whether the criminal is healed after being punished.

Raskolnikov's division of humankind into Napoleons who have the right to step over obstacles, on the one hand, and old pawnbrokers who can be exterminated like lice, on the other, dramatizes the confusion about human nature in Coleridge's time. Coleridge foresaw that the removal of a gap or chasm separating human beings from animals would lead to increasingly vicious treatment of persons (see Taylor, *Coleridge's Defense* 9–60). As *Crime and Punishment* brings the perception of human beings as insects to its logical conclusion (exterminating the brutes), so Kafka's *Metamorphosis* internalizes the confusion that Coleridge worked hard to untangle. As Christabel becomes a "reptile soul," fixed in her compulsions, so Gregor becomes an insect soul by relinquishing his human nature, yielding to a self-loathing that may finally be seen as freely willed. In the late work *Opus Maximum* Coleridge writes at length on the freedom of human beings to choose whether they move up or down on the scale of species, becoming worse than any beast or slug or rising to fully human status by exercising the will, imagination, self-consciousness, and yearnings for perfection that distinguish human beings from animals (Taylor, *Coleridge's Defense* 145–99).

In prose and verse Coleridge worries about how "the imp of the perverse" can be controlled or redeemed. Poe, in the essay of that name, uses the term to refer to "an innate and primitive principle of human action" through whose "promptings we act without a comprehensible object . . . for the reason that we should *not*" (269)—a principle recalling the motiveless malignity that spurs the Mariner's deed. At the end of the semester, when we read D. H. Lawrence's "Snake" and see how it revises the assumptions of Coleridge's *Ancient Mariner*, students pounce with delight on the direct reference to the albatross. They write about the differences between the reasons for cruelty in each poem. In doing so, they confirm their discovery that the literary tradition is an active dialogue among styles, ethical and spiritual values, and ultimately persons. Coleridge's prophetic examination of the illness of his time and the possible cures illuminates the entire survey of European literature.

Teaching the Fragment:
Christabel and "Kubla Khan"

Patricia L. Skarda

Students sit down to read *Christabel* and "Kubla Khan" as if they were the complete poems Coleridge had originally planned to write. Dismissing the apologies and explanations Coleridge included in his preface to each poem, students fasten on the possibilities for closure or resolution suggested by the imagery and themes in the poems themselves. They come to class mystified if not disappointed. I attempt to show them that by being fragments these poems exemplify irreconcilable tensions that cannot be resolved or definitively interpreted. The imagination can and does exceed Coleridge's power of representation, and the imaginations of students can be freed to do the same. When their imaginations are fully exercised, students experience for themselves something of the longing that Thomas McFarland regards as essential to Romanticism (*Romanticism* 7). After a few words of introduction on the publication history of both poems, I invite students to articulate their expectations and to exercise their imaginations in analyzing these poems as fragments.

Neither *Christabel* nor "Kubla Khan" appeared in the 1798 or 1800 editions of *Lyrical Ballads*. From the beginning, however, Coleridge intended *Christabel* for *Lyrical Ballads*, saying that in it he "should have more nearly realized [his] ideal" than in *Ancient Mariner* or the "Dark Ladie," begun at the same time (*CC* 7.2: 7). Wordsworth was the first to recognize the incompleteness of *Christabel* and, for the 1800 edition, replaced it with his "Michael," which has completeness among its virtues. Coleridge regarded *Christabel* as an advance over *Ancient Mariner* in that *Christabel* is concerned not so much with the supernatural as with the preternatural, not with what is above nature but with what is outside of nature. He planned to write a prefatory essay for each poem clarifying this important distinction, but, like so many of Coleridge's proposed projects, the essays were never written, and, more important, *Christabel* was never finished, though part 2 was added in 1800, and the conclusion to part 2 in 1802, long before its eventual publication in 1816, over eighteen years since the first flush of enthusiasm initiated his vision. "Kubla Khan" was never finished either, and it appeared, also in 1816, in Coleridge's volume of fragments, *Christabel; Kubla Khan, a Vision; The Pains of Sleep*.

It is useful for students to respond as a class to these two fragmentary poems by seeing them first in relation to *Ancient Mariner*, which they have just studied and which Coleridge was completing when he began *Christabel*. Noting the significance of dreams and the movement from hope to despair, from innocence to shame in *Christabel*, they see the resonance of the spell of silence as the obverse of the Mariner's "woeful agony" to tell his "ghastly tale," and they see the likeness of control and the contrast of purpose in

Geraldine's "serpent's eye" and the Mariner's "glittering eye." With some prodding, they see that Christabel, likened to a dove by Bard Bracy and like the albatross itself, seems to be betrayed and even violated for her innocent trust and openheartedness. A bard of a different order appears at the end of "Kubla Khan," a figure of mystical, magical passion, inspiring "holy dread," to which anyone like Sir Leoline is bound to be immune. Compared with *Ancient Mariner*, "Kubla Khan" has a similar incantatory rhythm and a haunting power, but its lyricism reflects on itself when the poetic "I" in the third strophe aligns himself with the decreeing Kubla Khan. Students sense but cannot explain the transcendence of the structural self-reflexivity of "Kubla Khan," but they know already that Coleridge distinguishes between the understanding of the concrete world, the literal, and the reason of the universal insight, the imaginative; few, however, are willing to risk a reading combining the two. Fewer still are satisfied with G. W. Knight's reading of the three poems as "Coleridge's Divine Comedy" with *Christabel* as hell, *Ancient Mariner* as purgatory, and "Kubla Khan" as paradise, provocative though such a reading is in its fullness. The fact remains that *Christabel* and "Kubla Khan" are fragments and are thus more open to interpretation than is the complete *Ancient Mariner*.

The early reviewers of the 1816 volume commented often on the question of incompletion. I distribute a list of reviewers' remarks drawn from Donald H. Reiman's *Romantics Reviewed*, inviting students to explore the question of fragmentation represented by both poems. Hazlitt complained, saying, "The fault of Mr. Coleridge is, that he comes to no conclusion" (Reiman 2: 530). Francis Jeffrey made his personal frustrations known by declaring the volume "one of the boldest experiments that has yet been made on the patience or understanding of the public" (2: 473). Josiah Conder compared *Christabel* to "a mutilated statue, the beauty of which can only be appreciated by those who have knowledge or imagination sufficient to complete the idea of the whole composition" (1: 373). A reviewer, perhaps Charles Lamb, for the *Times* of London, says the work "interests more by what it leaves untold, than even by what it tells," suggesting that *Christabel*, though unfinished, has "a fragmental beauty" that "lays irresistible hold of the imagination" (2: 891). Lamb was one among many readers to say that "Kubla Khan" is "nonsense" (Lucas 2: 190). "Kubla Khan," Hazlitt said, "only shews that Mr. Coleridge can write better *nonsense* verses than any man in England. It is not a poem, but a musical composition" (Reiman 2: 531). Despite the similarities between the codas of *Christabel* and "Kubla Khan," the incompleteness of the poems differs in kind; and with the class as a whole, I try to elicit various determinants of the apparent fragmentation. I distribute a handout that includes comments of earlier reviewers, reports of how Coleridge thought *Christabel* might be concluded, the sentences missing from the preface to *Christabel*, and a sentence from the Crewe manuscript of "Kubla Khan."

Armed with these materials, the class (usually numbering between thirty and forty) breaks up into four groups of students. One group (the completers) tries to identify what is left untold and to determine how, if at all, *Christabel* and "Kubla Khan" could have been completed. They are instructed to move from plot to characterization to morality on *Christabel* and to imagery and theme on "Kubla Khan." Since they will report first, they need to raise the major issues that other groups can rely on for their reports. Another group (the preface group) focuses on the prefaces as part of each poem in an effort to see the relation of vision to poetic language, of inspiration to poetic process, and of prose formulations to poetic articulations. A third group (the coda group) studies the last section of each poem, having been reminded to look carefully at the narrator in *Christabel* and the speaker of "Kubla Khan." And a fourth group (the fragmenters) attempts to argue for the incoherence of both poems by listing the various contradictions and inconclusive lines of inquiry found throughout them. While the students work, I circulate, providing information and asking and answering questions.

Each group selects a recorder-reporter, two functions in one student, who naturally directs the discussion so that the group will have something to share with the entire class. By experience, I have found that students eager to record are not eager to contribute, and students eager to report may not be willing to listen to others. Recorder-reporters, however, both lead and listen, involving themselves in the seriousness of the questions under discussion while struggling to find the felicitous phrases that represent the best thoughts of the group. If all the groups are working well, reports can be postponed to the next class hour, so that groups can continue discussion outside class and reporters can formalize the sometimes inchoate responses of other students. But I try to confine the discussion, if not the reports, to the seventy-minute class period to urge students to some sort of closure, however formless or Coleridgean. What follows here approximates the reports of the various groups, including the additions made by other members of the class or by me.

The group considering what is left untold wants to know whether Christabel escapes from the spell of silence, regains Sir Leoline's love, and is at last reunited with her lover. Of Geraldine, they ask whether she returns to Tryermaine, with or without Sir Leoline or Lord Roland de Vaux, and whether she releases Christabel from the spell. They question Leoline's refusal to believe Bard Bracy's dream and wonder if he will ever extricate himself from Geraldine's apparent seduction, and they ask if Bard Bracy does obey Sir Leoline's order to race to Roland de Vaux of Tryermaine to tell him his daughter Geraldine is safe in Langdale hall. In short, the surface narrative receives most of the students' attention.

The completers examine Coleridge's several statements about how he intended to complete the story. The longest of these, one of two readings included in the 1838 biography of Coleridge by James Gillman, contains a series of vanishings and reappearances, impersonations and magical transformations:

> Over the mountains, the Bard, as directed by Sir Leoline, "hastes" with his disciple; but in consequence of one of those inundations supposed to be common to this country, the spot only where the castle once stood is discovered,—the edifice itself being washed away. He determines to return. Geraldine being acquainted with all that is passing, like the Weird Sisters in Macbeth, vanishes. Re-appearing, however, she waits the return of the Bard, exciting in the mean time, by her wily arts, all the anger she could rouse in the Baron's breast, as well as that jealousy of which he is described to have been susceptible. The old Bard and the youth at length arrive, and therefore she can no longer personate the character of Geraldine, the daughter of Lord Roland de Vaux, but changes her appearance to that of the accepted though absent lover of Christabel. Next ensues a courtship most distressing to Christabel, who feels—she knows not why—great disgust for her once favoured knight. This coldness is very painful to the Baron, who has no more conception than herself of the supernatural transformation. She at last yields to her father's entreaties, and consents to approach the altar with this hated suitor. The real lover returning, enters at this moment, and produces the ring which she had once given him in sign of her betrothment. Thus defeated, the supernatural being Geraldine disappears. As predicted, the castle bell tolls, the mother's voice is heard, and to the exceeding great joy of the parties, the rightful marriage takes place, after which follows a reconciliation and explanation between the father and daughter.
>
> (301–02)

The improbability of this account reduces the poem to melodramatic story, dispelling many mysteries of the action without providing the source of Geraldine's evil or the point of Christabel's suffering. Students, like critics, invariably mistrust it, though they vie with one another in producing other fanciful conclusions, all more or less improbable.

Another account recorded by Gillman says only:

> The story of Christabel is partly founded on the notion, that the virtuous of this world save the wicked. The pious and good Christabel suffers and prays for "The weal of her lover that is far away," exposed to various temptations in a foreign land; and she thus defeats the power of evil represented in the person of Geraldine. This is one main object of the tale.
>
> (283)

Students work out various narrative alternatives consistent with this contradictory possibility, but ultimately they see the triumph of good over evil as thinner than the ambiguity in Coleridge's fragment is.

One last account, written by the poet's son Derwent for an edition of his father's poems in 1870, wholly exonerates Geraldine:

> The sufferings of Christabel were to have been represented as vicarious, endured for her "lover far away"; and Geraldine, no witch or goblin, or malignant being of any kind, but a spirit, executing her appointed task with the best good will, as she herself says:—
>
> > All they, who live in the upper sky,
> > Do love you, holy Christabel, &c. (227–32)
>
> In form this is, of course, accommodated to "a fond superstition," in keeping with the general tenor of the piece; but that the holy and the innocent do often suffer for the faults of those they love, and are thus made the instruments to bring them back to the ways of peace, is a matter of fact, and in Coleridge's hands might have been worked up into a tale of deep and delicate pathos.
>
> (Qtd. in Fruman 356–57)

Like Gillman's two accounts, this one emphasizes the romance at the expense of the mystery, but it alone raises the issue of the conclusion to part 2, where "love's excess" is expressed in "words of unmeant bitterness" (664–65).

Finding none of these Romantic or gothic possibilities wholly satisfactory, students turn to characterization, including that of the tale's teller. They note that the narrator interrupts his story throughout to ask interpretive questions, pushing beyond the literal without any clear answers. The inquiring narrator asks no questions that could not have been asked by Christabel, and many of the questions sound like paraphrases of Christabel's own doubts and fears: "Is it the wind that moaneth bleak?" (44); "What sees she there?" (57); "And what can ail the mastiff bitch?" (153); "Alas! what ails poor Geraldine? / Why stares she with unsettled eye?" (208–09). Like Christabel's own questions, "And who art thou?" (70) and "How camest thou here?" (76), the narrator's inquiries indicate a fragmented awareness that reflects the mystery of what is contemplated. But the mystery remains unsolved even to the last question, addressed clearly to Sir Leoline: "And wouldst thou wrong thy only child, / Her child and thine?" (634–35).

When focusing on the issue of morality, students generally agree that Bard Bracy's dream, which he told to delay his ordered departure for Tryermaine, makes clear the dovelike innocence of Christabel and the snakelike evil of Geraldine, but the consistency of characterization becomes suspect with

Geraldine's desire for "delay" (259) and with Christabel's prayer to be cleansed of "her sins unknown" (390). Why Geraldine pauses before lying down with Christabel and why Christabel admits to sins, albeit "unknown" ones, precipitate an active discussion of the possible transgressions committed by both characters. Students cannot find sufficient evidence within the poem to support their identification of Geraldine as sorceress, though I give them Coleridge's canceled description of Geraldine's "bosom and half her side" (252) as "lean and old and foul of hue," the marks of a sorceress. They ally the "serpent's eye" (585) with the lamia and "the touch and pain" (453) with the lesbian possibilities, but they cannot come to firm agreement, except to note that Geraldine clearly threatens Christabel's innocence. The narrator's prayers and exclamations do not seem adequate support for reading Christabel solely as victim or even martyr, though Coleridge told Thomas Allsop that he had Crashaw's lines on Saint Teresa's martyrdom in mind when writing the poem (Allsop 117–18).

The name Christabel includes two well-known victims, betrayed respectively by friend or brother, but Christabel herself is more naive than merely innocent. For unstated reasons, she "stole" (31) to the wood at midnight to pray for her lover, "stole to the other side of the oak" (56), and once in the castle says to Geraldine, "we will move as if in stealth" (120), clearly indicating the illicit nature of her activities. She willingly stretches forth her hand (75, 102, 104), openly invites Geraldine to her bed (122), painstakingly carries Geraldine over the threshold (132), and with truly incredible generosity gives Geraldine the "cordial wine" made by her mother (191–93). One student, perhaps unaware of the laws of hospitality, quipped querulously, "How much of her mother's wine can she be hoarding? A cellarful or but one last bottle?" The dead mother, "wandering" (205) for reasons not given, might have helped Christabel to notice the many signs of danger: Geraldine refuses to cross the threshold unaided or to pray to "the Virgin all divine" (139); as the women pass, the mastiff uncharacteristically makes "an angry moan" (149) and the brands flare up (158–61), but Christabel notes only "the lady's eye" (160), well before the actual curse excuses such mesmerism. Christabel clearly invites the seduction, if that is what happens, and by her explicit neglect to heed the various warnings, she commits enough sins of omission to suggest that innocence carries the seeds of its own destruction. With such fuzzy character definition, Coleridge shows something less than the usurping of one consciousness by another, though that description of evil by Henry James can be useful in looking at part 2 of the poem.

The group of completers struggles with what is left untold in "Kubla Khan," for they see at once that the untold has little to do with narrative and more to do with imagery and theme. The line ending the description—"Ancestral voices prophesying war!"—promises action and perhaps even destruction of the improbable "sunny pleasure-dome with caves of ice!" But no action of any kind intervenes before the strange coda, with its injunction to "Beware! Beware!" not of war but of the visionary speaker himself. At the very least, history is left untold, unfinished, for despite the consistent past tense throughout the description of Xanadu, "ancestral voices" must be heard from an even earlier time. Besides the temporal and spatial discontinuities, "Kubla Khan" interrupts itself stylistically, metrically, and thematically. Marjorie Levinson calls the manner of lines 1–36, "removed, authoritative, even authoritarian," with "epic scope and lyric treatment" (98, 99). The exotic setting of this earthly paradise recalls not only Purchas's Pilgrimage but also the more familiar Garden of Eden in Milton and the happy valley behind Mount Amara (the manuscript version for "Abora") in Johnson's Rasselas. The "deep romantic chasm," however, admits a note of ominous danger out of keeping with paradise though in keeping with human trials like that of "woman wailing for her demon-lover" to which the chasm's savagery, holiness, and enchantment is oddly compared. The civilizing effects of the English landscape in the first eleven lines seem to be opposed by the volcanic fountain flinging up "the sacred river." Kubla Khan cannot do more than decree the "stately pleasure-dome" and enclose within fortresslike walls the primitive violence of forces beyond his control. Pleasure, repeated three times (2, 31, 36), and versions of sun (5, 11, 36) enjoyed above are undermined by repeated images of imponderable, empty infinity in "measureless" caverns, "sunless sea," "lifeless ocean," "caves of ice." One subject drifts into another without demonstrable logic or progression, but the profusion of contradictory images seems introductory to something even larger, more momentous even than Kubla Khan's "miracle of rare device."

The preface group, having been provided with the sentences missing from the preface to Christabel, looks first at this new information for ways to proceed. Following the date and place of composition, Coleridge wrote:

> Since the latter date [1800], my poetic powers have been, till very lately, in a state of suspended animation. But as, in my very first conception of the tale, I had the whole present to my mind, with the wholeness, no less than the liveliness of a vision; I trust that I shall be able to embody in verse the three parts yet to come in the course of the present year.

The use of "vision" is especially worth noting, for here Coleridge clearly regards "vision" as tantamount to a metaphor for completeness, despite the incompleteness of the narrative. Irene Chayes goes further, saying that "vision" is already a metaphor for completeness of artistic intention (" 'Kubla Khan' " 2). But the "vision" is clearly larger than the poem that follows.

This group must also be told of the 1934 discovery of the Crewe manuscript of "Kubla Khan" (see Shelton) with its brief note:

This fragment with a good deal more, not recoverable, composed in a sort of Reverie brought on by two grains of Opium, taken to check a dysentery, at a Farm House between Porlock and Linton, a quarter of a mile from Culbone Church, in the fall of the year, 1797.

Students usually ignore the discrepancy in the dating revealed by the Crewe manuscript; fall or summer makes little difference to them. I accord students the right to their own ignorance of this complicated matter, except to point out the flap caused by Dorothy Wordsworth's enigmatic journal entry on carrying "*Kubla* to a fountain in the neighbouring market-place" (1: 34). Students rather like thinking the Wordsworths playful enough to name their water jug "Kubla," but they can, I think, be spared the arguments on the dating of the poem. They ought to notice, however, that "Reverie" from the Crewe manuscript disappears in the 1816 preface, in favor of the "profound sleep" in which, as the subtitle makes clear, the poet enjoys "a vision in a dream." This "vision" becomes, as the subtitle also makes clear, "a fragment." The use of "vision" refers not merely to the poet's state but also to some aspects of the subject matter that follows, certainly of the poem and possibly of the preface as well. Students considering the full prefaces of 1816 note the repeated emphasis on the fragmentary nature of both poems, but they focus first on the striking self-justification and defensive apologies of the poet. Instead of completing the poems before publication in 1816, Coleridge gives the time when and the place where he wrote the two parts of *Christabel* and all of "Kubla Khan," as though genesis would in and of itself illuminate the poems. He had, by 1816, reason to deflect attention from yet two more unfinished projects, for he had embarrassed himself by promising so much and completing so little. Besides, he had spoken often of *Christabel* in letters from 1799 on, and he had made the poem known by frequent recitation long before its official publication. "Kubla Khan" came to the public without nearly so much advance advertising, though Byron among others had apparently heard it recited by Coleridge, and Byron did instigate publication by asking his publisher to visit Coleridge in April 1816. When the work was finally published on 25 May 1816, the new preface became an integral part of the poem itself.

Had Coleridge not delayed the publication of *Christabel*, he would not have had to defend himself against plagiarism of Sir Walter Scott and Lord Byron, the "celebrated poets" to which he refers, but his defense of his own originality results from real and increasingly more serious accusations of plagiarism (the most acrimonious coming from Thomas De Quincey in 1834 [2: 138–228] and J. F. Ferrier in 1840), especially regarding his *Biographia Literaria*. In the first chapter of the *Biographia*, which Coleridge had been working on while writing the preface to *Christabel*, he expresses unequivocally what Norman Fruman summarizes as his "moral disapproval of plagiarists, imitators, and otherwise intellectually dishonest persons, and his own singularity in professing scrupulously all intellectual obligations" (73). The issue had long been of interest to Coleridge; in fact, he translated the quoted Latin hexameters—

> 'Tis mine and it is likewise yours;
> But an if this will not do;
> Let it be mine, good friend! for I
> Am the poorer of the two.

—in November 1801, long before he found it desirable or necessary to defend himself from critics who would "derive every rill they behold flowing, from a perforation made in some other man's tank." In the fountain imagery, students recognize an allusion to Wordsworth's definition of poetry, and they rightly seize on the suggestion that Coleridge was wounded by Wordsworth's refusal to publish the fragmentary *Christabel* in *Lyrical Ballads*. Given the fact that Coleridge owes the publication of the whole volume *Christabel; Kubla Khan, a Vision; The Pains of Sleep* to Byron's intercession with John Murray, Byron's own publisher, the fear that *Christabel* might be seen as derivative of Byron seems natural. Nonetheless the discussion of plagiarism deflects attention from the poem itself even as it highlights the originality of the new verse form, which Coleridge forever after regarded as being perhaps the most successful part of the poem. By mentioning the accentual rather than syllabic measure, Coleridge does draw attention to his variations, said to mark "some transition in the nature of the imagery or passion." Students look for such transitions within the poem, finding shorter lines in the narrator's "Ah wel-a-day!" (264), Geraldine's curse (271–75), the revised setting in the conclusion to part 1 (282–85), and at the narrator's last question of Sir Leoline, whose name alone fills the shortened line 633: "And wouldst thou wrong thy only child, / Her child and thine?" (634–35). Each moment does mark a transition that the students can identify and explain to their peers. Despite the distractions, then, the preface to *Christabel* reveals an important clue about how the poem is to be read. But even this clue remains part of the prevalent mystery of irresolution.

The elaborate discursive preface to "Kubla Khan" emphatically announces the poem as a fragment, but the reasons for incompletion are presented by an anecdote that is probably more fiction than fact. Again Coleridge defends himself extensively, this time by blaming a visitor for interrupting his poetic record of his dream. Apologizing for the "*poetic* merits" of the poem to follow, Coleridge draws our attention to "Kubla Khan" as "a psychological curiosity." "Psychological" leads most students and many critics to excuse the strangeness of "Kubla Khan" because it was allegedly an opium dream. At the time of writing the poem, however, Coleridge was not yet an addict to laudanum, the alcoholic tincture of opium, but he, like others, used laudanum as a convenient "anodyne" to any number of minor ailments including the "dysentery" mentioned in the Crewe manuscript. Only a few years later, when Coleridge could be fairly called an addict, opium gave him the corrosive nightmares described in "The Pains of Sleep" (1803), but in 1797 his experiences with opium were essentially pleasurable, soothing, and creative. In her book-length study, Elisabeth Schneider describes the effects of the occasional use of opium as "euphoria" (40), and Alethea Hayter says that its action "can uncover that imagination while it is at work in a way which might enable an exceptionally gifted and self-aware writer to observe and learn from his own mental processes" (335). Indeed, mental processes do fascinate Coleridge, and his associations and transformations become the subject of the preface, as well as of the poem itself.

While in a deep sleep, Coleridge says emphatically that "all the images" read in "Purchas's Pilgrimage" "rose up before him as *things*, with a parallel production of the correspondent expressions, without any sensation or consciousness of effort." With this in mind, students cling to the notion that at least the first part of the poem is, then, the product of the subconscious, free of the "waking intelligence," as John Livingston Lowes puts it in his famous *Road to Xanadu* (401). The passivity implied by such a reading of "psychological curiosity" makes it possible to read "Kubla Khan" psychoanalytically, but it encumbers the reading of "Kubla Khan" as a poem about poetry and the poetic process, if that is "the general purport of the vision," which the poet says he retained even after the visit of the "person from Porlock." The reliability of the preface is called into question by the number of qualifying adverbs—"instantly and eagerly," "unfortunately called out" —and by the explicit excusing of the incompletion when with "no small surprise and mortification" the poet could remember nothing but "scattered lines and images." It is not, perhaps, incidental to note that Coleridge had few business dealings and none we know of with a "person from Porlock," who carries the burden of the blame for Coleridge. But the fact remains that the preface rehearses for us much of the creative process and the difficulties that beset it for Coleridge. Whether he accurately presents us the facts of the composition of "Kubla Khan," he raises the central issues of completeness, unity, structure, and meaning in a prose statement that anticipates the poem. Students see the parallel movements of the preface and poem as proceeding generally from enthusiasm for the possibilities of art through to loss, disappointment, and deferred effort (Chayes, " 'Kubla Khan' " 4). The inclusion of the quotation from his own poem "The Picture: Or, The Lover's Resolution," coupled with the quotation from Theocritus, "but the to-morrow is yet to come," resoundingly reminds us that the loss is unpredictable and that the poet gives us finally but a fragment of "the dream of pain and disease."

Students in the coda group puzzle long and hard over Coleridge's description of images as "*things*," bearing in mind the incredible exactness of the poetic descriptions both of place and of the figure of the poet. The creation of Kubla Khan, when likened to the creation of the "damsel with a dulcimer" and of the poet figure, the "I" in the coda, makes the creation into an emblem of mind meditating, the "symphony and song" of the Abyssinian maid, the poet poeticizing. The reflexivity of the poetic act, commenting on the commentator, is, of course, exactly what is going on in the preface, regardless of whether it is fact or fiction or some mix of the two. Students in the group considering the final verse paragraph of "Kubla Khan" see at once the threat and the joy of creation to the creator, much as Kubla Khan himself hears of war and "mingled measure / From the fountain and the caves." The speaker usurps by analogy the role of Kubla Khan when he says, "I would build that dome in air, / That sunny dome! those caves of ice!" He does not complete the vision of the landscape with its civilized savagery or the history of Kubla Khan's creation but replaces Kubla Khan with himself, a creator with an audience, "all," capable of hearing, seeing, crying and capable of demanding action, weaving "a circle round him thrice," closing "eyes with holy dread." The coda responds to the first two stanzas of the poem by seeing an analogy to creation itself, duplicated in the descriptive stanzas by the flowing of the "sacred river" to the "sunless sea" and "lifeless ocean," and again in the coda by the song of the Abyssinian maid, which if "revive[d] within" the speaker would precipitate a new version of the figure of Kubla Khan and a new creation as paradoxical as Kubla Khan's. The fragment completes itself by the reader's perception of its circular movement, finding "meaning in its partiality," as Marjorie Levinson suggests (49), and combining the first and second stanzas, the "stately pleasure-dome" of the first with the "sunny pleasure-dome with caves of ice" of the second into "That sunny dome! those caves of ice!" in the remarkable third. Without closure, there is, nonetheless, an experience of closure to the gifted reader. The speaking "I" goes one better than Kubla Khan, who "did decree" the "stately pleasure-dome"; the speaker says he "would build that dome in air," presumably by himself, without need of others. The context makes it clear that it is not only the dome but the poem itself that he would "build," consciously now rather than in dream, reverie, or anything short of poetic crafting, word by word, phrase by phrase, stanza by stanza. Although the "damsel with the dulcimer" was discovered "in a vision," this image is described clearly not as merely recalled but as seen, "once I saw," and heard, "Singing of Mount Abora." Only part of the vision is needed to revive the bard, to empower him, to make him prophetic and, of course, poetic. So, too, what is recorded of the vision of Kubla Khan, even in its fragmented state, is enough to make not only this poem but also the poet himself.

The coda to *Christabel* remains less satisfactory for students, since the expectations of the story seem to be all but abandoned. Of course, they see the father-child relationship and even the echo of his confused "rage and pain" (676) with the confusion of Sir Leoline's "rage and pain" (638), but the child of the coda is a far cry from Christabel, and the father's expression of "his love's excess / With words of unmeant bitterness" (664–65) pales next to Sir Leoline's offense. The tragic tone of what has gone before can scarcely be answered by the realism of the conclusion to part 2, the coda. There is more missing here than there was in closure of *Ancient Mariner*, for despite the unsatisfying reductive moralism of the memorable stanza beginning "He prayeth best who loveth best," the Mariner himself does return home to tell his tale, even if he tells it again and again. Uncanny though the motivations be in the killing of the albatross and the blessing of the snakes and the sailing of the ship back to England, the poem ends conclusively, certainly. But in *Christabel*, Coleridge shifts his apparent purposes dramatically from plot to human nature, from serious seduction to slight misspeaking. Mention of the "world of sin" (673) in the coda does, however, provoke a parenthetical response in the voice of the sometimes querulous, sometimes sympathetic, narrator "(O sorrow and shame should this be true!)" (674), providing the merest suggestion that the speaker is still around and still concerned with larger, more imponderable transgressions than speaking bitter words, even out of "rage and pain." In the domestication of the tragic emotions, the perversity of the human heart is universalized. Satisfaction remains unrealized, particularly with the blithe suggestion, appropriately qualified from the beginning, "Perhaps 'tis pretty to force together / Thoughts so all unlike each other" (666–67). Students sometimes shout, "No, it's not pretty. It's avoiding all the important issues." The speaker repeats his own hesitation with another qualification, with another reach toward some universal principle: "Perhaps 'tis tender too and pretty / At each wild word to feel within / A sweet recoil of love and pity" (670–72). "Perhaps," students sometimes respond, "we are meant to love the poem and pity the poet who couldn't finish the last three parts of this extraordinary poem." But the coda to *Christabel* ends the poem without finishing it, stopping the poem with an afterthought.

The last group, the fragmenters, generates a long list of contradictions ranging from the paradisiacal/infernal, ascent/descent, intermittency/continuity, peace/war, suggestiveness/concreteness, past/future in "Kubla Khan" to the good/evil, reality/dream, victim/victor, passivity/activity, innocence/guilt, silence/speaking, tragedy/romance, lover/mother, transcendence/transgression, ideal/actual in *Christabel*. Their list has, of course, grown longer as a result of the reports of other groups. Oppositions like these cannot be easily resolved in either narrative or lyric, but in fragments the oppositions can exist in uneasy, even perilous, balance. Perhaps, then, the fact of fragmentation is, whether intended or not, a ploy, a device, to maintain irresolvable tensions, to stymie those readers and reviewers who think that parts must necessarily be less than the whole. From these poetic examples, fragmentation can be seen as more useful than completion, for by seeing only the part, the reading cannot ever be completed. Incoherence comes to be seen as useful in itself, for it contains all oppositions, including by implication the complementarity of fragmentation and completion. We turn then to Coleridge's description of the power of the imagination, which reveals itself

> in the balance or reconciliation of opposite or discordant qualities: of sameness, with difference; of the general, with the concrete; the idea, with the image; the individual, with the representative; the sense of novelty and freshness, with old and familiar objects; a more than usual state of emotion, with more than usual order; judgement ever awake and steady self-possession, with enthusiasm and feeling profound or vehement; and while it blends and harmonizes the natural and the artificial, still subordinates art to nature; the manner to matter; and our admiration of the poet to our sympathy with the poetry.
>
> (CC 7.2: 16–17)

The very disappointment, even dismay, that students experience when reading *Christabel* and "Kubla Khan" proves in fact that their admiration of the poet has been subordinated to their sympathy with the poetry. The vision of the poet overpowers the language to embody it, and the poems cannot end because the vision they aspire to cannot be embodied in language. The resolution students seek need not be found in the meeting of their expectations or in the satisfying of their longings, but it can be found in the recognition that they have exercised their imaginations without Coleridge doing more than exercising his, however inconclusively. There is, then, as Coleridge said there should be, "*method* in the fragments" (*The Friend* [*CC* 4.1: 449]). Romantic poetry need not accord with set genres of narrative and lyric, romance or tragedy, for, as Friedrich Schlegel insisted in his own fragments, every poem is its own genre. It need not describe the poet to the exclusion of the poem, for it can "hover at the midpoint between the portrayed and the portrayer." It need not end with a definitive bang or even with an indecisive whimper, for "[t]he romantic kind of poetry is still in the state of becoming; that, in fact, is its real essence: that it should forever be becoming and never be perfected" (Firchow 116). And what we have done in this class is to certify that *Christabel* and "Kubla Khan," like other Romantic poems, are not so finished as to be capable of being fully analyzed. Instead, we have just begun to respond to Coleridge's fragments with the full powers of our own reconciling imaginations. But at least we have begun.

Coleridge and the Mysterious (M)other

Anne Williams

In 1797 Coleridge expressed reservations about the contemporary fashion
for the gothic: "The horrible and the preternatural," he wrote in a review
of *The Monk*, ". . . can never be required except by the torpor of an un-
awakened, or the languor of an exhausted mind" (Raysor, *Miscellaneous*
370). Yet three of his own major works begun the same year—"Kubla Khan,"
Christabel, and *The Rime of the Ancient Mariner*—offer a virtual catalog of
gothic conventions (including a haunted castle, an archetypal wanderer,
ghosts, family curses, fatal women). These poems invite us into an otherworld
"where more is meant than meets the ear," and yet they stubbornly resist
interpretation. I suggest that Coleridge's use of the gothic shows that these
poems constitute cultural rather than merely personal nightmares; they exemplify the kind of writing contemporary feminist theorists call *l'écriture
féminine*.

Speculation about this concept may be found in the writings of recent
French feminist theorists, notably Luce Irigaray, Hélène Cixous, and Monique Wittig. *L'écriture féminine* is not necessarily the creation of women
but may rather be the work of those who "refuse to identify with [the] father
and the laws of paternal discourse" (Jones 362). (Cixous cites Joyce, Genet,
and Kleist as among the few authors of this mode of writing.) Like *woman*
itself, *l'écriture féminine* is a concept defined by its divergence from a dominant cultural norm, by its status as other. (It is, therefore, perhaps more
readily available to women, who have traditionally found themselves kept
outside various modes of male-dominated discourse.) Psychologically it may
be understood as a return to "the pleasures of preverbal identification with
the mother" (Jones 363). Specifically, this identification is manifested in the
primacy of the image over the idea and of the concrete over the figurative/
symbolic; it is akin to those modes of meaning that Freud calls "primary
process" thought. For some, the Freudian hysteric (whose body "writes"
the "message") is the perfect example of such "feminine" communication
(Hunter 98–103). Such alternative modes of meaning are understandably
threatening to the dominant culture inextricably rooted in the laws of its
language. Elaine Showalter summarizes the debate by saying that *l'écriture
féminine* "undermines the linguistic, syntactical, and metaphysical conventions of Western narrative" (9). There is no certainty, however, about what
this mode of writing *is*, since by definition it resists the concept of *definition*;
hence one interesting consequence of reading Coleridge's Mystery poems
in this context is to increase our experience of this paradoxical writing that
is not writing as the word is usually understood.

I devised this approach to Coleridge's three poems for an undergraduate
feminist analysis of the gothic tradition. My students had first learned some-

thing of Freudian dream theory and other basic psychoanalytic concepts. (I had assigned the chapters on Freudian and archetypal criticism in Guérin et al., *A Handbook of Critical Approaches to Literature*, as well as Freud's summary of his dream theory, "On Dreams" (*Interpretation* 633–86), and Brenner's chapter on the subject in his *Elementary Textbook of Psychoanalysis*.) Many of my students had already studied "Kubla Khan" and *Ancient Mariner* and were thus partially familiar with New Critical readings of these poems, such as the notion that "Kubla Khan" concerns the primary and secondary imagination and that *Ancient Mariner* is a Christian allegory of sin and redemption.

In the classroom I first lead my students through a fairly conventional close reading of each text, emphasizing a search for some principle of orderly coherence—in fact, a reading that posits Coleridge's own principle that good poems have "organic unity." We also discuss psychoanalytic readings which argue that the poems express Freudian themes. Several emphasize Coleridge's presumed problems with his mother (Beres; Durham; Schapiro). After we have done our best to achieve a coherent interpretation, I ask students to find problems in the text that cannot be resolved, questions that cannot be answered—the incongruities, disjunctions, and inconsistencies that the interpretations we have considered ignore or elide. I encourage some analysis of the things we take for granted in "reality" and in "fiction." In the following discussion I group comments about all three poems under topics relevant to a presentation of the concept of *l'écriture féminine*.

The Metaphysical Conventions of Western Narrative

To introduce the concept of *metaphysical* conventions, I give students a copy of Aristotle's paradigm in the *Metaphysics* (A_3) which organizes reality into the following ten pairs of opposites:

male	female
limit	unlimited
odd	even
one	plurality
right	left
square	oblong
at rest	moving
straight	curved
light	darkness
good	evil

The terms in the column beginning with "male" are sometimes referred to as the "line of good," whereas those in the column introduced by "female" are called the "line of evil" (Maclean 2).

In *The Newly Born Woman*, Cixous expands Aristotle's list, adding the following pairs of opposites: activity, passivity; sun, moon; culture, nature; day, night; father, mother; head, heart; intelligible, palpable; logos, pathos (Cixous and Clément 63). The terms in the line of good are the culturally central ones, often what linguists call "unmarked" words; those in the line of evil are defined in relation to the first, and that relation is often constituted as the opposite or the absence of the first.

The fundamental feature of this Aristotelian schema is its dualistic structure. Cixous surmises that the reason patriarchal culture subjects thought to binary systems of irreconcilable opposites may be founded on recognition of " 'the' couple, man/woman":

> Everywhere (where) ordering intervenes, where a law organizes what is thinkable by oppositions . . . and all these pairs of oppositions are *couples*. . . . We see that "victory" always comes to the same thing: things get hierarchical. Organization by hierarchy makes all conceptual organization subject to man. . . .
>
> (64–65)

Similarly, Irigaray argues that a "dream of symmetry" is the telling sign of patriarchy itself, the founding assumption of our culture (*Speculum* 11–112).

This entire system of imagery and language (and hence thought) privileges the male, the light, the static, the unified. Our model for creativity (and power) is the image of God the Father, eternal and unchanging, three in one, who created the universe by speaking and who dwells in light. "Man" may see him by the light of reason. But the Coleridge texts under consideration appear to be preoccupied with the terms in the second column, with nature, the female, pathos, passivity, the palpable, the irrational. (One may also note that the first column lists qualities associated with a classical aesthetic, while the second one suggests the romantic—or even, more specifically, the gothic.)

The privileging of unity has in itself important effects on our artistic criteria. With some encouragement, students can usually articulate some of these effects. Asked to think about what makes a good plot, they may suggest (Aristotelian) notions such as the principle that a good story should have a beginning, a middle, and an end; that events should be plausibly related by cause and effect; and that characters should act according to some discernible rationale of motivation. It is readily apparent, however, that in different ways all three Coleridge poems deny or at least frustrate such expectations; indeed, his decision to publish "Kubla Khan" and *Christabel* as fragments can itself be seen as a subversion of conventional demands.

In this context *Ancient Mariner*, ostensibly complete, appears curiously inconclusive. To facilitate discussion of the plot and the conventional expectations it arouses, I hand out a graph of the poem (fig. 1). The plot is

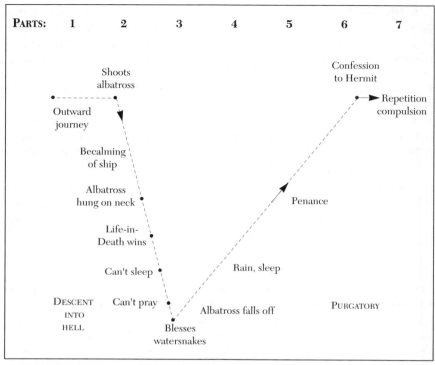

Figure 1. The structure of Coleridge's *Rime of the Ancient Mariner*

apparently comic—in fact, like Dante's *Divine Comedy*, it describes a descent into hell, followed by an uphill journey through a purgatorial realm of expiation. But there emphatically is no *Paradise*—nor is there the familiar conclusion to more earthly comedies: marriage. The Mariner is trapped in a purgatory of repetition compulsion, while his chosen interlocutor, the Wedding Guest, is not exactly edified by the tale—"He went like one that hath been stunned, / And is of sense forlorn" (622–23); it seems that the Mariner's message has had an effect ("A sadder and a wiser man / He rose the morrow morn"), but it is one that evades ordinary modes of linguistic communication. The "meaning" of the Mariner's tale is experienced first as physical sensation that only belatedly finds expression as intellectual response. The Mariner remains homeless and companionless; the Wedding Guest misses the wedding. M. H. Abrams's comment that the Guest is singled out as one who "needs to be instructed in the full significance of love and union" (*Natural Supernaturalism* 273) glosses over the peculiar violence of the love and the incomprehensibility of the union that appear to prevail in the Mariner's world. Implicitly, the human institution (or metaphor) of the wedding is irrelevant or inadequate.

Ancient Mariner also revises our patriarchy's root myth, the story of Adam and Eve. Here the fall is associated with the sacrifice of the albatross on the crossbow, while the redemption is effected by serpents (many rather than one). The Mariner breaks no consciously known law (as Adam and Eve did), and his salvation comes mysteriously from within himself, not through the intervention of an external divinity. As many readers have noticed, good things tend to happen in the moonlight, while sunlight alternately comforts and afflicts the Mariner. Bostetter's discussion of the poem as a revelation of a "random" universe is insightful; he is also right in noting that the Mariner continually experiences "an arbitrary exhibition of power" (116). But one can go even further. Certainly Coleridge and the Mariner and the implied author of the glosses attempt to force the events of the narrative into a coherent, conventional shape. (From this perspective the term *gloss* may mean not only an old-fashioned footnote but also "a purposefully misleading interpretation or explanation" [*American Heritage Dictionary*, New College ed., 1976].) The Mariner's neat summary ("He prayeth best who loveth best") could testify to this attempt to order, and to its failure. The point is that language, with its impulse to order, always and necessarily fails to comprehend or apprehend the reality it attempts to grasp. A verbal criticism founded on assumptions of coherence also participates in this partly doomed effort. But one might say that the action of *Ancient Mariner* takes place in a world not ordered by a logos; it implies the troubling hypothesis that our assumptions about meaning and order (including those of language itself) are part of the problem.

When asked to contrast this poem with "Kubla Khan," students generally suggest that the first poem approaches through an act of violence an otherworld recalcitrant to principles of order, while the second begins with the premise of order and proceeds to imagery of birth. But the familiar notion that "Kubla Khan" is a poem about the poetic imagination (which manifests "a reconciliation of opposites or discordant qualities") has partly distracted attention from the extraordinary instability of Kubla's garden, apparently subject to something like natural cycles and processes. Like the Garden of Eden, it is "spoken" into being, but in it the word may be uncreating as well; Kubla hears "ancestral voices prophesying war." This "creative father" seems haunted by fathers himself. Kubla's creativity is more tenuous than Jehovah's, however. He causes nature to participate in his building the dome of pleasure, but he co-opts rather than preempts the prior creative powers of nature, and his "encircling" of natural phenomena is temporary. Furthermore, nature as it is represented in the garden cannot adequately be described according to cultural expectations. The narrator perceives that the opposites exist but registers the limitations of that descriptive vocabulary: though things are opposed, they are also one in a way that defies language. (The disjunction between the second and third stanzas and the sudden emergence of the "I"—apparently marking the transformation of a narrative into a lyric—could equally be seen as enacting this linguistic inadequacy.)

Nor does *Christabel* allow us to rest within our usual metaphysical, psychological, or aesthetic categories. Geraldine (whose name is a feminine version of "spear-bearer") violates the principle that one character cannot be several disparate things at once—evil spirit, fatal woman, mother surrogate, vampire, damsel in distress. Christabel herself is a mixture of heroine and victim, at once initiator of her own downfall and innocent object of evil. Similar is Sir Leoline's ambivalence about his daughter (whom he dearly loves and perhaps dearly hates as the cause of her mother's death, a death he speaks of every morning). Certainly his affections are easily swayed by the Lady Geraldine, who may, or may not, be telling the truth when she identifies herself as the daughter of his old friend. Coleridge's lyrical conclusions to the narrative sections add a further bafflement: these comments appear to be interpreting and summarizing the story but in fact simply complicate it. (One thinks of similar disjunctions between the text of *Ancient Mariner* and its marginal gloss.)

Speaking Nature's (M)other Tongue

The paradoxical possibility of a nonverbal language or of communication that evades words fascinated all the Romantic poets. Students may recall Keats's "La Belle Dame sans Merci" (a text that could also be taught here) or Wordsworth's "Solitary Reaper." Thus I ask them to examine speech in the Mystery poems, the causes and effects of directly quoted language that attempts to articulate what may be beyond words. All three poems imply the inadequacies of speech in relation to experience; all these poems take place in the realm designated as other by the structures of language and thought. This duality—that some experience should be beyond language— is inherent in language and culture. Indeed it may be caused by language.

According to Freud and his interpreter Jacques Lacan, the child's (son's) entry into culture occurs when the father interrupts the preoedipal mother-child relation; the father (representing patriarchal culture) demands that the child turn away from all that the mother represents (the unconscious, the preverbal paradise where desires are met and communication is wordless). Lacan emphasizes that the "symbolic order" (language and the culture created by that language) offers the child a substitute for the mother; but her absence is unconsciously felt for the rest of his life (281–91). Speech is thus paradoxical. It is all one has to compensate for the loss of the mother and the preverbal paradise, but that one has it at all signifies her absence. And since in the infant's unconscious the mother has two contradictory and omnipotent aspects (as all-satisfying and all-rejecting), the female presence unconsciously sought is thus infinitely desirable and terribly frightening.

Coleridge's Mystery poems consistently reflect such anxiety about the female principle and contradictory images of both fatal woman and benevolent mother. The ancient Mariner separates the Wedding Guest from the apparently attractive bride of the frame narrative ("Red as a rose is she"), later substituting the bride of death, "The Night-mare Life-in-Death" (193) who gambles for the Mariner's soul and wins it. But, confusingly, the archetypally female moon presides over certain redemptive events in the poem, and the Mariner attributes the gift of sleep to "Mary Queen" (294), called "holy Mother" in the glosses. In "Kubla Khan" the ominous "woman wailing for her demon lover" is balanced by the muselike "Abyssinian maid," who facilitates a rebirth of the paradise.

In *Christabel* the ambiguity of the female is a central theme. Geraldine is alternately "evil," dangerous, lamialike, and an apparently conscience-stricken fatal woman. Nor is Christabel entirely the innocent victim. She seeks out her "Mother Nature." Significantly, she also chooses to pray under the branches of the "huge, broad-breasted, old oak tree" (42). Having left the protection of her father's house, she actively carries Geraldine over the threshold. It is true that evil spirits must have aid to enter. But brides (and sometimes children) are carried over thresholds as well. The vampire is frequently a figure for nature as terrible mother; and the serpent-goddess Lamia's career as a vampire (as Coleridge apparently knew) originated in her frustrated motherhood.

The essentially ambiguous power and appeal of the maternal is thus apparent in all three poems, as is the problem of the limits of language. The ancient Mariner is forever controlled by the necessity he feels to wander throughout the world telling and retelling his story. His confession to the Hermit near the end of his adventure does not absolve his need to keep talking; one may suspect that this need reveals that his "talking cure" is never efficacious. During the Mariner's adventure, speech is often beside the point, if not harmful. The shipmates' superstitious "interpretations" are apparently fatal, and in the depths of despair the Mariner is tortured by the "wicked whisper" (246) that intrudes on his efforts to pray; during his long penance he hears pronounced a sentence of further suffering. Similarly, the turning point occurs when the "spring of love" gushes from his heart and he blesses the snakes "unaware" (283, 284)—which among other things seems to imply "inarticulately."

In "Kubla Khan" the king's "decree" causes something to be effected, the reordering or rearrangement of what is already present in nature; it is as if the Khan temporarily succeeded in re-creating the preverbal paradise of things rather than of words, of natural rather than of human sounds. But the termination of this paradise is signaled by something like the Word of the Father ("Ancestral voices prophesying war"). And in *Christabel* Geraldine's speech is alternately seductive, enigmatic, and mendacious, while her spell makes it impossible for Christabel to express what she knows.

Finally, all three poems show adequate expression to be the result of consuming some natural substance; in the Mariner's case, it is blood; for the frenzied poet, "honey-dew" and "the milk of Paradise"; for Geraldine, the cordial wine Christabel's mother had made "of wild flowers" (191–93).

Writing the Body

Writing the body is a theme that is particularly debated among theorists of *l'écriture féminine*. Monique Wittig, for instance, asserts that such writing would shun what she sees as a patriarchal habit of metaphorizing the body, above all the female body; Cixous declares that true female writing might be written in the "white ink" that is "mother's milk" (94). Some theorists agree, however, that a simple inversion of patriarchal "écriture" will not furnish an adequate model.

Similarly, though the Mystery poems "belong" to the realm of the other as posited by a patriarchal culture, one should not read them simply as an inversion of the familiar hierarchies, privileging dark rather than light, the moon rather than the sun, and so on. Instead, the concept of *l'écriture féminine* implies an entirely different mode of signification, one that attempts to reconstitute preverbal communication with the mother. Dianne Hunter explains, "Before we enter the grammatical order of language, we exist in a dyadic, semiotic world of pure sound and body rhythms, oceanically at one with our nurturer" (98–99). Such a language might be suggested by emphasis on the literal or concrete rather than on the figurative and by puns or other wordplay.

In initiating this stage of the discussion, I ask students to look for examples of meaning that is "embodied" or where the image supersedes the idea. I point out that Coleridge's descriptions of ideal poetic language often seem to be striving toward this notion. In the preface to "Kubla Khan" he exclaims at the power of the dream in which "images rose up before him as *things*." Similarly, in struggling to articulate the reasons that the "symbol" is superior to "allegory," he seems to be groping toward the primacy of the concrete as communication:

> In looking at objects of Nature while I am thinking, as at yonder moon dim-glimmering thro' the dewy window-pane, I seem rather to be seeking, as it were *asking*, a symbolical language for something within me that already and forever exists. . . . I have always an obscure feeling

as if that new phænomenon were the dim Awaking of a forgotten or hidden Truth of my inner Nature.

(CN 2: 2546)

This description of "meaning" in the concrete may be discussed in terms of the significance that preverbal experience may have to a mind that has acquired language. These texts may in various ways unconsciously allow us to share something of the perspective of the preverbal infant, which helps us understand their supernaturalism, as well as the curious passivity of their central consciousnesses. From the infant's point of view, the world is controlled by infinitely powerful and irrational forces completely beyond the control of the self. Camille Paglia calls the Mariner "a male heroine" (321). In fact, it might be more accurate to call him a helpless infant in the lap of Mother Nature who alternately, and bewilderingly, punishes and succors her son.

As Freud points out, in dreams the image is prior to the word. The organization of *Ancient Mariner* suggests this principle. At the point at which the Mariner shoots the albatross, the mode of the poem changes; it is as if the motive of the Mariner, who seemingly does the deed just for the hell of it, were abruptly "realized." In the subsequent events, he experiences pure consciousness as an absolute. No other being, natural or supernatural, impinges on that being. He cannot even lose himself in sleep. The setting of the narrative is oddly reminiscent of the imagery psychologists use to describe the preverbal state—that sense of the "oceanic"—but the Mariner knows what it is to be aware of the ocean and yet divided from it. From this perspective the poem may be seen as an allegory of consciousness and of imagination, which in Coleridge's system is patriarchal and imperial, a "repetition in the finite mind of the eternal act of creation in the infinite I AM" (CC 7.1: 304).

In "Kubla Khan" the concrete vividness of the imagery is one of the poem's greatest strengths; as in dreams juxtaposition supplants sequential cause and effect as ordering principle of the imagery, and a curious indeterminacy occurs in the boundaries between concrete and figurative. One is always surprised to be reminded that the powerful image "As e'er beneath a waning moon was haunted / By woman wailing for her demon-lover" is a figure of speech, a simile. The incantatory rhythms of the verse bring it increasingly near to the inarticulate expressions of nature, which also appear in all three poems. Not only do we have the "woman wailing" and the Maid's singing, there are the cries and whistles of Life-in-Death and Christabel's snakelike hisses. At the conclusion of "Kubla Khan" the frenzied poet's vocation is manifested not so much in a language of words as in a kind of body language; his "message," like the Freudian hysteric's, is "embodied" in "flashing eyes and floating hair."

Indeed, Richard Gerber suggests that the name *kubla* may itself be a pun on the name *Cybele* (pronounced in Greek kub'la), the familiar name of the Great Mother of Asia Minor, who was frequently portrayed wearing a mural crown (of "walls and towers"). If the landscape is unconsciously associated with this mother goddess, of "the wild forests and the hills," who wailed for her dead lover Attis (328), the various aspects of the landscape may have a hidden affinity after all.

One may speculate that the fragmentary state of *Christabel* and "Kubla Khan" is in fact congruent with this mode of writing. If these poems imply a theoretical *écriture féminine*, they are by definition "incomplete," for completeness is a standard of patriarchal language and culture.

But having considered the ways these poems imply this kind of writing, one may also speculate about Coleridge's attraction, perhaps need, for gothic conventions. In the 1790s the gothic was a literary discourse of the other— of there rather than here, of then rather than now, of the supernatural rather than the natural. However ludicrous or merely silly most "gothick" narratives were, the conventions of the mode were well adapted to expressing and exploring new realms of imagination, a sort of colonizing of the "unnameable," the "unspeakable." From this perspective the Romantic artist, like the preverbal child, feels what cannot be spoken or thought; the artist must, however, somehow express this experience in language.

As Norman Fruman suggests in a footnote to *Coleridge, the Damaged Archangel,* Coleridge had an uneasy relation with the "feminine" side of himself (572); his fears of madness and of nightmares may be related to this anxiety. But it is important to remember that "femininity" is a cultural construct, not a biological absolute. In Western culture it has been associated with powerlessness, wordlessness, and incapacity. Paradoxically, though Western metaphysics tends to deny women power over language, cultural stereotyping mocks women as speakers. Interestingly, Coleridge was also famous for his loquaciousness, as well as for his fragmentary works. If the Mystery poems seem to exemplify *l'écriture féminine,* what we know about Coleridge's life makes it plausible that he was unconsciously led into this mode. Psychoanalytic readings of his dreams and the fragments of his dreams have sketched a portrait of the artist as a neurotic—beset by nightmares, tortured by conscious and unconscious conflicts (see, e.g., Fruman 353–420)—an artist who is like a stereotypical woman.

Finally, this reading of the Mystery poems uncovers the disturbing implications of the common Romantic trope, the marriage of mind and nature. Coleridge struggled in his faith that mind and nature may be, must be, wed, for human beings to live at their best in this world. But "mind" and "nature" are themselves conceived within the structures of Western patriarchal thought; imagination is a male "shaping spirit" ("Dejection," line 86); nature is female, passive—mater/matter. If the creative (paternal) spirit imbues her with life, the wedding becomes possible, but in taking on life, she takes on power as well (including the power of death) and may turn into a witch, a femme fatale, a terrible mother. According to Freud, to marry one's mother is the most desirable and most horrible of circumstances. (This is a fear and a desire worked out in much of the gothic tradition.) Coleridge's poems celebrate that mystery as well.

Coleridge's Mystery Poems and Their Critics

Jeanne Moskal

I designed this sequence of assignments for an undergraduate honors seminar in British Romanticism at the University of North Carolina at Chapel Hill. Students in such honors courses usually plan to write a thesis within the next two years; the course gives them a writing assignment from which the thesis can be developed. Twice I have adapted the assignment sequence for my regular upper-division Romantics course, which has thirty-five students in each section. To build a store of common knowledge among the class members, I focus the writing assignments on the work of one poet, though we devote a more or less equal amount of class time to each of the six major poets. A seminar naturally generates common knowledge as students share ideas and library materials. In a survey course, I try to approximate the experience of a seminar by suggesting that students form small study groups consisting of all the students working on the same poem. Unfortunately, my class time for small groups is limited, so I give them ten minutes at the end of a lecture period to meet, exchange phone numbers, and arrange for sharing library materials or for scheduling future meetings. Some students take advantage of this chance; some don't.

The first assignment is a standard close reading of *The Rime of the Ancient Mariner*, *Christabel*, or "Kubla Khan" that asks students to analyze theme and form in one stanza or section of a poem. The purpose is to give them a good possession of a text and an acquaintance with some of its cruxes. Honors students and seniors usually have no trouble producing a close reading. In the Romantics survey course, I teach some principles of close reading early on, usually when we read Blake's *Songs of Innocence and of Experience*. The second assignment, the descriptive bibliography, introduces them to some landmarks of the critical and scholarly landscape and teaches them to think analytically about secondary literature.

Many research assignments send students to the library first. My sequence reverses the usual process. I am convinced that this initial paper, written without secondary sources, gives students a provisional thesis that keeps them from being overwhelmed by scholarship and criticism. It gives them a defined point of view from which to examine the secondary sources. In addition, students are more generous to critics once they know the complexity of the critical task. In grading these close-reading assignments, I keep the following guidelines in mind. First, I identify the students' interests. For example, if a student writes a perfunctory paper, with one enthusiastic paragraph about Coleridge's alleged opium dream, I identify that interest as psychological or biographical. Then I suggest allies—critics or scholars —who share that interest (in this case, Elisabeth Schneider). Second, I point out cruxes in the poem that students may have missed. One ambiguity ignored by the student may call into question the total interpretation the student has proposed. I use a dialogue format, asking, for example, "How do you respond to someone who points out the compulsiveness and repetition of the Mariner's confession?" Students often think they should ignore evidence that contradicts their main point, and this dialogic approach helps them prepare for the give and take they'll see in the best professional scholarship. I sometimes mention an issue that is widely disputed in the secondary literature, relating it to their close reading. On a student's paper I might write, "Your reading of 'Kubla Khan' depends on the assumption that Coleridge finished the poem; you might be interested in reading Lowes's work, which assumes it isn't finished, and see what you think of that approach."

Having completed a paper of explication, the students begin working on the descriptive bibliography. This assignment consists of written reviews of secondary literature on *Ancient Mariner*, *Christabel*, or "Kubla Khan." For each review students must (1) provide the correct MLA bibliographic citation, (2) summarize the writer's argument, (3) identify the writer's presuppositions, and (4) briefly evaluate the writer's contribution. In addition, students write a two- or three-page introduction to the reviews for the reader, providing an overview of the critical issues involved.

I prepare students for the second assignment by one or two class periods of lecture on the varieties of critical approaches. Often one full class period is devoted to the distinction between scholarship and criticism and to M. H. Abrams's familiar diagram of critical orientations: mimetic, didactic, expressive, and objective (*Mirror*). Honors students have often heard these distinctions before, but it is useful to review them. A second lecture quickly covers the critical movements that have become popular since 1965: Marxism, structuralism, deconstruction, psychoanalysis, feminism, and new historicism. Instead of asking the students to label the critic properly, I suggest that they discern values through recognizing the writer's goal or heroes (e.g., the writer's quoting of Freud as authoritative). I also mention some goals in contemporary criticism, such as the undermining of a privileged status for "literature" in Marxism and in deconstruction, and the assumption that poets do not know their complete intentions, a position that is common to those theories called "hermeneutics of suspicion" (Ricoeur). A useful approach is to ask, What counts as truth for this writer? or, as Hazard Adams says, Where does the critic "locate" reality? (1). As a practical example, in another class session, I distribute a short work of criticism on Shelley or Byron, whom we are studying by this point in the semester. We examine its presuppositions, performing a "close reading" of the critic's prose. One critical essay on Shelley that I have used a couple of times is Irene H. Chayes's "Rhetoric as Drama." Students often find "Ode to the West Wind" a difficult poem, so Chayes's essay helps them with Shelley by linking the ode with Coleridge's Dejection Ode, which they already know, and by providing a close reading focused on the speaker's shifting attribution of power to the west wind and to himself. Chayes's essay also helps them with the bibliography assignment by giving them a model essay of the New Criticism in its insistence on the difference between speaker and poet and its stress on rhetoric and drama. Sometimes I explain that the speaker-poet differentiation was needed by the New Critics to rehabilitate Shelley's literary reputation after the attacks of T. S. Eliot and others. Usually it is not necessary to spend class time close-reading a work of historical scholarship to discern its theoretical assumptions. The assumptions, such as the one that verifiable biographical information counts as truth for the scholar, are generally straightforward. Students tend to like the concreteness of historical scholarship and to be convinced by facts. If I have time, however, I distribute photocopies of the introduction to Louis Crompton's biography of Byron, *Byron and Greek Love*. We read it in class and talk about how a scholar's choice of which facts to write about can be guided by extraliterary concerns and commitments.

With respect to presuppositions and commitments, the assignment itself assumes the New Critical position that the individual poem is the proper unit of study. Most of my students take this New Critical position, in a more or less articulate way. I warn them that many critics and scholars do not share this assumption; consequently, the student may be frustrated if a secondary source doesn't say anything about a particular poem. For example, a student reading *The Road to Xanadu* may be frustrated that John Livingston Lowes does not tell him what *Ancient Mariner* "means." I anticipate and try to prevent this frustration by pointing out that in this assignment, the individual poem is a provisional starting point only. It is fine if the student becomes intrigued by issues of literary biography, archetypes, or feminism.

To choose their six secondary works, the students consult Max F. Schulz's bibliographic essay on Coleridge. I place several important books and articles described by Schulz on reserve at the undergraduate library. I offer a few guidelines for selecting the secondary works: (1) Students should include works that Schulz describes as central and influential. For example, students who write about *Ancient Mariner* must include both Robert Penn Warren and Edward E. Bostetter ("Nightmare"). (2) Students should aim for variety in approach. They should read some scholarship and some criticism. And two of the six articles must have been written in the last fifteen years. For students who already have a sense of what interests them, Schulz's essay is the best place to begin, since it describes the content of most secondary literature. These students, relying on Schulz, can easily follow the thread of their own concerns. Students who need more guidance usually depend heavily on the reserve list, following a standard plan of research. The exciting thing for me is to see a student who starts out with the regimented approach suddenly become interested in an issue that requires a specialized, focused set of readings.

In the overview of the six secondary works, which provides the reader with a map of the scholarly and critical landscape, I encourage students to focus their remarks on one issue in criticism or one crux in the poem. As I said, I identify the student's own interest and suggest allies as I grade the first paper. Often, however, no particular issue emerges, so I suggest some standard ones, some pertinent to most literature and some pertinent to these poems in particular. One issue of general interest is the authority of a poet's statement of intention. Is it less reliable, for example, if written several years after the poem? There is another crux that students frequently write about, with good results: How does the critic handle multiple meanings? Is he or she determined to pin down the poem, or a symbol in the poem, to one meaning? If so, how does the critic adjudicate which is a better interpretation? If the critic wants to allow multiple or even contradictory meanings, what rubric is used to justify them? (One good example here from the *Christabel* critics is Elizabeth M. Liggins, who writes about Coleridge's use of folklore and uses folklore as a rubric for multiple meanings: "In folklore there is often no consistency in the interpretation of signs: they vary from place and may even be contradictory. . . . Critics attempting to solve the riddle of Geraldine sometimes try to be needlessly specific about her nature. In folklore there are no sharp distinctions between witches and fairies, between fairies and devils, and between fairies and the dead" [92].)

Students who focus on *Ancient Mariner* usually begin their scholarly reading with John Livingston Lowes's *Road to Xanadu*. For this assignment they read only Lowes's first chapter and one or two of the chapters from book 2, the book that focuses on *Ancient Mariner*. Chapter 1 describes Coleridge's Gutch Memorandum Book and shows the logic of searching for sources in travel literature. Students usually choose a chapter in book 2 on the basis of their interests in the first writing assignment. Lowes's tireless research and his knowledge of William Bartram and Samuel Purchas impress students, but in their reviews, some students express a certain disquietude with Lowes's desire to find an antecedent for every image in *Ancient Mariner*. It is difficult to square his exhaustive source study with his admiration for Coleridge's creativity.

Students concerned with authorial intention consult Mark L. Reed's scholarly article on the "plan" of *Lyrical Ballads*. Reed carefully assesses the reliability of Coleridge's and Wordsworth's later accounts of the division of aesthetic labor involved in *Lyrical Ballads*. He concludes that the "plan" for *Lyrical Ballads* emerged sometime after many of the poems were written. His work suggests to students that even poets may at times misrepresent themselves, though this judgment should not be made lightly. Reed's article has the further advantage of putting *Ancient Mariner* in its original context, *Lyrical Ballads*, rather than in the more usual grouping with *Christabel* and "Kubla Khan."

Several students become intrigued by the gloss. Usually I ask my students in class how they read *Ancient Mariner*: Do they alternate between poem and gloss? read the poem, then the gloss? skip the gloss completely? Students with this interest need first to know the historical facts about the gloss, so I suggest the two scholarly articles by B. R. McElderry, Jr., and Huntington Brown. McElderry points out the significance of the lateness of Coleridge's addition of the gloss in 1817. Moreover, McElderry notices that the gloss presents moral themes far more explicitly than the poem itself does. Brown's useful essay provides a scholarly examination of the historical epochs of the minstrel and the glossist. The discovery of multiple layers and narrators paves the way for later discussion.

Criticism on *Ancient Mariner* is ideal for this assignment, because of the apparently irreconcilable interpretations offered by Warren and Bostetter and their followers. Warren appeals to students because he directly addresses the question they often ask: Why did the Mariner shoot the albatross in the first place? Many students come to the first class session on *Ancient Mariner* sensing the themes of sin and redemption. Warren provides an elegant, articulate version of their impression, and his close reading of the albatross's likeness to Christ shows the students a model formalist analysis. Moreover, Warren's is a good example of close reading organized around a particular purpose—a good corrective for students who tend to produce laundry-list close readings. (A few astute class members are puzzled by Warren's emphasis on "sacramentality." This is a good opportunity to talk about some of the theological agendas in the American New Criticism.)

Bostetter often meets with students' resistance because he questions the benevolence of the Mariner's God—or, more precisely, of Warren's God. Bostetter also deflates Warren's sacramentalism by holding that the Mariner does not act like a forgiven person but is subject to "unrelenting sense of guilt [and] a compulsion to confession" (114). Bostetter's introduction to *The Romantic Ventriloquists* clearly states his skeptical approach to the Romantic poets' optimism and idealism. The usefulness of pairing Warren and Bostetter in this assignment is that both employ the same method, close reading, to support diametrically opposed views. For the purposes of *Ancient Mariner*, the students must choose between them. For the purpose of looking critically at criticism, the opposition of the two writers calls into question the objectivity of the New Critics.

Raimonda Modiano's article provides a very careful rubric for reconciling Warren's and Bostetter's readings. She explains the reasons for the Mariner's contradictory signals, that the Mariner uses the public language of religion in his appeal for the Wedding Guest's approval, while the essential inexpressible experience remains fundamentally arbitrary and isolating. In reading her article, the student sees criticism make a genuine advance. Another article that makes sense of the Warren-Bostetter impasse is Jerome J. McGann's wide-ranging discussion, which takes the new-historicist view that *Ancient Mariner* should be reexamined as a product of Coleridge's time and ideology. Without such examination, McGann argues, acts of criticism become mere "vehicles for recapitulating and objectifying the reader's particular ideological commitments" ("Meaning" 55). This contention comes with some force to a student confronted, often for the first time, with contradictory and bewildering interpretations.

Scholarship and criticism on *Christabel* tend to center on the issue of what the poet leaves unsaid about Geraldine herself and about her midnight encounter with Christabel. Much of the scholarship seeks to discern exactly what species of creature Geraldine belongs to, and the students get a good example of this tendency in Arthur H. Nethercot's *Road to Tryermaine*, from which all later criticism draws. The first four chapters present the thesis that Geraldine is a vampire. In the last chapter, Nethercot applies his research to the poem and reveals his own critical bias, namely, that his goal is to re-create the moment of creation in the poet's mind: "I believe that by some good luck my eye has caught a glimpse of the glow, the illumination, which was in a poet's mind. . . . I shall therefore feel more than compensated if my adventures among the vampires, lamias, serpents, and demons of the air should afford other persons a similar insight" (214). As with Lowes, we have the curious paradox that a scholar who admires Coleridge's imagination must so thoroughly attribute all the poetic material to some other source. Other useful works of scholarship are John Adlard's and Elizabeth M. Liggins's discussions of folklore sources for Geraldine. Some students react to the precise categorization of Geraldine in historical scholarship with a sense of relief, as if to say: "Ah! that explains the horror!" Others think there might be a significant rhetorical reason that the poet left out this information. By this time in the course I have usually mentioned the traditional distinction between belles lettres and popular literature. One student became interested in the gothic and folklore motifs in *Christabel* in the light of this traditional distinction, asking what made Coleridge's presentation of a "vampire" more interesting than the vampire sources cited by Nethercot. It was an exciting paper to read.

When they turn to criticism of *Christabel*, many students find that central concerns are the continuity (or lack of it) between parts 1 and 2 and the unfinished state of the poem. A provocative psychoanalytic hypothesis is provided in James Twitchell's " 'Desire with Loathing Strangely Mixed.' " Twitchell attributes the ambivalence in *Christabel* to Coleridge's identification with Christabel, who enacts Coleridge's simultaneous desire for his mother (Geraldine) and revulsion from such a feeling. This essay clearly addresses the concern of the unfinished state of the poem and the problem of the unsaid by postulating that Coleridge could not continue to confront this desire. The author's use of Freud is straightforward, so the students can easily identify Twitchell's critical presuppositions. It is harder for them to identify their objection to Twitchell, namely, that such an approach challenges their idealized image of the poet.

Wendy S. Flory's essay analyzes the characters, especially Geraldine, as psychological subjects. Her effort, like Nethercot's, is to name the unsaid. Flory posits a homosexual affair between Sir Leoline and Roland de Vaux as a natural explanation of Geraldine's self-hatred. Many students find the idea farfetched. Barbara A. Schapiro's essay ("*Christabel*") focuses on the poet as psychological subject. She rigorously analyzes the ambivalence toward the mother in Coleridge, mirrored in Christabel's attitude toward the dead good mother and the evil Geraldine. (Schapiro's introduction to *The Romantic Mother* clarifies her approach and should be assigned in addition to the section on *Christabel*.) Schapiro, like Twitchell, provides a psychological answer to the question about the poem's fragmentary status. When students review two works with the same general approach, they can better judge the individual critic's carefulness and persuasiveness.

In descriptive bibliographies on "Kubla Khan," students often focus on the question of whether the poem is a fragment or a complete whole. The scholarship reflects different answers to the question. Lowes accepts Coleridge's claims that "Kubla Khan" is a fragment and that it was given whole in an opium dream. As with *Ancient Mariner* Lowes examines travel literature for antecedents of Coleridge's imagery in "Kubla Khan." Lowes presents multiple threads of historical allusion and influence but does not posit any aesthetic unity for the poem, as created by a conscious, deliberate Coleridge. Instead he postulates a brief, magical moment of creativity induced by opium, which unifies "Kubla Khan" through simultaneity of composition. Elisabeth Schneider, another historical scholar, wants to put "Kubla Khan" into the realm of the interpretable. She does so by Lowes's own method, historical scholarship, offering the reader medical information about opium addiction. She shows in chapter 1 that opium does not itself produce extraordinary dreams, though diseases or withdrawal symptoms might produce them. Schneider's fifth chapter provides the resulting interpretation of the poem, discussing the orientalism of many works of literature Coleridge knew, such as those by William Collins and Thomas Gray and, most important, John Milton. For Schneider, Coleridge belongs in the company of the central poets, not of Bartram and other eccentric explorers. Thus the interesting question becomes not, What critical orientation does Schneider use? but, What is Schneider trying to achieve? Her debunking of the opium myth and her citation of belletristic sources for Coleridge's poem both serve to mainstream "Kubla Khan," to place it under the kind of scrutiny devoted to canonical works.

Let me mention two other works of scholarship on "Kubla Khan." Elinor S. Shaffer's *"Kubla Khan" and* The Fall of Jerusalem discusses orientalism, linking it to the higher criticism of the Bible that understood the Old Testament as oriental literature. She documents Coleridge's knowledge of higher criticism and contends that "Kubla Khan" is a distilled version of a projected epic on the fall of Jerusalem. Another work of scholarship, Donald Pearce's, finds important analogues to Xanadu in the landscape of Ottery St. Mary, where Coleridge grew up. He associates many of Kubla's characteristics with those of the boy Coleridge as evidenced in his overnight escape from his parents after he fought with his brother Frank. Fundamentally, however, the debate between Lowes and Schneider is the most important thing for the students to discern, for when they examine critical interpretations of "Kubla Khan," they should notice that the critic often needs to assume that the poem is an aesthetic whole before interpretation can take place.

Richard Harter Fogle's article provides a good example of criticism completing scholarship. In Fogle's view, Schneider has provided a scholarly justification for abandoning Lowes's assumption that "Kubla Khan is *sui generis* and, hence, ironically, marginal to literature." Fogle justifies this shift through critical tools, not scholarly tools. Fogle borrows back the New Critical theme, borrowed from Coleridge in the first place, of "reconciliation of opposites." Therefore, he argues, no matter how much pleasure of Lowes's sort we derive from "Kubla Khan," it must be significant and hence interpretable. Fogle clearly states his use of New Criticism in the introduction to *The Permanent Pleasure*: explication, or "concrete interpretation, provides the closest and most vital contact with literature" (xi). Fogle explicitly distances himself from the evaluative battles of the New Critics, including the denigration of Romanticism. Yet Fogle's disagreements with them occur in the context of a fundamental agreement about method. Another interpretation, A. C. Goodson's "Kubla's Construct," takes a structuralist approach to "Kubla Khan." It is quite a difficult essay for most undergraduate students. Bewildered students can find their way by noticing who Goodson's heroes are: Michael Riffaterre, Ferdinand de Saussure, and Roman Jakobson all are quoted as authorities. Curiously, Goodson's map of the oppositions in "Kubla Khan" is derived in part from Fogle's reading, so the acute student might comment on this odd alliance.

Students find that, in general, studies of "Kubla Khan" fall into two distinct historical stages. In the first stage, scholars assumed that the poem was a fragment and traced its biographical and historical sources. In the second stage, critics regarded "Kubla Khan" as an aesthetic whole and sought to interpret its meaning. An exception to this two-stage pattern is provided in the myth criticism of G. Wilson Knight, an interpretation that disregards the concept of aesthetic wholeness by taking canonical literary tradition as the object of study, along the lines of Northrop Frye, whose ideas were later developed in *Anatomy of Criticism*. Some students get lost in Knight's constant references to other literary works. They tend to quote Knight's odd statement that *Christabel* is Coleridge's *Inferno*, *Ancient Mariner* his *Purgatorio*, and "Kubla Khan" his *Paradiso*, without really knowing what Knight means. (Many of them seem to think I'll know what Knight means, even if they don't.) The students who probe more deeply recognize that, by linking the three poems, Knight constructs a subject of analysis larger than the individual poem. This chapter can be a very good corrective to the New Critical bias toward the individual poem. Yet Knight shares the New Critical belief that poetry offers a transcendent experience for the reader: "poetry, in moments of high optimistic vision, reveals . . . a new and more concrete perception of life here and now, unveiling a new *dimension* of existence" (93).

There are some definite short-term goals for this assignment, available to students majoring in a field other than English. In writing a descriptive bibliography, students benefit by exposure to skillful readers. They accumulate numerous observations about the details of the poem. They observe scholarly and critical methods, and their writing often improves by exposure to good models. Moreover, they learn to judge the persuasiveness of an interpretation. Those who previously scorned literary interpretation as "all a matter of opinion anyway" come to recognize informed critical judgment when they see it.

There are longer-term goals for students who are majoring in English, especially if they are planning on writing an honors thesis or going to graduate school. I have mentioned a few questions as central to the critical and scholarly debate on Coleridge's Mystery poems: the issue of theology central to the Warren-Bostetter debate on *Ancient Mariner*, the issue of the unsaid in *Christabel*, and the question of the fragmentary status of "Kubla Khan." My hope in making this assignment is that every English major through doing the assigned reading will understand these particular controversies. It remains for those writing honors theses to acknowledge the contributions of past critics and scholars of Coleridge along the way to making new observations of their own.

CONTRIBUTORS AND SURVEY PARTICIPANTS

While some colleagues wrote encouraging and advisory private letters about this project to enhance the teaching of Coleridge, the following scholars and teachers contributed by responding to a challenging questionnaire that preceded the preparation of this volume:

Joseph Thomas Barbarese, Friends School; J. Robert Barth, S.J., Boston Coll.; Don H. Bialostosky, Univ. of Toledo; G. Kim Blank, Univ. of Victoria; David V. Erdman, State University of New York, Buffalo; William R. Evans, Kean Coll. of New Jersey; Mary Favret, Indiana Univ., Bloomington; Norman Fruman, Univ. of Minnesota, Minneapolis; Elizabeth Harden, Wright State Univ.; John A. Hodgson, Harvard Univ.; Kenneth R. Johnston, Indiana Univ., Bloomington; Laurence S. Lockridge, New York Univ.; Paul Magnuson, New York Univ.; Robert M. Maniquis, Univ. of California, Los Angeles; Richard T. Martin, Ohio State Univ., Columbus; Richard E. Matlak, Coll. of the Holy Cross; Fleming McClelland, Northeast Louisiana Univ.; James Holt McGavran, Jr., Univ. of North Carolina, Charlotte; James C. McKusick, Univ. of Maryland, Baltimore; Jeanne Moskal, Univ. of North Carolina, Chapel Hill; John T. Ogden, Univ. of Manitoba; Donald H. Reiman, New York Public Library; Max F. Schulz, Univ. of Southern California; Patricia L. Skarda, Smith Coll.; Karen Swann, Williams Coll.; Anya Taylor, John Jay Coll. of Criminal Justice; Gordon K. Thomas, Brigham Young Univ.; Anne Williams, Coll. of the Holy Cross; P. M. Zall, California State Univ., Los Angeles.

WORKS CITED

Primary Coleridge Texts and Abbreviations

CC The Collected Works of Samuel Taylor Coleridge. Gen. ed. Kathleen Coburn. Bollingen Series 75. Princeton: Princeton UP, 1969–.

    CC 1: *Lectures 1795 on Politics and Religion.* Ed. Lewis Patton and Peter Mann. 1971.

    CC 2: *The Watchman.* Ed. Lewis Patton. 1970.

    CC 3: *Essays on His Times in the* Morning Post *and the* Courier. 3 vols. Ed. David V. Erdman. 1978.

    CC 4: *The Friend.* 2 vols. Ed. Barbara E. Rooke. 1969.

    CC 5: *Lectures 1808–1819 on Literature.* 2 vols. Ed. R. A. Foakes. 1987.

    CC 6: *Lay Sermons.* Ed. R. J. White. 1972.

    CC 7: *Biographia Literaria.* 2 vols. Ed. W. Jackson Bate and James Engell. 1983. Rpt. as 1-vol. paperback, 1984.

    CC 10: *On the Constitution of the Church and State.* Ed. John Colmer. 1976.

    CC 12: *Marginalia.* 2 vols. Ed. George Whalley. 1980, 1984. 3 more vols. forthcoming.

    CC 13: *Logic.* Ed. J. R. de J. Jackson. 1981.

CL Collected Letters of Samuel Taylor Coleridge. Ed. Earl Leslie Griggs. 6 vols. Oxford: Clarendon–Oxford UP, 1956–71.

CN The Notebooks of Samuel Taylor Coleridge. Ed. Kathleen Coburn. 3 vols. to date. New York: Pantheon, 1957–.

CPW The Complete Poetical Works of Samuel Taylor Coleridge. Ed. Ernest Hartley Coleridge. 2 vols. Oxford: Clarendon–Oxford UP, 1912.

PW Coleridge: Poetical Works. Ed. Ernest Hartley Coleridge. 1912. Oxford: Oxford UP, 1967.

Books and Articles

Aarsleff, Hans. *From Locke to Saussure: Essays on the Study of Language and Intellectual History.* Minneapolis: U of Minnesota P, 1982.

———. *The Study of Language in England, 1780–1860.* Princeton: Princeton UP, 1967.

Abrams, M. H., ed. *English Romantic Poets: Modern Essays in Criticism.* 2nd ed. New York: Oxford UP, 1975.

————. *The Milk of Paradise: The Effect of Opium Visions on the Works of De Quincey, Crabbe, Francis Thompson, and Coleridge.* 1934. New York: Harper, 1970.

————. *The Mirror and the Lamp: Romantic Theory and the Critical Tradition.* New York: Oxford UP, 1953.

————. *Natural Supernaturalism: Tradition and Revolution in Romantic Literature.* New York: Norton, 1971.

————, gen. ed. *The Norton Anthology of English Literature,* 5th ed. 2 vols. New York: Norton, 1986.

————, gen ed. *The Norton Anthology of English Literature: Major Authors Edition.* 5th ed. New York: Norton, 1987.

————. "Structure and Style in the Greater Romantic Lyric." *From Sensibility to Romanticism: Essays Presented to Frederick A. Pottle.* Ed. Frederick W. Hilles and Harold Bloom. New York: Oxford UP, 1965. 527–60.

Adams, Hazard. Introduction. *Critical Theory since Plato.* New York: Harcourt, 1971. 1–10.

Adlard, John. "The Quantock *Christabel.*" *Philological Quarterly* 50 (1971): 230–38.

"Aeolian Harp." *Encyclopaedia Britannica.* 1910.

Allsop, Thomas. *Letters, Conversations, and Recollections of S. T. Coleridge.* New York: Harper, 1836.

Aristotle. *The Basic Works of Aristotle.* Ed. Richard McKeon. New York: Random, 1941.

Auerbach, Erich. "Odysseus' Scar." *Mimesis: The Representation of Reality in Western Literature.* Trans. Willard R. Trask. 1946. Garden City: Anchor-Doubleday, 1957. 1–20.

Bacon, Francis. *The Advancement of Learning.* Ed. G. W. Kitchen. London: Dent, 1973.

Barfield, Owen. *What Coleridge Thought.* Middletown: Wesleyan UP, 1971.

Barrell, John, ed. *On the Constitution of the Church and State.* By Samuel Taylor Coleridge. London: Dent, 1972.

Barth, J. Robert, S. J. *Coleridge and Christian Doctrine.* Cambridge: Harvard UP, 1969.

————. Rev. of *Coleridge's Variety: Bicentenary Studies,* ed. John Beer. *Wordsworth Circle* 7 (1976): 239–43.

Bate, Walter Jackson. *Coleridge.* New York: Macmillan, 1968.

————, ed. *Criticism: The Major Texts.* New York: Harcourt, 1952.

Beer, John. *Coleridge's Poetic Intelligence.* London: Macmillan, 1977.

————, ed. *Coleridge's Variety: Bicentenary Studies.* London: Macmillan, 1974.

————. *Coleridge the Visionary.* London: Chatto, 1959.

Belsey, Catherine. *Critical Practice.* London: Methuen, 1980.

Beres, David. "A Dream, a Vision, and a Poem: A Psychoanalytic Study of the Origins of *The Rime of the Ancient Mariner.*" *International Journal of Psychoanalysis* 32 (1951): 97–116.

Bialostosky, Don H. "Coleridge's Interpretation of Wordsworth's Preface to *Lyrical Ballads*." *PMLA* 93 (1978): 912–24.

Blake, William. Preface. *Milton: A Poem in Two Books. The Complete Poetry and Prose of William Blake*. Ed. David V. Erdman. Rev. ed. New York: Anchor-Doubleday, 1982.

Blank, G. Kim. "Coleridge Now: A Survey." *Coleridge Bulletin* 3 (1990): 3–15.

Bleich, David. *Readings and Feelings: An Introduction to Subjective Criticism*. Urbana: NCTE, 1975.

Bloom, Harold. "Coleridge: The Anxiety of Influence." *New Perspectives on Coleridge and Wordsworth*. Ed. Geoffrey H. Hartman. New York: Columbia UP, 1972. 247–67.

———, ed. *Romanticism and Consciousness: Essays in Criticism*. New York: Norton, 1970.

Booth, Wayne C. *The Rhetoric of Fiction*. Chicago: U of Chicago P, 1961.

Bostetter, Edward E. "The Nightmare World of *The Ancient Mariner*." *Studies in Romanticism* 1 (1962): 241–54. Rpt. as pt. 4 of "Coleridge" in Bostetter, *Romantic Ventriloquists* 108–18.

———. *The Romantic Ventriloquists: Wordsworth, Coleridge, Keats, Shelley, Byron*. Seattle: U of Washington P, 1963.

Boulger, James D., ed. The Rime of the Ancient Mariner: *A Collection of Critical Essays*. Englewood Cliffs: Prentice, 1969.

Brenner, Charles. *An Elementary Textbook of Psychoanalysis*. New York: Doubleday, 1957.

Brett, R. L., and A. R. Jones, eds. Lyrical Ballads: *Wordsworth and Coleridge: The Text of the 1798 Edition with the Additional 1800 Poems and the Prefaces*. London: Methuen, 1965.

Brisman, Leslie. *Romantic Origins*. Ithaca: Cornell UP, 1978.

Brooks, Cleanth, and Robert Penn Warren. *Understanding Poetry*. 3rd ed. New York: Holt, 1960.

Brown, Huntington. "The Gloss to *The Ancient Mariner*." *Modern Language Quarterly* 6 (1945): 319–24.

Burke, Edmund. *A Philosophical Enquiry into the Origin of Our Ideas of the Sublime and the Beautiful*. Ed. J. T. Boulton. New York: Columbia UP, 1958.

Burton, Robert. *The Anatomy of Melancholy*. Ed. Holbrook Jackson. New York: Vintage-Random, 1977.

Calleo, David P. *Coleridge and the Idea of the Modern State*. New Haven: Yale UP, 1966.

Carlyle, Thomas. "Coleridge." *The Works of Thomas Carlyle*. Centenary Edition. Vol. 11. London: Chapman, 1897. 52–62.

Carpenter, Maurice. *The Indifferent Horseman: The Divine Comedy of Samuel Taylor Coleridge*. London: Elek, 1954.

Cavell, Stanley. "In Quest of the Ordinary: Texts of Recovery." *Romanticism and*

Contemporary Criticism. Ed. Morris Eaves and Michael Fischer. Ithaca: Cornell UP, 1986. 183–239.

Chambers, E. K. *Samuel Taylor Coleridge: A Biographical Study.* Oxford: Clarendon–Oxford UP, 1938.

Chayes, Irene H. " 'Kubla Khan' and the Creative Process." *Studies in Romanticism* 6.1 (1966): 1–21.

———. "Rhetoric as Drama: An Approach to the Romantic Ode." Reiman and Powers 621–25.

Christensen, Jerome C. *Coleridge's Blessed Machine of Language.* Ithaca: Cornell UP, 1981.

———. "Coleridge's Marginal Method in the *Biographia Literaria.*" *PMLA* 92 (1977): 928–40.

———. " 'Like a Guilty Thing Surprised': Deconstruction, Coleridge, and the Apostasy of Criticism." *Critical Inquiry* 12 (1986): 769–87.

Cixous, Hélène, and Catherine Clément. *The Newly Born Woman.* Trans. Betsy Wing. Theory and History of Literature 24. Minneapolis: U of Minnesota P, 1986.

Clifford, James. " 'Hanging Up Looking Glasses at Odd Corners': Ethnobiographical Prospects." *Studies in Biography.* Ed. Daniel Aaron. Harvard English Studies 8. Cambridge: Harvard UP, 1978. 41–56.

Coburn, Kathleen, ed. *Coleridge: A Collection of Critical Essays.* Englewood Cliffs: Prentice, 1967.

———, ed. *Inquiring Spirit.* Toronto: U of Toronto P, 1979.

Coleridge, Ernest Hartley, ed. Christabel, *Illustrated by a Facsimile of the Manuscript and by Textual and Other Notes.* London: Frowde, 1907.

Coleridge, Samuel Taylor. *Christabel; Kubla Khan, a Vision; The Pains of Sleep.* London: Murray, 1816.

Colmer, John. *Coleridge: Critic of Society.* Oxford: Clarendon–Oxford UP, 1959.

Cooper, Lane. "The Abyssinian Paradise in Coleridge and Milton." *Modern Philology* 3 (1906): 327–32.

Cottle, Joseph. *Early Recollections, Chiefly Relating to the Late Samuel Taylor Coleridge, during His Long Residence in Bristol.* 2 vols. London: Longman, 1837.

———. "John the Baptist." *Poems.* 2nd ed. Bristol, 1796.

Crawford, Walter B., ed. *Reading Coleridge: Approaches and Applications.* Ithaca: Cornell UP, 1979.

Crompton, Louis. *Byron and Greek Love: Homophobia in Nineteenth-Century England.* Berkeley: U of California P, 1985.

Deen, Leonard W. "Coleridge and the Radicalism of Religious Dissent." *Journal of English and Germanic Philology* 61 (1962): 496–510.

Dekker, George. *Coleridge and the Literature of Sensibility.* New York: Barnes, 1978.

De Quincey, Thomas. *The Collected Writings of Thomas De Quincey*. Ed. David Masson. 14 vols. Edinburgh: Black, 1890.

Derrida, Jacques. "Plato's Pharmacy." *Dissemination*. Trans. Barbara Johnson. Chicago: U of Chicago P, 1981. 63–171.

Dobrée, Bonamy, ed. *Thomas De Quincey*. New York: Schocken, 1965.

Durham, Margery. "The Mother Tongue: *Christabel* and the Language of Love." Garner et al. 169–93.

Eagleton, Terry. *Marxism and Literary Criticism*. Berkeley: U of California P, 1976.

Edgeworth, Maria. *Belinda*. London: Pandora, 1986.

Empson, William, and David Pirie, eds. *Coleridge's Verse: A Selection*. New York: Schocken, 1972.

Emslie, MacDonald, and Paul Edwards. "The Limitations of Langdale: A Reading of *Christabel*." *Essays in Criticism* 20 (1970): 57–70.

Erdman, David V. "Coleridge as Editorial Writer." *Power and Consciousness*. Ed. Conor Cruise O'Brien and William Dean Vanech. New York: New York UP, 1969. 183–201.

———. "Coleridge on Coleridge: The Context (and Text) of His Review of 'Mr. Coleridge's Second Lay Sermon.' " *Studies in Romanticism* 1 (1961): 47–64.

Erdman, David V., et al. *The Romantic Movement: A Selective and Critical Bibliography*. New York: Garland, 1979–.

Ferrier, J. F. "The Plagiarisms of S. T. Coleridge." *Blackwood's Edinburgh Magazine* Mar. 1840: 287–99.

Firchow, Peter, trans. *Friedrich Schlegel's "Lucinde" and the "Fragments."* Minneapolis: U of Minnesota P, 1971.

Fish, Stanley. "Literature in the Reader: Affective Stylistics." *Self-Consuming Artifacts: The Experience of Seventeenth-Century Literature*. Berkeley: U of California P, 1972. 383–427. Rpt. in *Reader-Response Criticism: From Formalism to Post-structuralism*. Ed. Jane P. Tompkins. Baltimore: Johns Hopkins UP, 1980. 70–99.

Flory, Wendy S. "Fathers and Daughters: Coleridge and *Christabel*." *Women and Literature* 3 (1975): 5–15.

Fogle, Richard Harter. *The Permanent Pleasure: Essays on Classics of Romanticism*. Athens: U of Georgia P, 1974.

———. "The Romantic Unity of 'Kubla Khan.' " *College English* 13 (1951): 13–18. Rpt. in Fogle, *Permanent Pleasure* 43–52.

Freud, Sigmund. *The Interpretation of Dreams*. Vol. 5 of *Standard Edition of the Complete Psychological Works of Sigmund Freud*. Trans. and gen. ed. James Strachey. London: Hogarth, 1953.

———. *New Introductory Lectures on Psychoanalysis*. Trans. and ed. James Strachey. 1933. New York: Norton, 1965.

———. *On Creativity and the Unconscious: Papers on the Psychology of Art, Literature, Love, Religion*. Selected by Benjamin Nelson. New York: Harper, 1958.

Fruman, Norman. *Coleridge, the Damaged Archangel.* New York: Braziller, 1971.

Frye, Northrop. *Anatomy of Criticism: Four Essays.* 1957. New York: Atheneum, 1966.

———. *The Educated Imagination.* Bloomington: Indiana UP, 1964.

Gardner, Martin, ed. *The Annotated* Ancient Mariner: The Rime of the Ancient Mariner *with an Introduction and Notes.* Illus. Gustav Doré. New York: Potter, 1965.

Garner, Shirley Nelson, Claire Kahane, and Madelon Sprengnether, eds. *The (M)other Tongue: Essays in Feminist Psychoanalytic Interpretation.* Ithaca: Cornell UP, 1985.

Gérard, Albert S. *English Romantic Poetry: Ethos, Structure, and Symbol in Coleridge, Wordsworth, Shelley, and Keats.* Berkeley: U of California P, 1968.

Gerber, Richard. "Keys to 'Kubla Khan.' " *English Studies* 44 (1963): 321–41.

Gettmann, Royal A., ed. The Rime of the Ancient Mariner: *A Handbook.* San Francisco: Wadsworth, 1961.

Gilbert, Sandra M., and Susan Gubar. *The Madwoman in the Attic: The Woman Writer and the Nineteenth-Century Literary Imagination.* New Haven: Yale UP, 1979.

———, eds. *Norton Anthology of Literature by Women.* New York: Norton, 1985.

Gillman, James. *The Life of Samuel Taylor Coleridge.* London: Pickering, 1838.

Goodson, A. C. "Kubla's Construct." *Studies in Romanticism* 18 (1979): 405–25.

Guérin, Wilfred L., et al., eds. *A Handbook of Critical Approaches to Literature.* 2nd ed. New York: Harper, 1979.

Haven, Richard. *Patterns of Consciousness: An Essay on Coleridge.* Amherst: U of Massachusetts P, 1969.

Hayter, Alethea. *Opium and the Romantic Imagination.* Berkeley: U of California P, 1970.

Hazlitt, William. "Bentham." *The Spirit of the Age. Selected Writings of William Hazlitt.* Ed. Christopher Salvesen. New York: NAL, 1972. 293–304.

———. "My First Acquaintance with Poets." 1823. *The Complete Works of William Hazlitt.* Ed. P. P. Howe. Centenary Edition. Vol. 17. London: Dent, 1933. 106–22.

Heath, William, ed. *Major British Poets of the Romantic Period.* New York: Macmillan, 1973.

Heilbrun, Carolyn G. *Toward a Recognition of Androgyny.* New York: Harper, 1974.

Heninger, S. K., Jr. "A Jungian Reading of 'Kubla Khan.' " *Journal of Aesthetics and Art Criticism* 18 (1960): 358–67.

Holmes, Richard. *Coleridge: Early Visions.* New York: Viking, 1989.

Hort, F. J. A. "Coleridge." *Cambridge Essays.* London: Parker, 1856. 292–351.

House, Humphrey. *Coleridge: The Clark Lectures, 1951–52.* London: Hart-Davis, 1953.

Hunter, Dianne. "Hysteria, Psychoanalysis, and Feminism: The Case of Anna O." Garner et al. 89–115.

Hutcheon, Linda. *A Theory of Parody: The Teachings of Twentieth-Century Art Forms.* New York: Methuen, 1985.

Irigaray, Luce. *Speculum of the Other Woman.* Trans. Gillian C. Gill. Ithaca: Cornell UP, 1985.

———. *This Sex Which Is Not One.* Trans. Catherine Porter, with Carolyn Burke. Ithaca: Cornell UP, 1985.

Jackson, H. J. "Coleridge's 'Maxilian.' " *Comparative Literature* 33 (1981): 38–49.

———, ed. *Samuel Taylor Coleridge.* Oxford Authors. New York: Oxford UP, 1985.

Jackson, J. R. de J., ed. *Coleridge: The Critical Heritage.* London: Routledge, 1970.

Jacobus, Mary. *Tradition and Experiment in Wordsworth's* Lyrical Ballads *(1798).* Oxford: Clarendon–Oxford UP, 1976.

Jones, Ann Rosalind. "Writing the Body: Toward an Understanding of *l'écriture féminine.*" Showalter 361–78.

Jordan, Frank, ed. *The English Romantic Poets: A Review of Research and Criticism.* 3rd and 4th eds. New York: MLA, 1972, 1985.

Jung, Carl Gustav. *Aion: Researches into the Phenomenology of the Self.* 2nd ed. Trans. R. F. C. Hull. *Collected Works of Carl G. Jung.* Vol. 9, pt. 2. Princeton: Princeton UP, 1968.

Kant, Immanuel. *Kritik der reinen Vernunft.* 2nd ed. Riga, 1787.

Katz, Marilyn. "Early Dissent between Wordsworth and Coleridge: Preface Deletion of October, 1800." *Wordsworth Circle* 9 (1978): 50–56.

Kissane, James. " 'Michael,' *Christabel,* and the *Lyrical Ballads* of 1800." *Wordsworth Circle* 9 (1978): 57–63.

Knight, G. Wilson. "Coleridge's Divine Comedy." *The Starlit Dome: Studies in the Poetry of Vision.* London: Methuen, 1941. 83–97.

Lacan, Jacques. *Ecrits: A Selection.* Trans. Alan Sheridan. New York: Norton, 1977.

Lamb, Charles. "Charles Lamb: His Last Words on Coleridge." *New Monthly Magazine* Feb. 1835: 198–99.

Leavis, F. R. "Coleridge." *The Importance of Scrutiny: Selections from* Scrutiny: A Quarterly Review, *1932–1948.* Ed. Eric Bentley. New York: New York UP, 1964. 76–87.

Lefebure, Molly. *Samuel Taylor Coleridge: A Bondage of Opium.* New York: Stein, 1974.

Levinson, Marjorie. *The Romantic Fragment Poem: A Critique of a Form.* Chapel Hill: U of North Carolina P, 1986.

Liggins, Elizabeth M. "Folklore and the Supernatural in *Christabel.*" *Folklore* 88 (1977): 91–104.

Lockridge, Laurence S. *Coleridge the Moralist.* Ithaca: Cornell UP, 1977.

———. "Explaining Coleridge's Explanation: Toward a Practical Methodology for Coleridge Studies." Crawford 23–55.

Lowes, John Livingston. *The Road to Xanadu: A Study in the Ways of the Imagination*. 1927. Princeton: Princeton UP, 1986.

Lucas, E. V., ed. *The Letters of Charles Lamb to Which Are Added Those of His Sister Mary Lamb*. 3 vols. New Haven: Yale UP, 1935.

Maclean, Ian. *The Renaissance Notion of Woman*. Cambridge Monographs on the History of Medicine. Cambridge: Cambridge UP, 1980.

Magnuson, Paul. *Coleridge and Wordsworth: A Lyrical Dialogue*. Princeton: Princeton UP, 1988.

———. " 'The Eolian Harp' in Context." *Studies in Romanticism* 24 (1985): 3–20.

Mahoney, John L., ed. *The English Romantics: Major Poetry and Critical Theory*. Lexington: Heath, 1978.

Martin, Jay. *Who Am I This Time? Uncovering the Fictive Personality*. New York: Norton, 1988.

Matlak, Richard E. "Classical Argument and Romantic Persuasion in 'Tintern Abbey.' " *Studies in Romanticism* 25 (1986): 97–129.

McElderry, B. R., Jr. "Coleridge's Revision of *The Ancient Mariner*." *Studies in Philology* 29 (1932): 68–94.

McFarland, Thomas. *Coleridge and the Pantheist Tradition*. Oxford: Clarendon–Oxford UP, 1969.

———. "Coleridge's Anxieties." Beer, *Coleridge's Variety* 134–65.

———. *Romanticism and the Forms of Ruin: Wordsworth, Coleridge, and Modalities of Fragmentation*. Princeton: Princeton UP, 1981.

———. "The Symbiosis of Coleridge and Wordsworth." *Studies in Romanticism* 11 (1972): 263–303. Rpt. in McFarland, *Romanticism* 56–103.

McGann, Jerome J. "The Meaning of the *Ancient Mariner*." *Critical Inquiry* 8 (1981): 35–67. Rpt. as "*The Ancient Mariner*: The Meaning of the Meanings." *The Beauty of Inflections: Literary Investigations in Historical Method and Theory*. By McGann. Oxford: Clarendon–Oxford UP, 1985. 135–72.

———. *The Romantic Ideology: A Critical Investigation*. Chicago: U of Chicago P, 1983.

McKusick, James C. *Coleridge's Philosophy of Language*. New Haven: Yale UP, 1986.

Mellor, Anne K. "Guilt and Samuel Taylor Coleridge." *English Romantic Irony*. Cambridge: Harvard UP, 1980. 137–64.

Mileur, Jean-Pierre. *Vision and Revision: Coleridge's Art of Immanence*. Berkeley: U of California P, 1982.

Mill, John Stuart. "Coleridge." *Collected Works of John Stuart Mill*. Vol. 10. Toronto: U of Toronto P, 1969. 117–63.

Milton, John. *Paradise Lost*. Ed. Merritt Y. Hughes. New York: Odyssey, 1935.

Modiano, Raimonda. "Words and 'Languageless' Meaning: Limits of Expression in *The Rime of the Ancient Mariner*." *Modern Language Quarterly* 38 (1977): 40–61.

Morley, Edith J., ed. *Henry Crabb Robinson on Books and Their Writers*. 3 vols. London: Dent, 1938.

Nethercot, Arthur H. *The Road to Tryermaine: A Study of the History, Background, and Purposes of Coleridge's* Christabel. Chicago: U of Chicago P, 1939.

Newlyn, Lucy. *Coleridge, Wordsworth, and the Language of Allusion*. Oxford: Clarendon–Oxford UP, 1986.

Noyes, Russell, ed. *English Romantic Poetry and Prose*. New York: Oxford UP, 1956.

Owen, W. J. B., ed. *Wordsworth and Coleridge:* Lyrical Ballads 1798. 2nd ed. Oxford: Oxford UP, 1969.

Paglia, Camille. *Sexual Personae: Art and Decadence from Nefertiti to Emily Dickinson*. New Haven: Yale UP, 1990.

Parker, Reeve. *Coleridge's Meditative Art*. Ithaca: Cornell UP, 1975.

Parrish, Stephen M. *The Art of the* Lyrical Ballads. Cambridge: Harvard UP, 1973.

————, ed. *Coleridge's "Dejection": The Earliest Manuscripts and the Earliest Printings*. Ithaca: Cornell UP, 1988.

Pater, Walter. "Coleridge." *Appreciations: The Works of Walter Pater*. Vol. 5. London: Macmillan, 1901. 65–104.

Pearce, Donald. " 'Kubla Khan' in Context." *Studies in English Literature* 21 (1981): 565–83.

Percy, Thomas, ed. *Reliques of Ancient English Poetry*. 3 vols. London: Dodsley, 1765.

Perkins, David, ed. *English Romantic Writers*. New York: Harcourt, 1967.

Piper, H. W. *The Active Universe: Pantheism and the Concept of Imagination in the English Romantic Poets*. London: Athlone, 1962.

————. *The Singing of Mount Abora: Coleridge's Use of Biblical Imagery and Natural Symbolism in Poetry and Philosophy*. Rutherford: Farleigh Dickinson UP, 1987.

Poe, Edgar Allan. "The Imp of the Perverse." *The Short Fiction of Edgar Allan Poe*. Ed. Stuart Levine and Susan Levine. Indianapolis: Bobbs, 1976. 268–71.

Potter, Stephen. *Coleridge and S. T. C.* London: Cape, 1938.

Preyer, Robert O. *Bentham, Coleridge, and the Science of History*. Bochum-Langendreer, Ger.: Poppinghaus, 1958.

Prickett, Stephen. *Coleridge and Wordsworth: The Poetry of Growth*. Cambridge: Cambridge UP, 1970.

Purves, Alan C. "Formal Structure in 'Kubla Khan.' " *Studies in Romanticism* 1 (1962): 187–91.

Raysor, T. M., ed. *Coleridge's Miscellaneous Criticism*. Cambridge: Harvard UP, 1936.

————, ed. *Shakesperian Criticism*. Vol. 1. Cambridge: Harvard UP, 1930.

Reed, Mark L. "Wordsworth, Coleridge, and the 'Plan' of *Lyrical Ballads*." *University of Toronto Quarterly* 34 (1965): 238–53.

————. *Wordsworth: The Chronology of the Middle Years, 1800–1815*. Cambridge: Harvard UP, 1975.

Reiman, Donald H. "Coleridge and the Art of Equivocation." *Studies in Romanticism* 25 (1986): 325–50.

———. *Intervals of Inspiration: The Skeptical Tradition and the Psychology of Romanticism*. Greenwood: Penkevill, 1988.

———, ed. *The Romantics Reviewed: A Collection in Depth of Periodical Reviews (1793–1830)*. 11 vols. New York: Garland, 1972.

———. *Romantic Texts and Contexts*. Columbia: U of Missouri P, 1987.

Reiman, Donald H., and Sharon B. Powers, eds. *Shelley's Poetry and Prose*. New York: Norton, 1977.

Richards, I. A., ed. *Portable Coleridge*. New York: Viking, 1950.

Richardson, Alan. "Romanticism and the Colonization of the Feminine." *Romanticism and Feminism*. Ed. Anne K. Mellor. Bloomington: Indiana UP, 1988. 13–25.

Ricoeur, Paul. *Freud and Philosophy: An Essay on Interpretation*. Trans. Denis Savage. New Haven: Yale UP, 1970.

Roe, Nicholas. *Wordsworth and Coleridge: The Radical Years*. Oxford: Clarendon–Oxford UP, 1988.

Rossabi, Morris. *Khubilai Khan: His Life and Times*. Berkeley: U of California P, 1988.

Rossetti, William Michael, ed. *The Diary of Dr. John William Polidori: 1816*. London: Matthews, 1911.

Ruoff, Gene W. *Wordsworth and Coleridge: The Making of the Major Lyrics, 1802–1804*. New Brunswick: Rutgers UP, 1989.

Sayre, Robert. "The Young Coleridge: Romantic Utopianism and the French Revolution." *Studies in Romanticism* 28 (1989): 397–415.

Schapiro, Barbara A. "*Christabel*: The Drama of Ambivalence." Schapiro, *Romantic Mother* 61–92.

———. *The Romantic Mother: Narcissistic Patterns in Romantic Poetry*. Baltimore: Johns Hopkins UP, 1983.

Schneider, Elisabeth. *Coleridge, Opium, and "Kubla Khan."* Chicago: U of Chicago P, 1953.

———, ed. *Samuel Taylor Coleridge: Selected Poetry and Prose*. New York: Holt, 1951.

Schulz, Max F. "Samuel Taylor Coleridge." Jordan, 4th ed. 341–463.

Shaffer, Elinor S. *"Kubla Khan" and The Fall of Jerusalem: The Mythological School in Biblical Criticism and Secular Literature, 1770–1800*. New York: Cambridge UP, 1975.

Shelton, John. "The Autograph Manuscript of 'Kubla Khan' and an Interpretation." *Review of English Literature* 7 (1966): 32–42. [Contains the Crewe ms.]

Showalter, Elaine, ed. *The New Feminist Criticism: Essays on Women, Literature, and Theory*. New York: Pantheon, 1985.

Smith, Fred Manning. "The Relation of Coleridge's 'Ode on Dejection' to Wordsworth's 'Ode on Intimations of Immortality.' " *PMLA* 50 (1935): 224–34.

Stauffer, Donald A., ed. *Selected Poetry and Prose of Samuel Taylor Coleridge*. New York: Random, 1951.

Stevens, Bonnie Klomp, and Larry L. Stewart. *A Guide to Literary Criticism and Research*. New York: Holt, 1987. Rev. ed. New York: Holt, 1992.

Sultana, Donald. *Samuel Taylor Coleridge in Malta and Italy*. Oxford: Blackwell, 1969.

Swann, Karen. "*Christabel*: The Wandering Mother and the Enigma of Form." *Studies in Romanticism* 23 (1984): 533–53.

Taylor, Anya. *Coleridge's Defense of the Human*. Columbus: Ohio State UP, 1986.

———. *Magic and English Romanticism*. Athens: U of Georgia P, 1979.

Thompson, E. P. Rev. of Coleridge, *Essays on His Times*, ed. David V. Erdman (*CC* 3). *Wordsworth Circle* 10 (1979): 261–65.

Twitchell, James. " 'Desire with Loathing Strangely Mixed': The Dream Work of *Christabel*." *Psychoanalytic Review* 61 (1974): 33–44.

Vlasopolos, Anca. " 'Deep Romantic Chasm': Woman as Textual Disturbances in Romantic Poetry." *Power, Gender, Values*. Ed. Judith Genova. Edmonton: Academic, 1987. 31–40.

Warren, Robert Penn. "A Poem of Pure Imagination: An Experiment in Reading." *Twentieth-Century Interpretations of* The Rime of the Ancient Mariner. Ed. James D. Boulger. Englewood Cliffs: Prentice, 1969. 21–47.

Watson, George, ed. *Samuel Taylor Coleridge*, Biographia Literaria. London: Dent, 1975.

Wellek, René. *Immanuel Kant in England, 1793–1838*. Princeton: Princeton UP, 1931.

———. *The Romantic Age*. Vol. 2 of *A History of Modern Criticism*. New Haven: Yale UP, 1955.

Wheeler, Kathleen M. *The Creative Mind in Coleridge's Poetry*. Cambridge: Harvard UP, 1981.

Willey, Basil. *Samuel Taylor Coleridge*. London: Chatto, 1972.

Williams, Raymond. *Culture and Society, 1780–1950*. New York: Columbia UP, 1958.

Wittig, Monique. *Les Guérillères*. 1969. Trans. David Le Vay. New York: Viking, 1971.

Woodring, Carl R. *Politics in the Poetry of Coleridge*. Madison: U of Wisconsin P, 1961.

Woolf, Virginia. *A Room of One's Own*. 1929. New York: Harcourt, 1957.

Wordsworth, Dorothy. *Journals of Dorothy Wordsworth*. Ed. Ernest de Selincourt. 2 vols. London: Macmillan, 1941.

Wordsworth, Jonathan, M. H. Abrams, and Stephen Gill, eds. *William Wordsworth: The Prelude 1799, 1805, 1850*. New York: Norton, 1979.

Wordsworth, Jonathan, Michael C. Jaye, and Robert Woof. *William Wordsworth and the Age of English Romanticism*. New Brunswick: Rutgers UP, 1987.

Audiovisual Aids

Iron Maiden. *Powerslave*. Capital, 4xJ, 12321, 1984.

Kiley, Richard, narr. *William Wordsworth and the Age of English Romanticism.* VHS. Ameritech, 1988. 28 min.

Prickett, Stephen. Lectures on *Biographia Literaria, Christabel,* and *Rime of the Ancient Mariner*. Everett/Edwards. Cassette Curriculum, 1973–74.

Richardson, Ralph. *Coleridge, Samuel Taylor: The Poetry of Coleridge*. Spoken Word Classic 1092. 1 cassette. Caedmon Records.

Russell, Ken, dir. *Samuel Taylor Coleridge:* The Rime of the Ancient Mariner. David Hemmings credits. Prod. Granada. Beta, VHS, 3/4U. Color. Films for the Humanities. 52 min.

Scofield, Paul, narr. *Coleridge: The Fountain and the Cave*. Prod. Bayley Selleck. Beta, VHS, 3/4U. Pyramid Film and Video, 1974. 57 min. or 32 min. ed. version.

INDEX OF NAMES

INDEX OF WORKS BY COLERIDGE